To Grace
For your
presence in this
author's life and
to one who may
rival Lord B. in
what she has
done for Greeee.
love,
Charles

Romanticism and Male Fantasy in Byron's *Don Juan*

A Marketable Vice

Charles Donelan

First published in Great Britain 2000 by
MACMILLAN PRESS LTD
Houndmills, Basingstoke, Hampshire RG21 6XS and London
Companies and representatives throughout the world

A catalogue record for this book is available from the British Library.

ISBN 0–333–76029–8

First published in the United States of America 2000 by
ST. MARTIN'S PRESS, INC.,
Scholarly and Reference Division,
175 Fifth Avenue, New York, N.Y. 10010

ISBN 0–312–22491–5

Library of Congress Cataloging-in-Publication Data
Donelan, Charles, 1960–
Romanticism and male fantasy in Byron's Don Juan : a marketable
vice / Charles Donelan.
 p.   cm. — (Romanticism in perspective)
Includes bibliographical references and index.
ISBN 0–312–22491–5 (cloth)
1. Byron, George Gordon Byron, Baron, 1788–1824. Don Juan.
2. Don Juan (Legendary character) in literature.   3. Epic poetry,
English—History and criticism.   4. Sexual fantasies in literature.
5. Masculinity in literature.   6. Seduction in literature.
7. Fantasy in literature.   8. Romanticism—England.   9. Men in
literature.   I. Title.   II. Series.
PR4359.D67   1999
821'.7—dc21   99–15892
                                                                  CIP

This book is printed on paper suitable for recycling and made from fully managed and sustained forest sources.

10   9   8   7   6   5   4   3   2   1
09   08   07   06   05   04   03   02   01   00

Printed and bound in Great Britain by
Antony Rowe Ltd, Chippenham, Wiltshire

For Liz

Contents

Acknowledgements

Thanks to my parents, Ann and Charles Donelan, and my siblings, especially James Donelan of UCSB. Thanks also to Professor Karl Kroeber for guiding this project through many stages and staying with it until the end. Thanks to Jonathan Arac, Elaine Scarry, Frances Ferguson and Stephen Greenblatt for advice and encouragement at crucial times. Thanks also to my original teachers of Romanticism: Harold Bloom, Alan Liu and Andrzej Warminski. Thanks to Marilyn Gaull for making this publication possible and to the Wordsworth Summer Conference in Grasmere for offering a unique experience of scholarly cooperation and exchange. Special thanks to Dorothy Mermin for valuable advice in the final stages.

Introduction: Romanticism and Vice in an Age of Reaction

On 1 June 1787, George III issued a royal proclamation 'for the Encouragement of Piety and Virtue, and for [the] preventing and punishing of Vice, Profaneness, and Immorality', which included a provision ordering the suppression of 'all loose and licentious prints, books, and publications dispensing poison to the minds of the young and unwary'.[1] While the proclamation of 1787 was not the first royal call for the suppression of vice, it was the first to act against the circulation of indecent literature. The implications of this addition to the agenda of British moral legislation were not lost on the young Evangelical layman William Wilberforce, then just twenty-eight years old and at the beginning of an extraordinary career of activism that would climax with his leadership in the abolition of the British slave trade in 1807. Following the announcement of the royal ordinance, Wilberforce formed a Proclamation Society to encourage public participation in the enforcement of the new laws against indecent literature. He wrote in his Journal that 'God Almighty has placed before me two great objects, the suppression of the slave trade and the reformation of manners.'[2] For more than a decade this group brought actions against those who published and distributed what the Proclamation Society considered to be obscenity. In 1802, the Proclamation Society was absorbed into another, larger group intent on the same mission, the Society for the Suppression of Vice. The campaign against indecent literature and seditious and blasphemous publications reached its high point in 1820, when the Duke of Wellington organized a third society, the Constitutional Society, to protect the British reading public from British publishers. It was in this final, most intense period of government censorship and publicly supported prosecution of publishers, authors and booksellers that Byron wrote and published his most important work, the comic epic *Don Juan*, which appeared in instalments from 1819 to 1824.

Don Juan is the Romantic period's most comprehensive defence of freedom of expression and liberty of the imagination. The poem satirizes and resists the state-sponsored evangelical censorship of

1

popular culture. In taking on the job of censorship, the evangelicals sought to cope with the unintended consequences of their own work of modernization, for it was the churches that had opened a new market for printed matter in the late eighteenth century by teaching working people to read. A sense of responsibility for the literacy they had bestowed combined with the pressure exerted by the circulation of revolutionary literature such as Tom Paine's *Age of Reason* led evangelicals to embrace censorship. The lay church's mission to teach reading became an even more fervent mission to contain and control what could be read. *Don Juan* responds to this political agenda of the societies for the suppression of vice. For Lord Byron and his liberal friends, the war on vice had become an attack on their right to address emerging problems of popular culture through literature in a time of political reaction.

How did the concept of vice come to occupy such a central place in cultural politics? The different senses of the word 'vice' in circulation at the time offer some clues. Originally, depravity and the corruption of morals were vices; so were habits perceived as immoral or degrading. 'Vice' covered activities as diverse as the abuse of alcohol, brothel-going and children playing on Sunday. Morality plays had personified Vice as a foolish character at the mercy of his appetites. Physical flaws or deformities could also count as vices – Chaucer's character Myda has the vice of long ass's ears. In the late eighteenth century, a rapid expansion in urban population made everything that could be termed a vice appear to be on the upsurge – corruption, bad habits, foolishness, appetite, even physical deformity. As a floating concept, moreover, 'vice' authorized speculation about the sources and symptoms of every kind of social deviancy. The societies for the suppression of vice and *Don Juan* both participate in the conflict of evangelical Puritan asceticism with an emerging hedonistic consumerism. The new level of social significance attached to vice at the end of the eighteenth century arose in response to what Colin Campbell has termed the 'puzzle' of modern consumerism:

> . . . a mystery surrounds . . . the behaviour of consumers in modern industrial societies. The mystery . . . concerns the very essence of modern consumption itself – its character as an activity which involves an apparently endless pursuit of wants; the most characteristic feature of modern consumption being this insatiability.[3]

Awareness of an increasing number and variety of vices, along with the invention of new, utilitarian virtues such as self-interest, allowed contemporary social critics to perceive the importance of modern consumerism. But in the aftermath of the Gordon Riots in 1780 and then of the French Revolution in 1789, the idea of vice in British culture became more vague just as its apparent consequences grew more drastic. The perception that a new dynamic range had been achieved in the sphere of ethics became commonplace, but this new dynamism was usually attributed to political rather than economic causes. The Whig statesman Sir James Mackintosh wrote that after the Revolution 'our sentiments, raised by such events so much above their ordinary level, became the source of guilt and heroism unknown before – and of sublime virtues and splendid crimes.'[4] The relation of the new 'range' in morals to new experiences in the economy remained for the most part unremarked; politicians on both sides of the Tory/Whig divide sought explanations in the sphere of ideas and allegiances for phenomena in fact generated in the adjacent sphere of goods and desires. The societies, by seizing on the Proclamation of 1787 as a licence to interfere with the production and sale of books, brought the blame for the perceived corruption of public morals closer to where something important was actually happening, in the marketplace where objects were bought and sold. Shakespeare could have Edgar announce in Act V of *King Lear* that 'the Gods are just, and of our pleasant vices / Make instruments to plague us', but by the end of eighteenth century the Gods had retired from the field. The evangelical societies were formed to take their places.

While they may not have succeeded in suppressing vice by their campaign against writers and publishers, the societies brought some important Romantic literature to trial, creating a threatening environment in which every act of literary creation had to be carefully vetted against their often unpredictable yet always stringent standards. By forcing Byron in particular into the position of the outlaw, they inadvertently cultivated his sense of the potential of literature to speak back to the law and the state.

Don Juan, Byron's best poem, gains in interest by being read as originating under this kind of overt political pressure. Familiar passages take on a new significance when read in the context of a culture of censorship and the cultural dialectic of Puritan and Romantic ethical positions that gave rise to it. Poetic language itself becomes identified in the poem with illicit desire. Two stanzas from Canto

1 ought to be read together in order to bring out the full meaning of the famous couplet that ends the first of them.

> 'Tis a sad thing, I cannot choose but say,
>   And all the fault of that indecent sun,
> Who cannot leave alone our helpless clay,
>   But will keep baking, broiling, burning on,   500
> That howsoever people fast and pray
>   The flesh is frail, and so the soul undone:
> What men call gallantry, and gods adultery,
> Is much more common where the climate's sultry.
>
> Happy the nations of the moral north!
>   Where all is virtue, and the winter season
> Sends sin, without a rag on, shivering forth;
>   ('Twas snow that brought St. Francis back to reason);
> Where juries cast up what a wife is worth
>   By laying whate'er sum, in mulct, they please on   510
> The lover, who must pay a handsome price,
> Because it is *a marketable vice.*

(I, st. 63–4, emphasis added)

   The idea that 'howsoever people fast and pray' in the countries of the South, the 'indecent sun ... cannot leave alone our helpless clay' recasts a commonplace of popular prejudice in explicitly religious terms. By invoking the language of the Gospels ('the flesh is frail') to assert the inadequacy of religious solutions to the pressures of climate and biology, the stanza implicitly mocks the efforts of colonial evangelists and their allies – the same people who formed the societies that strove to censor subversive poetry. By casting the work of colonial missionaries in the mocking light of an indecent sun, the stanza strikes at the evangelical movements' roots in missionary work and resumes one of Byron's initial positions in the ongoing public debate about the politics of empire.[5] The giddy fun of the concluding couplet's rhyme – 'sultry/adultery' – accentuates rather than diminishes the stanza's irreverence.

   Throughout his career Byron questioned the claims of religious belief in religious terms. By comparing the adulterous South to the moral North he necessarily alludes to public perception of his own notorious behaviour in exile. The poet's personal association with the moral laxity of the South makes the recurrence of religious texts and figures in this passage tantamount to blasphemy. Although Byron's tendency to indulge in scepticism amidst displays of biblical and Christian knowledge was threatening in itself, it was the additional element of humour in the case of *Don Juan* that most upset his pious critics. Thus the joke of the rhyme 'sultry/adultery' here operates on two levels. To an uneducated audience for whom the religious inflections are muffled, the couplet appeals as a 'harmless' jest. For pious readers more directly aware both of the specific references and the degree to which they have been torn from their context, this very appeal to the less well versed must seem like the flaunting of a covert act of corruption. The poem's profile as an act of political defiance stems from this perception that its 'irresistible' guise of high spirits and good humour was in fact a cover story for the poet's real mission: to spread disbelief among the impressionable. Robert Ryan calls attention to this aspect of Byron's reception when he states 'it was an acute cultural embarrassment that Britain's most celebrated modern poet was a persistent, mischievous critic of the national religion.'[6]

The following stanza pushes Byron's implicit criticism of the national religion further. The aside about St Francis repeats the now-familiar double strategy of religious allusion. By drawing the learned into a discussion of the relevance of an unusual episode from the life of St Francis, it potentially lulls them into a false sense of security about the propriety of the poem's frame of reference. But the saint in this instance only serves to set off another joke; this one aimed at the English themselves. Sin in England is shown as a naked woman, 'stripped' and driven into the snows of a culture bereft of human sympathy. By allowing religion to remain a persistent presence within the prurient discourse of narrator, the text calls the stability of religious claims about the efficacy of reading the Bible and the *Lives of the Saints* into question. If someone as spiritually lost as this speaker can remain intimately conscious of the language and imagery of the scriptures, then prayer and fasting alone cannot possibly save the reader or the colonials from the effects of the indecent sun. In this way the stanzas overturn the conventional polarities governing the 'light' of religious metaphor. The poem's language, like the human body in which it arises, has a tropism that attracts it to the natural light of the indecent sun, leading its readers away from moral north and into the broiling hothouse of Byron's poem. By branding the first idea of the sun as an indecent one, the poet articulates an identification that he will continue to develop throughout *Don Juan*: identification of language with human sexual desire.

The subtitle of this study, *A Marketable Vice*, draws attention to the darker side of the poem's identification of language with desire. Its satire of the coldly commercial social practices of England, the supposedly moral North, is a complexly necessary complement to its equally ironic celebration of the sunny, supposedly uncommodified and adultery-friendly climate of the Mediterranean. In addition, the poem is full of 'vice' and was itself not only supremely marketable, but also very actively marketed. This reflexive context qualifies yet again the irony of Byron's description of British social practices. From within the commonplace opposition of the moral North and the seductive South, commodification emerges as Byron's central subject, demonstrating an essentially modern principle of moral inversion. The 'sum, in mulct' mentioned in the marketable vice stanza is the fine that was imposed on men convicted of seducing married women, an amount that was paid to aggrieved husbands based on the jury's estimate of the value of their wives' fidelity. The stanza therefore implies that men in Regency England, if they could afford it, bought their way out of responsibility for this kind of sexual misbehaviour. By fining adulterers the law in effect established a market for adultery.

In coining the phrase 'a marketable vice' the poem gestures towards the central philosophical issues raised by modern consumerism, its uncertain relations to morality and utility. When considered from the point of view of utility, the insatiable demand for novelty characteristic of consumer behaviour is inexplicable, and can thus be grouped with other inutile pursuits such as fantasy and daydreaming. Not many men could expect to purchase a liaison with a married woman, yet the idea of adultery as something that can be bought might give hope to some pleasurable fantasies. But what is the moral status of an immoral fantasy? If the vice of adultery is available more as a fantasy than as a reality, is the fantasy sufficient to compromise morality? The apparent existence of vice as a pleasurable fantasy that may be marketed and thus transferred without ever actually occurring is what Colin Campbell refers to as 'modern autonomous imaginative hedonism':

> ... that distinctive cultural complex which was associated with
> the consumer revolution in eighteenth-century England, and which
> embraced the rise of the novel, romantic love and modern fashion,

is related to the widespread adoption of the habit of covert day-dreaming. The central insight required is the realization that individuals do not so much seek satisfaction from products, as pleasure from the self-illusory experiences which they construct from their associated meanings. The essential activity of consumption is thus not the actual selection, purchase or use of products, but the imaginative pleasure-seeking to which the product image lends itself, 'real' consumption being largely a resultant of this 'mentalistic' hedonism.[7]

'Byron' was the early nineteenth century's most successful, and the entire nineteenth century's most influential 'product image' in this sense. In the early nineteenth century, as modern consumerism displaced more traditional forms of consumption, and shopping sometimes ironically approached the status of a vice, the poetry of Byron repositioned 'letters' in the market as 'literature'. Arrayed among other suggestive commodities, literature could seem like an invitation to mental hedonism. Byron both went through the cycle of fashion and reflected on it from a uniquely detached position. But how did the poem's initial audiences receive ironies such as the notion of a marketable vice? Was the intensity of the poem's rhetorical performance appreciated at the time of its publication? All such questions finally come down to the simple problem, how did readers of *Don Juan* cope with the apparent disjunction of Byron's reputation, tone and matter?

The sporadic publication of *Don Juan* turned *Don Juan* into a recurrent event that created in its readers a sensitivity to the discontinuity of aesthetic and rational judgement. Each new canto, moreover, was introduced by an invocation to the poem's readers that examined and thwarted their habits and preconceptions. These invocations and digressions left many people who read the poem confused and upset. Because the poem is more than a narrative, with its form and matter in volatile interaction, it threatened an audience still in reaction to the rhetorical demands of a revolutionary era. Wordsworth hated the poem, as did Coleridge, who wondered how its author could be a genius yet lack any sense of morality. Reading it made Keats sick. The uproar over Byron's separation from and apparent abandonment of his wife and young child in 1816 caused many members of *Don Juan*'s initial audience to interpret its publication in 1819 as the poet's attempt to profit from his bad reputation by marketing it as literature. The narrator's observations were assumed to reflect the opinions of Lord Byron, a known adulterer. Even more upsetting, the strategy initiated in the poem's invocations for evading conventional expectations is developed in the narrative itself through the disjunction of the narrator and the hero. *Don Juan*, which provided neither the sensationalism of an erotic memoir, nor the reassurance of a coherent and sustained apology, turned out to be a very different work from what anyone, detractor or supporter, could have expected. For that reason, the 'Byron' it produces is a peculiarly powerful one.

I will now sketch the thematic foci of my five chapters portraying this powerful, surprising 'Byron', as well as how (and why) he was (and now may be) most rewardingly read. I will then offer a schematized presentation of the continuously criss-crossing threads of my argument that *Don Juan* is as valuable a poem today as it was when it was first published. That judgement is founded on my view that the significance of the poem depends on its perpetually ongoing interweaving: themes and ideas rise to prominence, disappear beneath others, then rise to visibility again in a different context created as the poem evolves. No mechanically structured critique can do justice to this intricate, open-ended texturing. My chapters roughly follow the sequence of the cantos. But my analyses of the poem's special efficacies must be responsive to its digressiveness, its revisiting and revising of earlier attitudes and observations, and above all to its developing challenges to central presuppositions determinative of its changing historical context.

Yet there is at least one constant in the poem: the traditional myth of Don Juan is transformed in Byron's version, both by conscious modification and by association with 'Byron'. Byron's *Don Juan* abandons the myth's original (exhausted) cultural function of re-enacting the ritual repression that founds monogamy and rejects a commercialized fetishization of monogamy as female chastity. All the women visited by Juan are portrayed realistically, while at the same time they are positioned as objects of male fantasy. So the narrative persistently explores the role women play in the establishment and maintenance of masculine identity. The poem's heroines, far from the unwitting victims of the traditional Don Juan's seductive duplicity, are represented as *already* living in various and complex relations to patriarchal constraint of their sexuality – which is why most of them are well aware of what they are getting into with Juan.

In the first chapter I describe the formal and thematic bases for the poem's claims on its audience, explaining how 'Byron' performs and *Don Juan* transforms the Don Juan myth to engage contemporary debates about gender, education, love and power. The poem begins with Don Juan's childhood, domesticating the familiar story of the figure's socially transgressive sexuality within an argument for the influence of environment on the formation of character, thus engaging its audience in a debate over the methods and results of the feminized educational culture to which middle-class British boys were increasingly subject in Byron's day. Juan's mother, Donna Inez, administers her son's education personally, displaying attitudes that coincide fully with those of her British and French counterparts of the late eighteenth century.

Chapter 2 reads the poem's most idealistic love story as a problematic and ultimately self-destructive fantasy identifying the process of narrative itself with a feminine pleasure principle. Juan is shipwrecked on a Greek island where the poem's most idealized woman, Haidee, saves his life. In a masterly revision and collation of the two principal moments in the direct action of the hero in the Odyssey, Juan is at first like Odysseus in Scheria, adopted by the local princess as her favourite, and then like one of the suitors whose courtship is so decisively interrupted by the return of the patriarch, in this case, Haidee's father, Lambro. The cantos devoted to Haidee are the poem's most extended meditation on the fundamental Oedipal relations and psychic environments that form the basis for our imaginative lives.

In Chapter 3 I examine the way fantasy in *Don Juan* is defined by its instability. The poem's most extreme male fantasy, that of the harem, precipitates its most convulsive and horrific transition, the arrival in Ismail of an invading imperial Russian army. The erotic daydream of endless male sexual prerogative represented by the imprisoned women of the harem is interrupted by its nightmarish anti-type, the equally dehumanizing and much more bloody superfluity of men required for imperial conquest. Juan, objectified as a slave and cross-dressed as a woman, escapes his fate as one of the girls by becoming one of the boys and joining the mercenaries and Russian soldiers in the destruction of the Ottoman city of Ismail. Unlike the journals of its day, *Don Juan* is not tied to the interests of the State by licence and regulation, and thus may depict war in all its graphic immediacy and horror. It may contextualize this horror as meaningless rather than glorious, complacent rather than valiant, and, most importantly, it may identify war as a specifically male form of applied fantasy. An applied fantasy appears that has outgrown, even overgrown, the epic context in which it arose.

Chapter 4 examines fantasy in relation to memory. The poem returns to and reconstructs memory in a tripartite structure – through the history of the time of the story of Don Juan, from 1788 to 1792; through the time of the narration, when Byron was writing the text, from 1818 to 1824; and through what Jerome McGann usefully terms the poem's 'memorial or recollective level', the period of Byron's London years of fame, from 1812 to 1816.[8] This tripartite structure arises out of a desire to inscribe the individual memory in its full range of historical contexts, and to oppose individual memory to the heavily regulated public records of experience. Byron transforms his earlier, grandiose self-contemplation and with it his relation to the age in *Don Juan*, cloaking his personal preoccupations in the antipathies, fantasies and favourite memories of an entire generation of European males. This is why in Chapter 4 I look closely at two accounts of murder in *Don Juan*. An historical assassination that took place outside of the poet's home in Ravenna during the poem's composition, and Juan's fictional murder in self-defence of a highwayman on Shooter's Hill near London provide points of departure for digressions on doubt, tacit belief and the objective existence of consciousness.

Though critical, *Don Juan*'s meta-discourse of collective memory is not a prescriptive process. Rather, like the processes of personal memory it seeks to influence, it is ruminative and reflective, shaped by and shaping in turn the moods to which it responds. The figure of 'Byron' reaches its limit in *Don Juan* in relation to the nineteenth-century practice of defining oneself against the paradigm of Byronic behaviour. Byron's influence on nineteenth-century culture initiated a reception of his work that can still prompt his readers to re-evaluate not only themselves, but also the images through which they have remembered the historical past.

The British reaction to revolution enunciated by Burke and embodied in the slide into Tory conservatism of Wordsworth and Coleridge tended towards a pseudo-feudalism of extreme patriarchy among the English gentry. Cantos X to the unfinished XVII are my concern in the final two chapters. They harbour the poet's most subtle, penetrating criticisms of the British social institutions of his day. Many of those responsible at the time for the maintenance of the boundaries of the emergent discipline of literature (the Reviewers, the Crown, the religious establishment) found Byron's tumultuous stirring of the collective memory, his insistence on examining the historical and psychological grounds of bourgeois individualism and the emergent institution of companionate marriage, painfully perverse. It seemed perverse because it revealed its author's cultural pre-eminence only by betraying this responsibility in what appeared to be a fit of demonic self-indulgence. This negative judgement of the basically affluent audience that had lionized Byron seems to have been a response to the poem's and the poet's increasing interest in and identification with the complex forms of subordination required of women in contemporary British society. *Don Juan* was more popular with the non-affluent than Byron's earlier verse, which had been celebrated by the affluent and powerful. Through its depiction of Adeline Amundeville and Aurora Raby, *Don Juan* offers some provocative final thoughts on the paradox of women's psychic mobility – their ability to conform their personalities to the needs and desires of those around them, while at the same time remaining emotionally and imaginatively detached by involving themselves in fantasy. Even within successful marriages British society produced masculine autonomy only by sanctifying an often-illusory state of feminine dependency. The paradox of an aristocratic criticism of privilege is deepened in Byron's case by the sense that his personal treatment of the women in his life stands in contradiction to his professions of sympathy for the plight of women in society. While it is important to examine the contradiction implied by this contrast, the significance of the social criticism in the poetry need not be held hostage to the poet's behaviour. This contradiction is another way in which the work troubles the construction of a coherent, unified 'Byron'.

The rise of women writers and a feminine-identified literary audience at the end of the eighteenth century precipitated fundamental changes in the masculine self-perceptions expressed in literature. While some Romantic writers consolidated their appropriation of the authority invested in women by their association with sensibility, Byron took a different course from his predecessors of the Lake School, Wordsworth, Southey and Coleridge. In response to the rise of women as an influential audience, to the spread of Romantic poetry and to his own prior success as a poet, Byron shaped his longest poem around an expressly masculine subject and viewpoint, with the result, *Don Juan*, becoming a uniquely valuable expression of Romantic concern with gender and genre, and as such, illuminating by contrast of contemporary attitudes towards their relation.

I turn now to a summary of the ideas to which my chapters most consistently return. Changing social relations in industrialized England put an unprecedented strain on the conventions of gender. As intellectual women began to articulate a distinctive sensibility and evolve a feminist politics, certain men began to fall out with the conventions of masculinity. Of the early nineteenth century's visible instances of male revolt against the patriarchal ideal of manhood, Byron's was perhaps the most complicated. His glamour, fame and reputation for and sense of his own creative genius were all bound up in the popular imagination with a carefully cultivated outlaw status. European travel and exile gave Byron a way to elaborate his youthful Whig opposition into a persona that was at once passive and active, permanently detached and eternally assertive.

The 'revolt' in *Don Juan* is against the literary tradition as well as against the conventions of gender, but here too Byron's revolt is an ambiguous one. *Don Juan* operates at times as an early modernist work, employing abstraction within the medium of narrative to make a social statement about 'poetry'. The poem is full of anti-literary devices and unpoetical prosaic contents, yet the end result is not entirely anti-epic or anti-art. Canto endings in particular heighten our awareness of the work's delicate balance between art and anti-art. Witness the end of Canto III, which breaks off the poem's most sustained romantic set-piece, an ode to the evening star, when it has created the sense that the trope of belatedness is becoming unbearably poignant for the exiled poet. After reflecting on the fact that even tyrants such as Nero are sometimes mourned when they are gone into the night of death, the narrator catches himself:

> But I'm digressing; what on earth has Nero,
>   Or any like such sovereign buffoons,
> To do with the transactions of my hero,
>   More than such madmen's fellow man – the moon's?
> Sure my invention must be down at zero
>
> (III, st.110)

The self-consciously performative manner of *Don Juan* continues the project Byron had begun in his Oriental tales and *Childe Harold's*

Pilgrimage, the lyricization of narrative forms, which was in the beginning mostly a matter of leaving things out. The task for his critics, as they understood it, was to integrate the disparate and fragmented materials of his art by constructing a 'Byron' who could be imagined as having intended their disjunction. This reading for 'Byron', or Byronism, is an exaggerated version of what is required by all literature, and the basis for the nineteenth-century phenomenon of self-definition in relation to Byron: it allowed each reader to imagine a 'Byron' of his or her own. For instance, the dispassionate, cavalier tone of the lines quoted above interrupts the sentimental flow of poetic association and introduces an extra-literary voice into the poem's mix that is neither entirely reducible to the narrator nor necessarily that of the poet in *propria persona*.

> Soft hour! Which wakes the wish and melts the heart
>> Of those who sail the seas, on the first day
> When they from their sweet friends are torn apart;
>> Or fills with love the pilgrim on his way
> As the far bell of vesper makes him start,
>> Seeming to weep the dying day's decay;
> Is this a fancy which our reason scorns?
> Ah! Surely nothing dies but something mourns!
>
> When Nero perish'd by the justest doom
>> Which ever the destroyer yet destroy'd,
> Amidst the roar of liberated Rome,
>> Of nations freed, and the world overjoy'd,
> Some hands unseen strew'd flowers upon his tomb;
>> Perhaps the weakness of a heart not void
> Of feeling for some kindness done when power
> Had left the wretch an uncorrupted hour.
>
> (III, st. 108–9)

In a canny use of poetic convention, these stanzas' metaphor for Juan's condition is nightfall. In the dark daylight boundaries disappear and poetic conventions break down. The evening star of the hero's belatedness is thus succeeded by the man-in-the-moon bathos of the narrator. One could read these final stanzas of this canto as flowers strewn on the grave of the tyrant of its own discourse, the melancholy male thinking of the evening star.

Byron's poetic strategies, like his poem, seemed to signal the nightfall of masculine discourse and with it of the nation itself. In early nineteenth-century England, a strong continuity between the conventions of manhood and the integrity of the nation was a central tenet of virtually all publicly available political positions, from Tory conservatism to agrarian radicalism. Jacobinism, the political philosophy of the French Revolution, was for the most part only accessible to the British public through a dense screen of counter-revolutionary male anxieties. Romantically reinventing Don Juan in an English poem in 1819, the dark side of Byron's wit and scepticism were thus, at first, as politically unintelligible to many radicals as to conservatives.

By 1819, however, the enormous cultural struggle over the status of women in British society had already come to stand synechdochally for a host of questions concerning those whose access to the public sphere was limited or denied by monopolies on effectual political expression. Within an already polarized political culture of men in and out of place, all alike threatened by the presence of revolutionary women, the figure of 'Byron' had come to stand for the desire, from wherever it emanated and for whoever held it, for a less tradition-bound, more exotic and passionate way of life. Having passed through the familiar initial stages of male revolt against convention by the time he turned thirty, Lord Byron wrote *Don Juan* in part to redirect the attention of his audience to those aspects of his experience of masculinity that were unsuited to the narrowly defined, politicized concept of manhood offered by contemporary cultural debate. This move, the step directing attention to that which made the specific political value of masculinity what it was in his day, is the one which renders *Don Juan* both enormously important and ambitious – as ambitious in its way as any comparably long poem in English.

Understanding how *Don Juan* explores the problematics of masculinity as defined in Regency England permits us to appreciate better the significance of Byron's resistance to the censorship of obscenity that I discussed earlier. Indulging in the vices one could afford came more and more to be taken as the potential right of every member of society. The phrase 'a marketable vice' captures the relation of the privileged status of masculinity in the Regency period to the fact that the licence of this status was as much idealized as feared by those excluded from its privileges. Male liberty from social responsibility thus often appeared as a form of vice.

The outrageous royal expenditures of the Prince Regent alarmed and fascinated working people, many of whom struggled to afford the artificially high price of bread. The utilitarian equation of economic reform with social justice implied that liberty could be purchased, and that an enfranchised consumer would be a free citizen accepting responsibility for his destiny. Yet, in his profligacy, the Prince Regent embodied anxieties about the mobility of capital, its potential for exacerbating inequities in the distribution of the social surplus. In an epoch so concerned with the imagination and the liberty of the individual, the Prince Regent's abdication of the role of the father, the spectacle of his royal revolt against the social strictures and responsibilities of traditional manhood, became an incentive for the public to excuse the pleasant vices and to tolerate improper behaviour on the part of other royals – even a woman. When the Prince Regent tried to divorce Princess Caroline for adultery, the working public sided almost entirely with his wife. The profligate Prince Regent had let them down and they wanted him to know it, but it was nevertheless a result of their acceptance of the prerogatives of wealth and status that led them to accord similar licence to Caroline.[9]

Politically, the 'selfish' liberty of the male revolt enacted by the Prince Regent and the dandies was both a contradiction and a necessity. As a result of *Don Juan,* 'Byron' became something more complex than other available icons of male privilege liberated from filial responsibility. In his most important and ambitious poem Byron makes a provisional but total statement of the aims and consequences of the male revolt against the social conventions of nationalistic domestic manhood. By undertaking to revive, alter and improve Don Juan, the abstract icon of male exploitation, *Don Juan* establishes a new relation between epic poetry – which shows male behaviour in a conventionally heroic style – and the philosophical importance of masculinity to nation and empire. Byron recognized that the 'marketability' of the vice of male privilege would not yield to pre-capitalist moral injunctions, and this recognition allows *Don Juan* to claim for *all* individuals and both genders a role in the social formation of the state.

Byron's analysis of the trouble with heroism in *Don Juan* proceeds from his own position as culture hero. Political and philosophical speculation about the viability of heroic ideals in the Romantic period was widespread and intense. In the absence of any reliable arena for heroic experience, men in the early nineteenth century

retreated into collective identities. Thus even extreme individual-
ists such as Byron and the dandy Beau Brummell were often seen
as the centres for hordes of imitators rather than as leaders of so-
ciety. But while for Brummell avoiding heroism was an acknowledged
goal of dandyism, Byron, despite his scepticism about conventional
heroes never relinquished heroic ambitions. The dandy's response
to a period of cultural transition was to heighten anxieties about
status to the exclusion of all other considerations, dropping from
the masculine repertoire any roles not conducive to composure.
Byron admired the aloofness and enjoyed the wit of the dandies,
but he could never fully identify with their deliberate lack of larger
ambitions or feel content adopting their remarkable policy of disa-
vowing all emotion.

The dandy's emotional autonomy is an essential part of the
multifaceted character of the narrator of *Don Juan*, but as a poet
Byron needed a wider and more challenging set of obstacles than
dandyism alone could provide. The attitudes and experiences of
the poem's hero Juan are those of a picaresque man of feeling, the
eighteenth-century masculine stereotype of emotional and empa-
thetic richness from which the dandies sought to escape. This is
the central structural principle of the poem: hero and narrator are
on opposite sides of a divide in sensibility, both of which are present
in the poem. The distance between the narrator and the hero ena-
bles the poem's characteristic interplay between intellectual and
empathetic responses to its own story. The text oscillates between
a subordination of every consideration to the discovery of fact, be
it of history, social practice or domestic economy, and a deploy-
ment of strategies for making the reader complicit with unexpected
attitudes towards the facts. The effect is to complicate and destabilize
authorial identity, charging the poem's many transitions – the begin-
nings and endings of cantos in particular – with nervous tension.

The sophisticated rhetorical performances that head many of the
cantos invite the reader to consider the contradictions of this unstable
authorial identity. For instance, here the narrator reflects on the
public reception of poem and poet in the first person.

> They accuse me – *Me* – the present writer of
>   The present poem – of – I know not what, –
> A tendency to under-rate and scoff
>   At human power and virtue, and all that;

And this they say in language rather rough.
Good God! I wonder what they would be at!
I say no more than has been said in Dante's
Verse, or by Solomon and by Cervantes;

By Swift, by Machiavel, by Rochefoucault,
By Fenelon, by Luther, and by Plato;
By Tillotson, and Wesley, and Rousseau,
Who knew this life was not worth a potato.
'Tis not their fault, nor mine, if this be so –
For my part, I pretend not to be Cato,
Nor even Diogenes. – we live and die,
But which is best, you know no more than I.

(VII, st. 3–4)

Byron, like Dante, is a part of his own poem, but without a name, foregrounding his lack of a socially coherent subject position. His tremendous fame made him an anomaly and detached him to some extent from his social class. In these stanzas he presents himself as self-created as a writer: 'the present writer of / The present poem.' The rhetorical constructs in his poem – the oscillations between detachment and empathy, fact and attitude to fact – model for their public an independent subjectivity *in excess of* any coherent social identity.

The idea of a 'romantic Don Juan', like that of a 'strong Superman' or a 'clever Genius', appears either redundant or ironic. An admirer of the seducer might see the adjective 'romantic' as appropriate but unnecessary, while a detractor of the Don's would surely object to describing him in any way that idealized or even connoted his sincerity. To say that Byron's character Juan is, of all the Don Juans, *the* romantic one does, however, make a kind of sense, and not merely because this poem is the major work of a writer officially classified as a Romantic. Although in a famous stanza the narrator disavows the poem's romanticism (and does so before the critical term had gained currency), the stanza still enacts the romantic story of affective disillusionment, though it does so as an overcoming of romanticism, rather than a succumbing to it.

As boy, I thought myself a clever fellow,
And wish'd that others held the same opinion;

They took it up when my days grew more mellow,
    And other minds acknowledged my dominion:
Now my sere fancy 'falls into the yellow
    Leaf', and imagination droops her pinion,
And the sad truth which hovers o'er my desk
Turns what was once romantic to burlesque.

(IV, st. 3)

Myths obtain new cultural lives by inverting as they migrate in history. The Don Juan myth in Spain described a phallic Lothario; in his cultural inversion of the Spanish myth Byron invests the hero with the feminine attributes of a passive sentimentalist. To imagine him as such was a wilful misreading of the tradition, a fantasy based on but opposed to the one which gave rise to the original version of the myth. This is why my study of Byron's *Don Juan* operates on the premise that male fantasy can contradict patriarchy as well as agree with it: because myths as they develop can contain their opposites. I use the theoretical concept of applied fantasy, moreover, to describe the phenomenon of fantasies that as they develop become active as social and political realities. In particular, *Don Juan* experiments with issues of gender roles and definitions in relation to narrative closure to open the possibility of imagining new relations between private fantasy and its application in public life.

To invert the Don Juan myth and expose its fantasies, the poem makes expert use of Romantic irony. As structures of feeling and patterns of behaviour, both romantic fantasy and romantic irony have historical roots in adventure. As early as the twelfth century, the appreciation of chaos, the cultivation of chance and a dialectic of self-mastery through simultaneous creation and destruction had been available to some European men as a life of adventurous travel and fortune hunting. The ideology of adventure is a merchant mentality modelled on chivalry. Michael Nerlich describes the semantic change in the word *aventure* effected by the courtly romances of Chretien de Troyes (*c.* 1150–90):

Aventure, which in its literary occurrences before the courtly romance means fate, chance, has become, in the knightly-courtly system of relations, an event that the knight must seek out and endure, although this event does continue to be unpredictable, a surprise of fate. The decisive factor, however, is that the surprising event, the *aventure*, is *sought*, and within the framework of this intentionality it is planned for and hence predicted.[10]

This revision of the meaning of *aventure* is re-enacted in another semantic shift at the end of the eighteenth century, when romantic irony was formulated as an intellectual version of 'knightly-courtly' adventure.

If irony denotes the tension between utterances and their significance to disparate auditors, romantic irony describes a technique of manipulating such tension surprisingly. The most systematic proponent of the term was Friedrich Schlegel, who posed romantic irony as a flexible intellectual response to an unpredictable world. Like the early modern adventurer, the romantic ironist *seeks* surprise, systematically extending his feelings beyond the bounds of any system. Historically, the continuity that underwrites this seeking depends on an assumption about gender. Just as adventure presumed the masculinity of the adventurer, most romantic irony assumes the male perspective. *Don Juan* uniquely employs a combination of romantic irony and the adventurous narrative, while turning both on their heads by examining their gendered presumptions.

Because it conflates the ironic distance it establishes towards itself with the adventure story it tells, male fantasy in *Don Juan* is marketable as a predictable, and therefore pleasurable, sense of surprise. The position of the enunciation, the way the text serves and structures the attention it engages, may at any moment lead the reader out of the fixity of any one point of view into a kind of adventure. Notice that as early modern adventure was an aspect of the development of commercial culture, the skills it promoted were increasingly determined by the profit motive. Don Quixote (an important figure of reference for *Don Juan*) lags behind in the development of ironic self-awareness precisely because he fails to keep pace with the modification of adventure skills into the social and political practices demanded by emergent capitalism. Given the extraordinary claims made for the social impact of *Don Quixote* in *Don Juan*, it is difficult to say whether Byron courted or avoided the effect he claimed for Cervantes.

> Cervantes smiled Spain's Chivalry away;
> A single laugh demolished the right arm
> Of his own country; – seldom since that day

>Has Spain had heroes. While Romance could charm,
> The world gave ground before her bright array;
>   And therefore have his volumes done such harm,
> That all their glory, as a composition,
>Was dearly purchased by his land's perdition.

(XIII, st. 11)

If the skills developed in the service of colonialism – navigation, shipbuilding, cartography and various refinements on intimidation – determined the tacit knowledge acquired by earlier modern adventurers, we might ask what skills the practice of romantic irony depended on or promoted. Schlegel provides an important clue in his Critical Fragment 26: 'Novels are the Socratic dialogues of our time, and this free form has become the refuge of common sense in its flight from pedantry.'[11] The valorization of new, previously sub-literary genres such as the novel parallels an epistemic shift from adventure as adventure to capitalism as adventure. In response to the essential multiplicity of narrative perspective in the emergent literary forms enunciating capitalism as adventure in the early nineteenth century, recent criticism of the novel has frequently focused on issues raised by narrative closure. Closure helps determine which details will count and whose perspective is perceived as most adequate to the totality of sense posited by the fiction. Closure creates the effect referred to by Schlegel as 'common sense', a sense that is common in so far as it knits disparate readers together into a perceived consensus about the data that the work presents. The interrogation of closure in the nineteenth-century novel undertaken by twentieth-century critics stems from their discontent with this commonality. *Don Juan* anticipates this discontent in its disavowal of novelistic closure, suggesting the possibility of genres less supposedly coercive and normalizing.

The logic of closure in nineteenth-century novels tends to underwrite social forms congenial to the stability of bourgeois domesticity and political economy. The best recent criticism thus reads these stories against the grain of their own plots. Contemporary critics show how, from 'subjectivities estranged from the generation of marriage plots and to sexualities exceeding or falling short of the organization of the couple', few nineteenth-century endings can solicit direct identification.[12] But, while such work has persuasively 'opened' great books of the nineteenth century, thus far it has left the greatest 'open' narrative of the period conspicuously closed. This is odd, because *Don Juan* disavows closure for many of the same reasons that contemporary critics do. The apparent predictability of the male fantasies that fill the poem sets off the real subject of its practice: the ironic recuperation of erotic catastrophe. Throughout *Don Juan* the narrator displays concern with 'the threat of a loss that would preclude any capacity to recover from it',[13] being above all obsessed with the problem of retaining the capacity to have meaningful feelings. Unlike the original Don Juan, Byron's Juan does feel things and does fear loss, making the most real threat to Juan the loss of his capacity to feel, because then he would be the old Don Juan, and not a new character. Which is the fantasy, the old Don Juan of unfeeling conquest and urge, or the idea of a Don Juan with feelings? The persistent subtext of this question precludes the possibility of closure in *Don Juan*.

Due to a critical bias dating back to Plato favouring mimesis as the paradigmatic function of serious literature, criticism lacks a comprehensive account of literary fantasy. Only recently have critics begun to acknowledge the role fantasy plays in literature other than that narrowly defined as such – fairy tales and science fiction, for example.[14] *Don Juan* demonstrates, however, that Byron understood fantasy as a constitutive element in all major works of the literary tradition. So only an inclusive critical account of fantasy will allow us to locate *Don Juan* within the range of the Romantic fantastic. While the other canonical Romantic poets mostly chose to write fantasy as fantasy, Byron took up the more challenging task of transforming the role of fantasy within genres perceived as primarily mimetic.

The Oriental tales, for instance, are full of fantastic touches like hidden identity, although they remain set in the natural historical world. The use of fantasy in Byron's tales corresponds to an overall shift in the Romantic period towards narrative verse. Hermann Fischer sees this change as an adjustment to demographic shifts in the reading public and a response to German drama, which combined to expand the range of available heroes to include 'the noble robber, the fascinating rogue, the rebel against the morals of society, ghosts, madmen, and similarly melodramatic fantasy figures'.[15] The unique contrast between the hero and the narrator of *Don Juan*, however, unsettles the structures of feeling that ordinarily accompany the experience of reading an adventure story. Byron does not simply take the sexually immoral figure and turn him into a conventional hero. For Juan is countered by another fantastic rogue – the narrator. The use of fantasy in *Don Juan*, therefore, represents a significant departure from its role in Byron's earlier poetry. No longer serving to heighten the reader's emotional involvement in the story, fantasy in *Don Juan* tends to *disrupt* the continuity of the audience's response. Fantasy in *Don Juan* often occurs as a failure to fulfil the standards of minimal probability set by narrative conventions of mimesis.

Where Romantic works of fantasy such as *Peter Bell*, *The Witch of Atlas*, *Lamia* and *Frankenstein* pose no real threat to the hegemony of novelistic mimesis, *Don Juan* profoundly challenges it. *Don Juan* foregrounds the notion that extraordinary things necessarily happen to a protagonist, regardless of what he wills or does.[16] By revising the crafty Don and his voracious appetite as Juan, whose leading characteristic is not his sexual insatiability but rather his susceptibility to emotion, the poem focuses attention on the structural function of the hero, thereby detracting significantly from our sense of his internal drive towards greatness, his 'heroism'. This innovative and iconoclastic use of fantasy did not pass unremarked: the outcry among his contemporaries against the poem's fluctuations in tone stemmed from their sense that crucial narrative conventions were being violated. They were right – *Don Juan* practises its fantasy as a deliberate failure to follow the rules of sentiment in adventurous narrative.

Fantasy possesses a tacit dimension. The successful fantasist achieves the paradox of having aroused surprise by deliberately telling a story compounded of the real and the imaginary. In the vocabulary of the psychological study of human development, this tacit skill is termed 'creative apperception'. Creative apperception refers to the way that individuality makes room for itself within larger social structures which demand a certain amount of specific compliance. By extending this psychological scheme into literary aesthetics, narrative itself can be seen as a 'transitional object'. This term, which object-relations psychology uses for favourite toys, security blankets and the like, can apply to anything an individual uses to establish psychic equilibrium yet which retains an aura of the fantastic or the unique. The transitional object is by definition neither real nor imaginary. As D.W. Winnicott asserts, 'is it real or imaginary?' is never the right question to ask about a transitional object.[17] The paradox of this undecidability must be accepted as paradox, and cannot be reduced to a representational relation.

In creative apperception one is conscious of one's self as a changing phenomenon with a variable content. Transitional objects train the developing mind to elaborate certain identities according to a logic of multiple determination of such binaries as outer and inner, self and other. This logic of 'both . . . and' is what allows the security blanket to be *both* a piece of fabric *and* a source of love. Through fantasy play with the object, the individual develops an ego flexible enough to recognize itself over the course of drastic changes in social role and situation. Recognition of self is therefore a function of ego-memory, and of ego-memory in relation to an object. This 'romantic' function of memory has been acknowledged at least since John Locke, who 'pointed, now some three centuries ago, to the importance of memory for anchoring a sense of individual continuity over time'.[18]

The protagonists of works of literature are perhaps our most sophisticated transitional objects. Through the play of the literary figure, literary form asserts the tacit dimension of experience which underlies our sense of life and the self as continuous, single and unified. Criticism has traditionally supported literature's role in human creative apperception, finding its justification in the identification of the patterns by which literature aids and encourages human self-fashioning. But if one puts more of the social context of literature back into the picture, creative apperception can be made to look more ominous. Feminist literary historians have found crucial points of convergence between literature and conventionalized behaviour and expectations in the outside world – in the courtship novel and the conduct book tradition.[19] Thus where readers and critics once located in the act of reading what appeared to be experiences of individuation, critics now often see in literature experiences of socialization and even coercion.

Don Juan is one step ahead of this critical game. Political liberalism and popular culture join forces in the poem to distinguish the tacit ethos of the fantasist from that of the nineteenth-century novelist or twentieth-century critic. In her study of Byron's heroines, Caroline Franklin identifies the signal departure of *Don Juan* from norms for the socialization of women in fictional narrative. In her reading, the poem rejects the efficacy of female chastity for securing the rights of property, a popular theme for the eighteenth-century novel:

> Byron himself was already being excoriated by the Tory reviewers as the corrupter of female morals in his poetry, and the epic

poem which he now writes should be seen as his considered attack on – not women themselves – but the notion of reforming society through propagating an ideal of female chastity.[20]

But, to return to the subject with which this introduction opened, *Don Juan's* criticism of society's treatment of women, specifically the commercial, ideological reification of their virginity, is a necessary criticism of precisely those barriers constructed to restrict the circulation of 'indecent' popular literature and literary experience that had been tolerated in the less repressive England of the early eighteenth century. When the rise of modern consumerism in the market for fictions exceeded the apparent bounds implied by existing literary practice, the societies for the suppression of vice were formed to oppose popular culture in the law courts. Byron's *Don Juan* resists that suppression.

The novel was not the only or even the primary source of instruction in self-fashioning available to the early nineteenth-century male, and before attempting an initial consideration of the text of *Don Juan,* we should consider another institution for the structuring of male consciousness: the military. In *The Historical Novel,* Georg Lukács posits the Napoleonic Wars as the material cause for the widespread development of historical consciousness in early nineteenth-century Europe.[21] The experiences of conscription and campaign that followed the advent of Napoleonic imperialism introduced among many European men new ideas about the role of the individual in world history.

Napoleon taught men in the early nineteenth century to imagine that one man could change history. He served as an embodiment of this new mythologized historical consciousness, but the changes in representation accompanying this paradigm shift were manifold. Scott's novels and Byron's poetry both appealed to and stemmed from a new sense of living in history that had roots in military experiences.[22] In the invocation to the reader at the beginning of this late canto, the narrator reflects on the young men of his age by making a comparison to Herodotus' account of the training of Persian soldiers:

> The antique Persians taught three useful things,
>   To draw the bow, to ride, and speak the truth.
> This was the mode of Cyrus, best of kings –
>   A mode adopted since by modern youth.

> Bows have they, generally with two strings;
>   Horses they ride without remorse or ruth;
> At speaking truth perhaps they are less clever,
>   But draw the long bow better now than ever.
>
> (XVI, st. 1)

On the face of it the final line of this stanza is an anachronism. Why would the narrator assert the skill of modern youth at drawing the long bow? The reference capitalizes on a familiar convention, the war between the sexes. Modern youths are less clever at speaking truth because they are duplicitous in love. Later nineteenth-century usage confirms the link, as 'two strings to his bow' was, by the time of Gilbert and Sullivan's *Iolanthe*, an idiomatic way of referring to double-dealing with women.[23]

The next stanza continues the metaphor and takes us further towards the analysis that *Don Juan* will attempt of the modern, militaristic consciousness as it operates in the war between the sexes.

> The cause of this effect, or this defect –
>   'For this effect defective comes by cause', –
> Is what I have not leisure to inspect,
>   But this I must say in my own applause,
> Of all the Muses that I recollect,
>   What e'er may be her follies or her flaws
> In some things, mine's beyond all contradiction
> The most sincere that ever dealt in fiction.
>
> (XVI, st. 2)

This is the Byronic mode of Shakespearean allusion that led G. Wilson Knight to claim that while Shakespeare merely wrote the plays, Byron lived them.[24] 'For this effect defective comes by cause' is from Polonius' speech describing the madness of Hamlet to Gertrude and Claudius in Act II, scene ii, line 103. Polonius is making his case for Hamlet's insanity ('What is't but to be nothing else but mad? ... That he's mad, 'tis true, 'tis true 'tis pity, / Pity 'tis, 'tis true –'). Byron alludes to Polonius' delusion that he is being analytical despite his absolute and tautological diagnosis. The defect of Hamlet's character that is his madness is not an accident, Polonius believes, and it may then be understood by relating it to its origin.

The allusion to Polonius thus undercuts the interpretive confidence the stanza expresses. Polonius' faith in a primitive form of the modern therapeutic paradigm, whereby madness is understood as the symptom of a trauma, must have amused Byron, who was himself somewhat victimized by the nascent science of mental health – and who better a model for the presumptuous analyst than Polonius? What would Hamlet's madness have meant to one who was famous for being 'mad, bad, and dangerous to know'? By laughing at himself through a Shakespearean guise, the narrator asserts self-doubt about the sanity and therapeutic value of his poem while at the same time laughing at self-doubt itself.

Whatever self-ridicule the allusion to Polonius communicates, the couplet compounds it by rhyming 'sincerity in fiction' with 'contradiction'. Sincere fiction may, for this narrator, *be* a contradiction, but one worth living with, even seeking out, because it allows us to recognize social fantasies for what they are. In the first of these stanzas we are asked to imagine modern youth as insincere lovers by an insincere poet. In the second the supposedly inept warriors of the first become the objects of an inept analysis. While the militarized historical consciousness of modern youth makes war on women, society mostly misses the method in this madness.

Sometimes the narrator pursues the paradox of sincerity in fiction by means of Latin allusions. Latin is the narrator's language of choice for expressing his artistic intentions. The allusion in the next stanza is a conflation of two titles from Aquinas, spliced so as to describe precisely the logic of the poem's fantasy:

> And as she treats all things, and ne'er retreats
>   From anything, this epic will contain
> A wilderness of the most rare conceits,
>   Which you might elsewhere hope to find in vain.
> 'Tis true there might be some bitters with the sweets,
>   Yet mixed so slightly that you can't complain
> But wonder why they so few are, since my tale is
> 'De rebus cunctis et quibusdam aliis.'

(XVI, st. 3)

'Of everything there is and a few other things' renders the principle at work throughout *Don Juan*, a principle by which the totality of the poem is conjoined to its ceaseless seriality. The meaning of

Don Juan is at once the fixed truth of what the poem as a whole says, and at the same time the possibility of its continuance and thus the transformation of that whole and its meaning. Because sincerity will no longer save the day, the poem must carry on with *and* without it.

Don Juan acts as its own background, surrounding itself with itself as if it could have no definitive shape or closure that was not also a subject of the poem's sequential commentary on itself.[25] The way the narrator appears to retell the single 'Don Juan' story in ever more elaborate variations suggests a self-critical poetry that can only know its intentions and raise them to consciousness through narrative analysis. This analysis, of course, reveals and enacts a compulsion to repeat, a reluctance to let go of the material and have done with what is at stake in its expression.[26]

Through the tension between Juan, whose continuing adventures result from the credulity of youth towards the truth of desire, and the less credulous narrator, the poem realizes the fundamental duality of narrative as a mode of self-knowledge. Byron's protagonist never arrives at a coincidence of perspective and consciousness with his narrator. Nor does fantasy in *Don Juan* ever achieve the final form of self-knowledge for the hero. It remains the ground and not the form of social identity. In Lacanian terms, the poem 'traverses' the fantasy, and the narrator identifies not with the hero, but with his symptom.[27]

In the poem's last completed canto, the narrator prepares his audience for the arrival of a ghost among the guests at Norman Abbey, and for his own brief appearance at the table with Juan and company. These twin impossibilities enact those aspects of fantasy which the poem so diversely insists on: that fantasy be a paradox accepted as such, and that this paradox be enacted through the telling of a story. One must enact the fantasy of one's specific existence through the skill of narrative representation:

> But of all the truths which she has told, the most
>   True is that which she is about to tell.
> I said it was a story of a ghost –
>   What then? I only know it so befell.
> Have you explored the limits of the coast,
>   Where all the dwellers of the earth must dwell?
> 'Tis time to strike such puny doubts dumb as
> The sceptics who would not believe Columbus.

> Some people would impose now with authority,
>   Turpin's or Monmouth Geoffrey's Chronicle;
> Men whose historical superiority
>   Is always greatest at a miracle
> But Saint Augustine has the greatest priority,
>   Who bids all men believe the impossible,
> *Because 'tis so.* Who nibble, scribble, quibble he
> Quiets at once with '*quia* impossible.'

>   (XVI, st. 4–5)

The narrator, like his readers, is an intellectual witness to his own fantasies, using them to evaluate the conventions of his society. He never seems far from some traumatic experience of the relativity of all values, yet he proceeds 'quia impossible'. Thus we tend to feel the weight of the narrator's experience in a way that we never do Juan's, despite the apparent pathos of Juan's serial perils. These experiments with literary perspective destabilize conventional identities and re-establish the literary as a disruptive category. They diminish the pseudo-objectification of works of art by presenting the literary as a form of attention as well as the endurance of its object.

I therefore believe that literary historians should not be so wary of the literary as to minimize inadvertently its role in the construction of modernity. Rather than relegate the experience of the aesthetic and the literary in the past to the past and its culture, we need to see the literary as instancing tendencies, the full consequences of which cannot be foreseen. *Don Juan* urges us to see that at times other things – religion, love, ambition, history, even politics – become as intense as art always is. In this *Don Juan* resembles historicist criticism, which also strives to establish the extra-aesthetic intensities present in the daily life in which art is embedded; yet the resemblance is so tight that it unfits much of New Historicism for the task of representing this poem. To 'work through' the political unconscious of *Don Juan*, to explain the ideologies and analogies that saturate each episode and digression, would be to do too much work and to ignore the work of the poem. No ideology, myth or ideal can maintain its totalizing force forever. Yet as *Don Juan* strips history of its illusory splendour, the poem revives the idea of grace in a modern form as intimacy, that is, as the situated emotions and desires occurring between imperfect people. This version of the literary claims to represent everyday life, but the *real* everyday, not the romanticized pastoral of Wordsworth. The reality of *Don Juan* is thus mostly in its emotions, paradoxes and contradictions, and not in its absurd situations, which mock history and conventional 'realism' in favour of something harsher and more insightful. The tripartite memory structure of *Don Juan* makes this revision of the literary possible, and is an important development in the history of narrative form. By constantly re-situating the reader, the narrative disrupts the unexamined systems of legitimation that uphold historical fiction and collective memory. For example, the same cantos that question the elements of wish-fulfilment and barbarism in the *Iliad* also offer the historical enigma of the Russian General Suwarrow's bureaucratic cut-throat character, and the equally surprising historical figure of General Boon of Kentucky (VIII, st. 61–7). Thus *Don Juan* illustrates the anxieties of its age through its fantasies and histories, establishing odd perspectives even on icons. *Don Juan* gives Regency England the collective memory it deserves, one rife with contradictions and catastrophes. As Laura Claridge puts it, Byron's stirring up of the collective memory offers 'the liberation of incomplete contemplation to the reader'.[28]

While incomplete contemplation may liberate us in life, in *Don Juan* it tends to result in catastrophe. Any encounter with another person, even in fantasy, endangers the established patterns of our desire. An apposite analogue to the narrative insights of *Don Juan* can be found in Freud's discussion of moral masochism, in which he describes the difficulty presented to analysts by their patients' identification of their parents with supernatural forces of fate and nature. *Don Juan*, one notices, is remarkable as a fantasy more for its consistent inclusion of the law of the father than for the exclusion of the oppressive patriarch. The poem offers an account of the psyche that goes beyond the death of the father to elaborate the lived experience of mutually exclusive gendered fantasies, fantasies variously arrayed in positions ranging from the obliviously coterminous to the expressly and mortally confrontational. *Don Juan* presents gender as historically specific, politically charged and socially constructed, and it addresses itself as much to women as to men.

The concerns that arose about *Don Juan*'s effect on public morality, as well as Byron's own remarks about his sense that a poem so apparently at odds with sentimentality could never be popular with women, point not to an absence of women readers, but rather to Byron's unprecedented awareness of the fact that women would read this poem and would inevitably make of it something differ-ent from men. The great question of Byron's marketable vice was whether or not intellect would have the same effect on women's morals it was presumed to have had on men's. What distinguishes the Haidee episode, for example, is not so much that Juan nearly vanishes into his reflection in Haidee's eyes (although that is what happens), but rather that the narrator slips out of his place in the scheme of gender identities imposed by the coherence of literary conventions. Here, as in so many places in the poem, the pleasure of Byron's verse reveals an effeminate sensibility that threatens the composure of the narrator's manly figure and voice. He concludes the Haidee episode by ceasing to speak of it 'for fear of seeming touch'd myself' – touched by something perhaps more threatening than madness: femininity.

1
Learning to Say Juan

Among the difficulties encountered by modern readers when start-
ing out with *Don Juan* the poem's anglicizing pronunciation of the
Spanish name 'Juan' is the one most apt to arouse mixed feelings.
Depending on where and when one has learned to speak English
(or Spanish), this detail may be perceived as anything from an
unremarkable cultural tic to an embarrassing and potentially in-
flammatory moment of linguistic violation. The pronunciation,
'Joo-en', with the emphasis on the first syllable, is something the
poem dictates. Its rhymes demand that the reader hear and recite
the word this way. As a result modern readers, particularly Ameri-
can ones, must assimilate to the anglicizing habits of pronunciation
prevalent in the Britain of Byron's day.[1] Compounding the diffi-
culty for some readers of learning to say Juan in this way is the
fact that the word in question is not just any word in the poem,
but rather the text's most prominent and essential syntactical marker,
the name of the hero. To understand better what is at stake when
a poet gets the name of his hero 'wrong', it may be useful to con-
sider the broader implications of name calling and miscalling. Before
doing so it will be necessary to introduce the poem in its initial
public appearance. Looking at what kind of event the publication
of this poem was will position us to return to the questions raised
by the poem's anglicizing pronunciation of Juan.

The first two cantos of *Don Juan* appeared together in a single
volume published anonymously in mid-July 1819. Byron's publisher,
John Murray, withheld both their names from the book's title-page,
leaving the text itself to make an enigmatic impression on the reading
public, something it continues to do to this day. Byron carried on
the poem's sporadic composition and serial publication for five years

despite considerable resistance from his friends and from Murray, who found the new poem too spirited for the times in an anxious, counter-revolutionary Britain with which they felt the poet had lost touch. The pirated editions and spurious continuations that followed immediately after the appearance of its first two cantos were the principle means by which the new poem found its audience, at least until Byron switched publishers after the release of Cantos III–V.

The initial volume offered readers a pair of love stories linked by a horrific shipwreck, all written in the eight-line Italian stanza form known as *ottava rima*. Although Byron was already well known for showing the life and mores of the Mediterranean to his British audience, playing on the broad popularity of the Don Juan legend in the entertainment marketplace was a departure from his earlier strategy of appealing primarily to the upper classes. Mixed in with the exotic settings and the familiar legend, the new poem also carried a bracing dose of radical satire and a great deal of sophisticated, teasing literary talk. All this was delivered by an amiable, chatty and digressive persona, the confident *ottava rima*-spouting narrator familiar to Byron's audience from his earlier effort in this verse form, the Venetian tale *Beppo*. In the spring of 1818 *Beppo* had made a strong impression on the poet's public and his publisher, who praised its natural speaking style and enjoyed its relatively gentle social satire. By returning to the *ottava rima* stanza in *Don Juan* Byron to some extent complied with Murray's request for more from him in this vein. He picked up where he had left off in exploring the persona he had developed in *Beppo*, that of a worldly-wise gentleman with a sharp wit and a vast fund of clever stories. Readers who heard in advance about the forthcoming work and who had been pleased with the sense that *Beppo*'s speaker was Lord Byron, were aroused by the news that his new poem would be about Don Juan. Byron would again take up the subject of comparative sexual morality, an irresistible source of controversy for the British reading public in the decades following the French Revolution.

Don Juan's most important character is thus Byron's flamboyant surrogate, the *ottava rima* narrator. While the narrator rarely figures as an active presence within the story, his performance dominates the experience of reading the poem and therefore must remain the first focus of its criticism. Byron's telling of *Don Juan* involves a bewildering range of rhetorical strategies and stylistic devices, strategies and devices that are also on display in the poem's frequent and sometimes prolonged digressions. These reflections and remarks defy easy containment by categorization, but employ at least one constant in their calculations: the familiar Romantic notion of the 'sense of history'. In Canto I the narrator apostrophizes his age and its wonders, chief of which in his account is a general acceleration of change in every aspect of life. While this feeling had roots for Byron in personal experience, his discourse about it corresponds to the advent of a more public 'sense of history' effect common to much of the literature of the era.[2] The rapid succession of heroes, 'new ones' but not 'true ones', invoked in the poem's opening stanzas thus serves two purposes. It is the point of departure for the poet's choice of 'our ancient friend Don Juan' as his protagonist, and the first example of the narrator's sense of recent history as a general acceleration of production.

> I want a hero: an uncommon want,
>> When every year and month sends forth a new one,
> Till, after cloying the gazettes with cant,
>> The age discovers he is not the true one;
> Of such as these I should not care to vaunt,
>> I'll therefore take our ancient friend Don Juan,
> We all have seen him in the pantomime
> Sent to the devil, somewhat ere his time.

> (I, st. 1)[3]

Notice how the poem's first stanza uses rhyme to force the reader to repronounce 'Juan'. 'Juan' appears at the end of the sixth line, the third of three 'b' rhymes, the others of which are 'true one' and 'new one'. The rapid-fire list of disposable heroes that follows in the next three stanzas forms an initial background for similar waves of historical observation that arise at intervals in the first two cantos and throughout the poem. In the process of further establishing the poem's concern with history, the proliferation of names in this opening sequence sets the stage for a more emphatic return to the name of the hero the poet *has* chosen. In this stanza the use of rhyme to dictate pronunciation moves from the sestet to the couplet.

> Brave men were living before Agamemnon
>> And since, exceeding valorous and sage,

A good deal like him too, though quite the same none;
  But then they shone not on the poet's page,
And so have been forgotten: – I condemn none,
  But can't find any in the present age
Fit for my poem (that is, for my new one);
So, as I said, I'll take my friend Don Juan.

(I, st. 5)

In this second instance the rhyme is stronger and more prescriptive. While Byron often closes a stanza with a skewed rhyme, he seldom clutters one with too many of them. In this stanza the attention goes to the sequence 'Agamemnon', 'same none', 'condemn none'. Confirming the pronunciation of 'Juan' implied by stanza 1, the couplet of stanza 5 leaves no doubt that in this poem 'Juan' will remain consistently disyllabic and anglicized. The disyllabic pronunciation has a number of things to recommend it on a practical level. Like many English proper names (e.g. Harold, Byron) it is a trochee. In iambic pentameter trochaic words are often split between feet, which makes them useful as a kind of syntagmatic glue. Trochees help the metrical units of a line cohere and lend to pentameter its characteristic counterpoint, in which the stresses of conventional intonation are more or less frequently in tension with the abstract pattern of the meter. By pronouncing the 'J' as a hard consonant Byron gains a stop and prevents unintentional liaison. This said, I again wish to postpone full consideration of the matter of repronunciation until I have laid out more of the thematic context for the choice.

An abundance of heroes is not the only prodigious aspect of the early nineteenth century that occupies the narrator. Later in the first canto the productive pressure of the age is imaged differently when the parade of 'heroes' shown at the outset is recast as its inventiveness.

Man's a strange animal, and makes strange use
  Of his own nature, and the various arts,
And likes particularly to produce
  Some new experiments to show his parts;
This is the age of oddities let loose,
  Where different talents find their different marts;
You'd best begin with truth, and when you've lost your
Labour, there's a sure market for imposture.

(I, st. 128)

This stanza has many of the typical elements one encounters in the mainstream of the poem's reflective passages. The innuendo in the fourth line, 'to show his parts' is picked up in the fifth and sixth by 'oddities let loose' and then 'different talents', but the real satire takes a target above the belt. In this instance the ironies are those of political economy engaged by the notion of losing one's 'Labour'. By the time the narrator resumes telling the story after this digression, the reader has been saturated with his vision of a prodigiously and perhaps fruitlessly productive world. In *Don Juan*, contemporary life continually speeds up, constantly pressing onwards towards novelty, and often leaving destruction and obsolescence in its wake. Confronted with the vast array of available human 'talents', Byron seeks a place to show his own parts. His poetic labour begins with the truth, then satirizes rather than adopts the marketable alternative of imposture.

The publication of *Don Juan* altered the dynamics of the expanding cultural interface between Great Britain and the wider world that Byron's own earlier poetry had in part created. In writing it Byron made it clear that he meant to compete with Wordsworth, Coleridge and the Poet Laureate Robert Southey for the attention of his audience and the admiration of posterity. In an odd way *Don Juan* is a testament to Byron's foresight – no one else of comparable satirical gifts appears to have understood quite so elementally as Byron did the canonical potential of Wordsworth's poetry. The vehemence of Byron's rejection of Wordsworth and the energy and passion of his competition with him is, if not the greatest, then at least the most backhanded testament to the power of Wordsworth's poetry of the era. In addition to making numerous direct attacks on the provincial attitudes of the group he called 'the Lakers', the poem also hints at the way Byron's quarrel with the emergent poetics of Wordsworthian Romanticism animated and sustained his own revised practice.

> 'Tis sweet to win, no matter how, one's laurels
>   By blood or ink; 'tis sweet to put an end
> To strife; 'tis sometimes sweet to have our quarrels,
>   Particularly with a tiresome friend.
>
> (I, st. 126)

While poetic ambition in *Don Juan* ordinarily returns to its immediate basis in living poetic rivalry, the 'sweetness' of Byron's quarrels with the Lakers stems from deeper sources in the changing social constitution of the literate public and the effect of these changes on notions of poetic decorum and canonical form. On one important level *Don Juan* was undertaken specifically to refute the theory and practice of Wordsworth, and the significance of this refutation has yet to be fully appreciated. No modern reader of the poem can miss the venom of the *ad hominem* attacks that punctuate the narrator's discourse, but the precise nature and significance of Byron's quarrel with what we have come to know as Romanticism has suffered from persistent critical misunderstanding.

The first obstacle to a proper appreciation of what is at stake in Byron's battle with Wordsworth has been Byron's own account of the dispute, which hinges on his defence of the poetry of Alexander Pope against what he perceived as an unfair and unwise conspiracy of denigration among Wordsworth and his followers. Recent scholarship on the problem of literary canon formation sheds important new light on the old problem of the 'Pope controversy'. In his 1993 book, *Cultural Capital*, John Guillory argues for a major revision of literary history in regard to the theory of poetic diction that Wordsworth set forth in his *Preface* to the *Lyrical Ballads*. Reviewing the problems raised by Coleridge in response to Wordsworth's notion of a purified 'rustic' language in the context of a longer, more complex history of the transition from the classical to the vernacular canon than has previously been available, Guillory finds in Wordsworth's supposed disavowal of poetic diction evidence of an anxiety about the very possibility of a distinction between poetry and prose. The point, however, is that the *language* of the novel and the *language* of poetry are, at this moment in literary history, virtually indistinct. It is this indistinction of language that Wordsworth unwittingly confirms in defending the language of prose, at the same time that he condemns the new reading public for neglecting poetry.[4]

By adapting the language, forms and social attitudes of radical popular culture to the central genre of the High Canonical lineage, Byron effectively collapsed the argument of the Preface to *Lyrical Ballads* at its most vulnerable point, the notion that the common language of ordinary people could be effectively 'purified' for any purpose whatsoever, never mind the establishment of a secular national scripture. As a move in the struggle for national poetic supremacy, *Don Juan* was calculated to outclass the crowded and morally intransigent field in at least two ways. It had to be more steeped in the poetic tradition *and* more sensationally popular than anything of which Wordsworth or Southey would be capable.

Byron confronts the Wordsworthian myth of the poetic character with a persona defined by instability and excess, thus endowing his satire with enough of an edge to cut the complacency of contemporary fashions in sensibility (i.e. Wordsworthian Romanticism). The principles that underlie the abundant energy and liberty of *Don Juan* are so deeply embedded in the work and its era, however, that they require careful attention to discover. Byron's ostensible appeal in his attack on the Lake Poets was to earlier norms of poetic achievement, but as is often the case with disputes over the content of the canon, his emphasis on the validity of Augustan values and method was a blind for more subversive, less socially acceptable innovations in poetic form and content. By invoking the precedent of Augustan satire in defence of *Don Juan* Byron managed to set the agenda for much useful future criticism of the poem. Many studies of this aspect of the poem have been made, and all of the more recent ones are to some extent indebted to George Ridenour's *The Style of Don Juan* (1960).[5] Ridenour identifies the central tenet of the Augustan satirical tradition as an overarching concern with and a classically derived feeling for the fit between poetic form and content.

> It would have been next to impossible to have read the Augustans as industriously and piously as Byron did without having absorbed a good deal of their thought on the subject of style. An eighteenth-century poet publishing a work of any magnitude was very likely to supply a preface explaining and justifying his use of a particular verse form and of particular kinds of language.[6]

While there can be no doubting the relevance of Augustan satirical conventions to the style of *Don Juan*, other recent scholarship on the poem and its milieu suggests that this approach may unnecessarily restrict critics from attending to popular contexts in which the poem participated and that contributed to the ferocity of its initial, largely negative, public reception. These approaches call on the history of mass culture to produce a version of *Don Juan* that, however indebted to Augustan poetics, looks more like a radical popular entertainment than a learned tract, while retaining important features of the latter. Byron's intentional fusion of the highest and the lowest cultural forms available confounded the critics and directly opposed the efforts of his contemporaries to contain literary performance within the scope of bourgeois propriety. In her study of the poem in the context of the popularity of the Don Juan legend at the time of its publication, Moyra Haslett makes a strong case against taking the poem as in any way standing above the fray of the popular versions of Don Juan.

> In choosing the Don Juan legend Byron ... adopted a theme which was connected with financial profiteering and indulgence to the market. ... a theme whose notoriety was due to it populist theatrical forms. [This choice] struck many of his previous readers as an unexpected and unwelcome development. ... the majority of his former readers would have disapproved of the choice of Don Juan. The Don Juan of the London stage ... was a figure created for the consumption of the crowd.[7]

The choice of a hero from the pantomime and other 'low' forms was not the only way in which the poem violated the expectations of readers who were used to the romantic style of Byron's earlier poetry. Several passages adopt satirical devices with specific political connotations that cannot be entirely reconciled with the Augustan tradition. First in the suppressed Dedication to the poem, where the narrator parodies the children's rhyme of the 'four and twenty blackbirds baked in a pie', then in the first canto when the poem parodies the ten commandments in six poetical commandments, the tools Byron uses to get at his poetic rivals are those identified with contemporary radical satire. The radical publisher William Hone stood trial three times between 1817 and 1822 for publishing satirical broadsides that used the forms of nursery rhymes and the Catechism of the Church of England to satirize the king and his government – almost exactly the period in which *Don Juan* appeared. Hone successfully served as his own counsel in each of the actions. Byron, whose close friend John Cam Hobhouse was imprisoned for a similar infraction, would have known of Hone's trials and his brilliant strategies of self-defence from accounts in the contemporary press. Hone was first prosecuted for adapting *The Late John Wilkes's Catechism of a Ministerial Member*, an eighteenth-century political satire. Byron made Wilkes one of the characters in what many consider to be his finest short satire, 'A Vision of Judgement'. By applying the method of parodying scripture used by Wilkes, Hone, Percy Shelley and even by earlier poets such as Dryden to

his own satirical targets, the other Romantic poets, Byron conducted
his campaign for the canon in a way that identified him with the
most politically subversive radical element on the contemporary
scene:

> Thou shalt believe in Milton, Dryden, Pope;
>   Thou shalt not set up Wordsworth, Coleridge, Southey;
> Because the first is crazed beyond all hope,
>   The second drunk, the third so quaint and mouthey:

(I, st. 205)

To discuss poetics in this idiom was at least to play at taking the
people's side in the ongoing struggle for political reform in Britain.
Byron's poetical commandments provoked some of the most strenuous
denunciations of his poem and character. The coy use of the phrase
'thou shalt not' as a comic device was particularly associated with
the popular hero Hone and his revision of Wilkes, as most contem-
porary English readers would immediately have recognized.[8] It is
important at this distance in time not only to acknowledge the
radical subtext these devices carried, but also to observe the way
poetic and political concerns overlap and interpenetrate one an-
other. In these poetical commandments Byron's commitment to the
Augustans and the poetic tradition of mock-heroic collapses into
an identity with Hone's commitment to revising and revitalizing
the eighteenth-century tradition of radical satire. They conflate the
parodic legacy of Wilkes to the patriotic legacy of Milton and Dryden.

By integrating the national poetic legacy into the radical idiom
of contemporary politics, *Don Juan* created a volatile situation in
which the internal contradictions of romantic poetic theory, Tory
rhetoric and evangelical education were brought to the surface at
once. Marcus Wood provides a useful analysis of the assumptions
underpinning the rhetoric of the evangelical leader William
Wilberforce, one of the founders of the Society for the Suppression
of Vice. After quoting from one of Wilberforce's addresses to the
Commons, Wood offers the following gloss on his conservative ideol-
ogy. According to Wood, Wilberforce thought that

> ... the only aim of reformers is the destruction of the social
> order and they will do anything to gain this end; the multitude
> are protected by their Church and their constitution, without

which they are helpless; the ruling class do not require religions because they have a code of honour which controls their behaviour, while without the constraints of state-administered religion the multitude would run riot. Adopting these attitudes it was possible to excuse the godless libertinism of the upper classes and to advocate the zealous imposition of morally strict state religion. This position could also be extended to justify the prosecution of any political figure who could be linked with the promulgation of blasphemy, defined in the broadest sense, among the poor.[9]

Whatever his earlier plans may have been, and however his initial fall from grace may have come about, with the publication of *Don Juan* Byron chose to be an incendiary figure. As the most ostentatious single public example of the godless libertinism of the upper classes he became, with the publication of *Don Juan*, the most patently blasphemous popular author yet to attempt the corruption of the morals of, if not the poor, at least the rapidly enlarging non-aristocratic reading public. This truly was an outflanking of the conservative ideology, attacking it on both sides and leaving no room for doubt about his intentions. To understand better what could have led to this aristocratic radicalism, it is necessary to look more closely at the form of *Don Juan* and its sources in Byron's earlier poetry.

Beppo, Byron's first attempt at composing in the *ottava rima* stanza, told the story of a wealthy Venetian woman named Laura who takes a Count for a lover after her husband is presumed lost at sea. When her husband returns after many years he surprises the by now established couple. Laura handles his reappearance very tactfully, and decorum is restored to the household without conflict or recrimination. The story was promoted as a slice of Venetian life and an antidote to the prudishness of the 'moral North'. Perhaps more important to the genesis of *Don Juan* than the moral relativism of *Beppo*, however, is the narrator's habit of acknowledging his involvement with the *ottava rima* stanza form as productive of the poem itself, in both plot and digression. In stanza 63 of *Beppo* the narrator enacts his difficulty in returning to the story once he has begun to digress.

> To turn, – and to return; – the devil take it!
> The story slips forever through my fingers,

Because, just as the stanza likes to make it,
  It needs must be – and so it rather lingers;
This form of verse began, I can't well break it,
  But must keep time and tune like public singers;
But if I once get through my present measure,
I'll take another one when next at leisure.[10]

With almost two centuries of reflexive art intervening, it is important to recover the impact of this passage at the time. However light and clever this stanza may sound, the gesture it makes undermines both moral and authorial authority. With the discovery of the *ottava rima* stanza, Byron had found the necessary formal complement to the radical content he wished to convey. Thus when the narrator claims that the *ottava rima* form affects his content, the wording of the remark suggests something other than an ordinary awareness of the 'verse contract'. The phrase 'as the stanza likes to make it' appears to impute agency to the verse form, adding an affective dimension to the mechanical ones of rhyme and metre and turning the conventional relation between form and content into a kind of intersubjective event.

Despite the disclaimer – 'But if I once get through my present measure, / I'll take another one when next at leisure' – the *ottava rima* stanza became the mature Byron's favourite poetic form. After revolving the lines and rhymes of each new stanza in his mind during the day, the poet would return to his rooms in the evening to copy down the latest batch. By breaking the flow of the narrative every eight lines, the form works equally well to prompt either a digression or a return to the story. Each stanza-break thus marks a potential transition to the other register – from plot to digression, or from digression to plot. The poet thus enjoys the advantage of never being locked into a scene or definitively cut off from the action. In Byron's hand the *ottava rima* stanza functions to decentre both the story and his narrator's commentary, ensuring that neither strand achieves an absolute precedence. While in *Beppo* this practice is said to have created a strain ('The story slips forever through my fingers'), in *Don Juan* the stanza's volatility augments the narrator's foregrounding of his own caprice as the basis for the poem's direction. The essential duality of *Don Juan*, the split between the poem as story and the poem as reflection, is captured in a remark made by a later poet who understood well the advantages of a suitable verse form. In his 'Adagia' Wallace Stevens wrote that:

> There are two arch-types of poets, of whom it is possible to take
> Homer as an illustration of the narrative type and Plato, regard-
> less of the consideration that he did not write in verse, as an
> illustration of the reflective type.[11]

In reading the relation of the narrator to his story and its form it
will be useful to keep in mind this archetypal duality of poetry as
the basis for the poem's two major modes: the narrative and the
reflective/digressive.

The poem's hero is Don Juan imagined first as a young boy. While
the legend of Don Juan provided the context in which the poem
was created and received, the decision to begin with his upbring-
ing departs from previous versions of the story. In Byron's version
Don Juan's mother is a punctilious woman named Donna Inez.
While Juan's father, Don Jose, is alive Inez reproaches him vigor-
ously for his infidelities, which are represented as numerous. The
couple are on the brink of divorce when Don Jose dies of the tertian,
a kind of malarial fever. Now the single mother of an only child,
Donna Inez turns her formidable energies to educating young Juan.
Her old campaigns against Don Jose find a new outlet in the super-
vision of her son's curriculum. The narrator exploits this turn in
the plot to lash out against some old enemies of his own, teasing
the intellectual women of his native country and mocking the ef-
forts of evangelical reformers to bowdlerize the classics. Beginning
with Don Juan's boyhood was a natural way to approach the task
of lampooning the evangelicals and the educational reformers of
the day. Byron's London circle saw in Inez a scandalous flyting of
Lady Byron, but Annabella's own reaction to her supposed por-
trayal as Inez was mild.

Donna Inez and her antagonist Donna Julia are distilled from
Byron's brooding on the ways in which eighteenth-century novel-
ists had tried to make sense of women. Elizabeth Boyd writes of
Byron that 'He studied feminine character as if he were in the lab-
oratory, using books as commentaries rather than as texts.'[12] The
education Juan receives is a synecdoche for all that was oppressive
and hypocritical about the bluestockings and evangelicals Byron
had left behind in England, and the result of that education is the
poet's ironic indictment of a culture that had lauded him early
only to reject him brutally later on. The elaborate restrictions and
censorship that Inez imposes on her son's curriculum thus leave
him predictably unprepared for what happens next.

This plot development hinges on a familiar male fantasy. When Juan turns sixteen, the poem's first erotic heroine makes her appearance. Donna Julia is the twenty-three-year-old wife of a Seville hidalgo, Don Alfonso. The narrator makes much out of the fact that Don Alfonso is fifty. Alfonso is thus closer in age to Juan's mother Inez than to his wife Julia, and Donna Julia is in turn closer in age to young Juan than to her husband Alfonso. The narrator suggests that Inez and Alfonso had once had an affair.

> Some people whisper (but no doubt they lie,
> For malice still imputes some private end)
> That Inez had, ere Don Alfonso's marriage,
> Forgot with him her very prudent carriage.

> (I, st. 66)

In any event, the usually vigilant Inez either misses or turns a blind eye to the attraction that develops between her son and Julia. Two issues focus the opening stages of this affair: speculation about the genesis of the attraction in the broader situation involving Inez and Alfonso, and the introspection and ambivalence of the two principals. Juan and Julia appear isolated, with Julia as the bored young wife home alone and Juan as a sheltered mama's boy with little experience of the world.

The satire thus shifts ground and takes for its new target the ways in which sexual attraction can be denied or repressed. Juan is the sudden victim of an attack of romanticism, taking long walks in the woods and pondering the universe during those moments in which he can distract himself from the image of Julia that keeps interrupting his reveries. Julia adapts to their situation by concluding that the relationship can remain Platonic, precipitating some of the narrator's most outrageous expressions of disbelief. The entire episode is related in a manner that promotes analysis and discussion of the situation from a psychological point of view. The narrator tells us that Inez must have 'had some other motive' for leaving the two so much alone, then backs away from his own suggestion, adding, 'But what that motive was, I sha'n't say here' (1, st. 101). An emotional forcefield too complex and in a way too obvious to be available either to Juan or to Julia is the cause of which the lovers' isolation is the effect. Theirs is not a personal isolation but rather a socially symptomatic loneliness.

The lonely lovers consummate their flirtation in the early evening of the sixth of June. When she is left alone in a remote bower with Juan, Julia's Platonic scruples slip away at the pressure of their first kiss. Neither Juan nor Julia is judged responsible for initiating the sexual phase of the affair. The audience's expectations would have been conditioned by the legend to expect that Don Juan would seduce Julia, yet the whole formula is to a degree upset by the fact that this Don Juan is doing it for the first time. The narrator artfully preserves the indecision, ambivalence and motivated unconsciousness of the physical contact that brings Juan and Julia together as lovers. While Julia considers her obligations to her husband, 'One hand on Juan's carelessly was thrown'.

> Unconsciously she leaned upon the other,
>   Which play'd within the tangles of her hair;
> And to contend with thoughts she could not smother,
>   She seem'd by the distraction of her air.
>
>   . . .
>
> The hand which still held Juan's, by degrees
>   Gently, but palpably confirm'd its grasp,
> As if it said 'detain me, if you please;'
>
>   . . .
>
> I cannot know what Juan thought of this,
>   But what he did, is much what you would do;
> His young lip thank'd it with a grateful kiss,
>   And then, abash'd at its own joy, withdrew
> In deep despair, lest he had done amiss,
>   Love is so very timid when 'tis new:
> She blush'd, and frown'd not, but she strove to speak,
> And held her tongue, her voice was grown so weak.
>
> (I, st. 109–12 passim)

The narrator cuts away from the scene and asks the reader to bear with him in supposing that six months pass in this way for Juan and Julia. Before resuming the story, however, he interrupts the forward flow of the narrative and introduces a set-piece in the Augustan manner, emphasizing the vast and contradictory nature of those things that can be classed under the category of pleasures. In a string of anaphoric verses beginning with the formula ''Tis sweet', the poem establishes the many contradictions that confound any simple account of what can be deemed pleasurable. At first sweetness is found in a gondolier's song and among conventional romantic images of nature – the evening star, creeping nightwinds and even in an ocean-based rainbow (I, st. 122). The sequence then moves into a domestic register, showing faithful dogs, birds and bees, and finally the 'lisp of children, and their earliest words' (I, st. 123). The satiric transformation of the motif begins when the formula twists away from simple assertion to statements of relation. Once the task of naming things that are sweet has been opened to include what is 'sweet to' others, the moral coherence and unity of pleasure is lost.

> Sweet is the vintage, when the showering grapes
>   In Bacchanal profusion reel to earth
> Purple and gushing: sweet are our escapes
>   From civic revelry to rural mirth;
> Sweet to the miser are his glittering heaps,
>   Sweet to the father is his first-born's birth,
> Sweet is revenge – especially to women,
> Pillage to soldiers, prize-money to seamen.
>
> Sweet is a legacy, and passing sweet
>   The unexpected death of some old lady
> Or gentleman of seventy years complete,
>   Who've made 'us youth' wait too – too long already
> For an estate, or cash, or country-seat,

>   (I, st. 124–5)

The comfort zone in this list, first breached with the mention of the miser, vanishes when the homicidal wish of 'us youth' for our legacies intrudes. By interpolating such 'insincere' examples as the legacy the narrator is using the Augustan satirical convention of the diminishing figure to thwart expectations and complicate the tone of his conclusion, in which first love is said to surpass all other pleasures.

> But sweeter still than this, than these, than all,
>   Is first and passionate love – it stands alone,
> Like Adam's recollection of his fall;
>   The tree of knowledge has been pluck'd – all's known –
> And life yields nothing further to recall

Worthy of this ambrosial sin, so shown,
No doubt in fable, as the unforgiven
Fire which Prometheus filch'd for us from heaven.

(I, st. 127)

At the end of this digression the narrator asks the reader to ac-
cept that six months of healthy, romantic, illicit first love have
now passed between Juan and Julia. The poem returns to the fan-
tasy of an older woman and a younger man and finds instead a
nightmare from the perspective of Alfonso. The sequence that fol-
lows builds on a number of familiar tales from the European tradition
as it describes the levee organized by Alfonso around his wife's bed
and his relative lack of success in discovering his wife's lover. Only
after all his allies and his lawyer have left does Don Alfonso find
what confirms his suspicions, an unfamiliar pair of men's shoes
standing empty in his wife's room. Juan escapes with nothing but
his life, running naked into the night after wrestling with Alfonso
for a few tense moments.

This bedroom scene is the canto's most elaborate production, and
as such it reveals some important elements in the overall pattern
of the poem's method. Julia's initial success in warding off her
husband and his posse comes from the facility with which she turns
the tables on him by means of a comic speech of outrage. The
device is familiar from countless precedents in the continental tra-
dition of the *fabliau*, but it gets a special twist in Byron's version
because of the way that his characters speak. Julia embarrasses Alfonso
when he cannot immediately locate the lover he expects to find
with her, but she does so in a voice that associates her too closely
with the tongue-in-cheek tone of the narrator. Her speech runs for
twelve stanzas, is full of the Augustan conceits the reader has come
to expect from the narrator's digressions, and makes few if any
concessions to verisimilitude as dialogue. The manner of the narrator's
digressions reappears in Julia's speech in such a way as to erode
the distinction between story and commentary. An example will
indicate the problem. Complaining bitterly that her virtue has been
questioned, Julia asks:

'Is it for this I have disdain'd to hold
The common privileges of my sex?
That I have chosen a confessor so old

And deaf, that any other it would vex,
And never once he has had cause to scold,
But found my very innocence perplex
So much, he always doubted I was married –
How sorry you will be when I've miscarried!'

(I, st. 147)

Adding to the mischievous oddity of this improbable speech's effect of turning aside Don Alfonso's suspicions is the narrator's own reaction to it, which is highly amorous. It is as though Julia has discovered the one way to the narrator's heart by lying so outrageously to her husband. Provoked by her energetic performance, the narrator shows his desire for her more openly than before.

She ceased, and turn'd upon her pillow; pale
    She lay, her dark eyes flashing through their tears,
Like skies that rain and lighten; as a veil,
    Waved and o'ershading her wan cheek, appears
Her streaming hair; the black curls strive, but fail,
    To hide the glossy shoulder, which uprears
Its snow through all; – her soft lips lie apart,
And louder than her breathing beats her heart.

(I, st. 158)

The intimation here is that the act of deceiving Don Alfonso is not without erotic interest, and it is confirmed just a few stanzas later when Juan and Julia find themselves aroused after Alfonso finally leaves the room. Acknowledging the involvement of the narrator's desire in the poem's production allows the scene to coalesce around an intelligible split between subject and treatment as it takes some of the pressure off Donna Julia, who otherwise would have to bear the entire burden of the narrator's lascivious bent as a mark of her own moral degradation.

If the initial effect of the bedroom sequence is comic, then its after-effects proved disquieting to contemporary critics of the poem. Francis Jeffrey thought the scene in Julia's bedroom 'indelicate but very clever, merely comic and a little coarse'. Others were not so tolerant, and even Jeffrey was taken aback by the shift in the poem's tone that follows Juan's discovery and permits Julia, now safely locked up in a convent, to write Juan a very memorable, entirely

conventional and deliberately quotable love letter at the end of
the canto (Canto I, 192–7).

> The poet chooses to make this shameless and abandoned woman
> address to her young gallant an epistle breathing the very spirit
> of warm, devoted, pure, and unalterable love – thus profaning
> the holiest language of the heart, and indirectly associating it
> with the most hateful and degrading sensualism. Thus our no-
> tions of right and wrong are at once confounded – our confidence
> in virtue shaken to the foundation – and our reliance on truth
> and fidelity at an end for ever. Of this it is that we complain.[13]

In provoking such persistent debate over the character of his erotic
heroine Byron was responding to and extending the influence of
politicized readings of the eighteenth-century literature of sensi-
bility he derived mainly from the women writers of the 1790s. The
contrast between Julia and Inez plays on his audience's familiarity
with the convention of opposing a heroine of sensibility with a
more proud and 'rational' woman. The affair of Julia and Juan shows
his metaphysical system of Romanticism fusing with a complemen-
tary unconscious drive towards masculine self-assertion, while her
'Platonism' finally splits away from any basis in physical inhibi-
tion. For a short time the couple appear to find the recognition
they crave in one another, thus compensating for what they have
been denied by their social positions. As a result of her affair with
Juan, Julia accepts her gender as her destiny, finding her own way
to be a woman despite the repressive circumstances of her marriage
to Don Alfonso. First in her bedroom speech, a miniature auto-
biography and self-justification, and later in her letter, she manages
to tell her own story, even if the manner of her telling betrays the
presence and interest of the poem's narrator. The final word, if there
can be one, on the curious inflection given her account of woman's
life of love by her letter's conspicuous materiality, its 'hue vermil-
ion', is that Julia remains what she has become – an individual in
possession of the means of erotic self-assertion.

This by no means sat well with the British public in 1819. The
public outcry against the poem was sustained and intense. Not only
Jeffrey, but also nearly every reviewer who chose to acknowledge
the poem did so in order to condemn it for its immorality. The
problem lay mostly in the poem's volatility of tone. It seemed at
once imperative and fruitless to piece together the disparate mo-

ments even within these two initial cantos into something resem-
bling a coherent point of view. This observation has been a truism
of Byron criticism, yet recent studies have found the question of
the poem's changing reception productive in new ways. As recently
as 1997 we find Moyra Haslett insisting that the problem has not
been adequately addressed:

> The contrast between contemporary and successive readings of
> the poem has therefore been considerable, while the causes of
> this difference have been overlooked. The vehemence of the con-
> temporary reviewers' attacks on the poem do [*sic*] not greatly
> surprise the modern reader, who explains it as a form of moral
> hegemony and premature 'Victorianism.' However, the program-
> matically suspicious interpretation of Don Juan reveals not a
> different moral perspective, but an entirely different 'hero.' This
> character is a rakish figure, such as that sketched in the inter-
> pretations of the poem's contemporary reviewers, who were
> scandalized by his behaviour, not just that of 'Byron', the author.[14]

Haslett's identification of the importance of the popular context of
the Don Juan legend to the poem's initial impression has made it
possible to hear again some of the lost or forgotten innuendoes
that provoked widespread anger in the early nineteenth-century
audience. Yet the recovery of an audience predisposed to read Don
Juan stories suspiciously goes only part of the way towards accounting
for the enormous differential of impact that the poem has encoun-
tered over the course of its continuing reception. For a better sense
of where the discomfort that caused this original and apparently
disproportionate affect could have come from it will be necessary
to explore sophisticated contemporary attitudes towards the modes
and aims of comedy.

In 1819, the same epochal year that Byron's *Don Juan* first saw
light, the attention of the era's best critic was also focused on the
social force of comedy, wit, and humour. In a series of public lec-
tures given at the famous Crown and Anchor, William Hazlitt offered
his observations on 'the English Comic Writers'. While it is not
clear whether Byron would have known the contents of Hazlitt's
lectures, there can be no doubt that they reflect, if not the most
conventional, then certainly among the most sophisticated ideas
about the nature and function of comic literature in English avail-
able at the time. The lectures may thus prove useful in establishing

the relative conformity or nonconformity of Byron's text to contemporary expectations. While M. Haslett has proven indispensable in tracing the echoes of lost innuendoes in the text of *Don Juan*, W. Hazlitt may help tell us where Byron adheres to and where he departs from recognizable modes of the comic.

Hazlitt's first major principle of the comic is the self-consistency within apparent chaos and absurdity involved in what he calls 'keeping in comic character':

> Keeping in comic character is consistency in absurdity; a determined and laudable attachment to the incongruous and singular. The regularity completes the contradiction; for the number of instances of deviation from the right line, branching out in all directions, shews the inveteracy of the original bias to any extravagance or folly, the natural improbability, as it were, increasing every time with multiplication of chances for a return to common sense, and in the end mounting up to an incredible and unaccountably ridiculous height, when we find our expectations as invariably baffled. The most curious problem of all, is this truth of absurdity to itself. That reason and good sense should be consistent, is not wonderful: but that caprice, and whim, and fantastical prejudice, should be uniform and infallible in their results, is the surprising thing.[15]

It would be hard, outside of Shakespeare and perhaps Sterne, to find a more effective illustration of this principle of comedy than the narrator of *Don Juan*. Yet the events and characters within the story he tells can be seen to violate another of Hazlitt's basic comic principles, and it is here that the problems of perception and interpretation arise. Hazlitt divides the comic into the laughable, the ludicrous and the ridiculous. The events of a farce such as the bedroom scene are the sort of thing that would ordinarily fall into the middle category, the ludicrous, which Hazlitt defines as arising from 'distress with which we cannot sympathize from its absurdity or insignificance'. Don Alfonso's absurd distress is presented as distinctly unsympathetic.

But the absurdity of the scene is tempered by another element, one not entirely compatible with a ludicrous effect. Although, as Hazlitt assures us, 'lying is a species of wit and humour' (thus saving the comic status of Julia's monologue), and 'we laugh at mischief', the important thing about the ludicrous is that 'we laugh at what

we do not believe'.[16] The question of the absurdity and insignifi-
cance of the action in *Don Juan* is never quite closed, precisely
because the narrator keeps his comic character so successfully. A
narrator able to concede even slightly more ground to a rational
consistency would allow the reader to fix the status of the events
that he relates within a moral framework, but in this instance the
consistency in absurdity of the narrative persona effectively blocks
our coming to any definitive conclusion about the status of the
events of the plot. Byron's adherence to one aspect of the comic
tradition leaves his text in an uncertain relation to another of its
principles, for however ludicrous Juan's many situations may be-
come, far too much narrative energy is invested in establishing their
believability for the distance implied in the maxim, 'we laugh at
what we do not believe' to hold. The mischief at which we laugh
in *Don Juan* comes couched in a commentary designed to render it
believable, even understandable, and the romanticism displayed by
Juan and Julia is hard ever to entirely gainsay. This is what really
upset Francis Jeffrey about Julia's letter – not that she was in any
essential way too shameless and abandoned a woman to have such
feelings, but on the contrary, that she was not shameless or absurd
enough to make her having such feelings genuinely ludicrous.

The British reading public had prepared for the publication of
Byron's poem with a combustible mixture of excitement and an-
ticipated disapproval. These mixed feelings testify to the extraordinary
currency of the Don Juan legend in early nineteenth-century England
and to the strength of popular associations of Byron with libertinism
and sexual immorality. One possible source for the uneasy expecta-
tions of the reading public is in the poetic tradition of libertine
verse as practised by Rochester and John Oldham. These aristocrats
and pseudo-aristocrats embraced and augmented their reputations
for sexual licence by composing verses that equated promiscuity
with more conventionally acceptable forms of adventurous behaviour.
The audience that assumed Byron would use *Don Juan* to defend
his sex life would have known poems such as Oldham's 'Satyr Against
Vertue' which deploys a conventional analogy between illicit sex
and imperial discovery.

> In Us [Sin's] a Perfection, who profess
> A studied and elab'rate Wickedness:
> We're the great Royal Society of Vice,
> Whose talents are to make discoveries,

> And advance Sin like other Arts and Sciences:
> 'Tis I, the bold Columbus, only I,
> Who must new Worlds in Vice descry,
> And fix the pillars of unpassable Iniquity.[17]

In *Don Juan* Byron was at once imitating the swaggering aristocratic posture of such forebears and mimicking its reception by the socially conservative bourgeoisie that comprised most of his contemporary audience. For the modern reader learning to say Juan in Byron's way allows a similar double act of assimilation, becoming both a surly libertine with no regard for conventional morality out to conquer new worlds and one of his provincial detractors, obliviously effacing linguistic difference.

The dialogical criticism and theory of Mikhail Bakhtin can help us understand the significance of this pronunciation. The laughter created by the poem is of the kind described by Bakhtin as the affect of comedy in the absence of closure. Using the Hellenistic Mediterranean as his initial historical model, Bakhtin theorized literary laughter as transformative, inter-generic, linguistic self-consciousness arising out of cultural conflict. When cultures laugh in this way, satires and parody displace the 'major' national genres, which rely too heavily on a monoglot consciousness to answer the needs of a more ambiguous cultural situation. When the value terms of a society cease to function reliably, 'laughter' forces 'men to experience beneath these categories [of identity] a different and contradictory reality that is otherwise not captured in them'.[18] *Don Juan* is an example of heteroglossic English laughter at the changes in early nineteenth-century gender boundaries that issued in what is now referred to as Victorianism. During the Regency renegotiation of gender, the maintenance of an integrated and stable sexual identity, especially for a bisexual such as Byron, became a matter of fantasy and humour.

Bakhtin also coined the term 'intonational quotation marks' to help locate this 'laughing', dialogical dimension of narrative consciousness. These hints allow the reader to know when a passage both represents and expresses the consciousness it gives voice to, creating a dialogic image of the language in which it takes shape. Like the Bakhtinian character – defined as 'a complex, internally dialogized image of a whole language' – intonational quotation marks recognize the difference between a self-conscious, laughing narrator and the unreliable figure of conventional interpretation.[19] To read repronunciation exclusively as an act of cultural imperialism, then, is to recognize only one moment in an ongoing process of linguistic interaction, to privilege the description of only one form of linguistic distinction. Understanding the anglicizing pronunciation of 'Juan' in Byron's *Don Juan* involves recognizing the ambiguous role of the pronunciation of names in linguistic imperialism. While the desire to get away from lazy and imperialist habits of anglicization has rendered this repronunciation alien to modern readers, identifying Byron's poetic choice as linguistic imperialism will not fully explain even our distance from it.

In the midst of what would prove to be Byron's final round of negotiations with his original publisher, John Murray, we find him indulging in a punning slur in the salutation of one of his best and most important letters. The letter was written from Pisa and is dated 3 November 1821.

> Dear Moray/ – The two passages cannot be altered without making Lucifer talk like the Bishop of Lincoln – which would not be in the character of the former.[20]

This is an important letter and I will return to it for other reasons, but for now the point is that Byron's increasing frustration with Murray's timidity and attempted censorship of *Cain*, added to the difficulty of pursuing a long-distance partnership by mail in the early nineteenth century, issues in the epithet 'Moray', an apt reminder that the eel-like publisher sometimes had a slippery way with his author's texts. Even (perhaps especially) in such rote conventions as salutations, playing with names qualifies the social acknowledgement implicit in their use. Byron uses the pun 'Moray' to make a point about what he feels is lacking in his relationship with Murray that a proper salutation would tacitly sanction. Such teasing cancels the assumed bond between letter-writer and addressee in order to establish it again on another, more consciously confrontational level.

In this light the repronunciation of 'Juan' takes on another aspect, materializing Byron's knowledge that merely by uttering a name one declares an allegiance, taking a side in what is sometimes an international conflict. The opening stanza of Canto IX remarks upon another particularly politicized repronunciation, demonstrating that Byron was very conscious of the potential there for nationalistic slur.

> OH, Wellington! (or 'Vilainton' – for Fame
>   Sounds the heroic syllables both ways;
> France could not even conquer your great name,
>   But punned it down to this facetious phrase –
> Beating or beaten she will laugh the same) –

(XI, st. 1)

When a proper name circulates in a foreign language it loses some of its integrity. Phonemes are linguistically inconsistent and the proper name, so dependent upon orthography for its identity, suffers more ignobly on foreign tongues than the common word. Even where transliteration is unnecessary, the fate of the travelling proper name is an uncertain one. For colonial subjects and their imperial masters, the abuse of names becomes symbolic; a cultural slur carried on the lips and tongues of entire peoples. Linguistic imperialism can, however, rebound unpredictably. The tendency to read all linguistic imperialism as colonial aggression disregards the necessarily double agency of actual tongues and sounds. Retaining the phonemic integrity of individual languages, be they imperial or indigenous, is as much about cultural nationalism as it is about respecting cultural difference. By getting foreign names right, we contain them in foreign sounds, simultaneously embracing their integrity as parts of another language and resisting their infiltration as potential elements in our own. Thus the slur may not always only express aggression, or the urge to dominate. Linguistic appropriation involves many scenarios, and might be less tendentiously described as repronunciation.

By beginning with an act of symbolic and pragmatic repronunciation *Don Juan* confounds its two main opposing lines of reception in a single aberrant figure. Byron's repronunciation is pragmatic in that a disyllable is more useful to a writer of iambic pentameter than a monosyllable, and symbolic in that it distinguishes this hero from the mythic Don Juan upon whom he is based. While previous critics have paid some attention to this detail, none has credited it as a revolutionary artistic decision, as I plan to do here. Requiring that the reader anglicize 'Juan', whether or not it registered as such when the poem was published, stands today as the poet's most distinctive aesthetic/linguistic innovation. It ties the linguistic identity of the poem's hero to its own discursive identity as rhyming poetry. If Byron's *Don Juan* were written in prose we would be able to choose for ourselves how to pronounce the hero's name. Out of the banality of a middle-class British provincialism Byron fashioned an icon of the pleasure the common reader takes in male fantasy. Learning to say Juan as this poem would have us do is nothing less than an initiation into a poetics as prophetic of postcolonial experience as anything to be found in nineteenth-century culture. The repronunciation of Juan is an incantation of mass culture, the signal that this poem departs from previous poetical systems and intends to evade the impasses of conventional romantic representations of the culturally other. In order to appreciate the consequences of this seemingly trivial poetic detail, we must attend to the process by which the poem prescribes this repronunciation, the reading experience that supports this unnatural name and the epistemology it represents.

As I said earlier, the way the reader learns to say Juan is simple – by hearing the poem's rhymes. While it is tempting to leave off here and submit only practical reasons for the repronunciation of 'Juan' as significant ones, the situation is not as simple as that. Peter Graham offers the pronunciation of Juan as an example of Byron's hostility to British insularity, avoiding the fact that Byron uses that which he ostensibly criticizes throughout this very long poem.[21] While retaining the Spanish pronunciation might have made the versification of the poem more difficult, we must still account for the symbolic content of the appropriation. In the most important literary precedents in English, Shakespeare's *Much Ado About Nothing* and Shadwell's *The Libertine* (1675), the name is rendered as 'Don John'. Perhaps the fact that Shadwell and Shakespeare had done this was reason enough for Byron not to, but if we look closely again at the two initial appearances of the name in Byron's poem I think we can develop a more satisfying and full account of his choice.

The repeated rhyme of 'Juan' with 'new one' has the most authority in the process of teaching us to say Juan, yet note that in neither instance does the phrase refer to the hero. In the first stanza 'new one' describes the bogus heroes of the press. In the fifth it refers to Byron's poem. Although Byron's Don Juan can be distinguished from the mythical one, he is still Don Juan, the legendary figure. This point is necessary to the sharp distinction between the production of heroes described as typical of the age at the beginning of the poem and the 'wanting' of one that the poem itself enacts. 'Wanting' characterizes a form of representation in which the desire of the narrator is taken to be the ground for the 'truth' of the work. In a conventional representational scheme the coherence of the figure, its consistency with itself, is what determines the success of the mimetic effect. In *Don Juan* the coherence not only of the hero but of virtually all the characters (and especially the women) derives not so much from their self-consistency as from their relation to the narrator's discourse of desire. This is a difficult and crucial concept, which I must illustrate with some care.

When the narrator introduces Donna Julia he gives an account first of her genealogy and then of her status as 'married, charming, chaste, and twenty-three.' A few stanzas later he makes the first of several remarks which will serve to characterize the 'wanting' mode of representation:

> Her eye (I'm very fond of handsome eyes)
>   Was large and dark, suppressing half its fire
> Until she spoke, then through its soft disguise
>   Flash'd an expression more of pride than ire,
> And love than either; and there would arise
>   A something in them which was not desire
> But would have been, perhaps, but for the soul
> Which struggled through and chasten'd down the whole.

(I, st. 60)

The parenthetical remark would not in itself constitute evidence of the specific rhetorical strategy and representational method I am interested in describing here were it not echoed in the very next stanza by another structurally identical remark of even more unequivocal meaning.

> Her glossy hair was cluster'd o'er a brow
>   Bright with intelligence, and fair and smooth;
> Her eyebrow's shape was like the aerial bow,
>   Her cheek all purple with the beam of youth,
> Mounting, at times, to a transparent glow,
>   As if her veins ran lightning; she, in sooth,
> Possess'd an air and grace by no means common:
> Her stature tall – I hate a dumpy woman.

(I, st. 61)

The narrator's involvement with his object of description, his desire for her, is not in itself unusual. What is remarkable here is that his description seems poised between that of an observer reporting on a woman he has seen and known and that of a fantasist revelling in the indulgence of his tastes. Her eyes are beautiful and her legs are long not so much because there was once some long-legged, dark-eyed beauty named Donna Julia but because the narrator happens to appreciate those particular traits. Description in Don Juan consistently bears traces of the narrator's desire, suggestions at the level of enunciation that the figure described is a composite one, not some particular woman either fictional or real, but a fantasy pieced together out of memory and myth, art and desire.

This rhetorical strategy of acknowledging what is traditionally suppressed in the interest of realism, the status of the narrative as wish fulfilment, characterizes those fictions that seek a dialogic relation with their audience. Dialogic fiction recognizes and exhibits the difference between the author and the producer of meaning as a subject position which may (in fact must, if the work is to be realized as a social act) be inhabited by a reader. At the level of enunciation the text is rendered as a material process rather than as a static icon or signifier. Enunciation is where such things as pronunciation take place, and one very obvious kind of dialogism occurs when a text prescribes pronunciation through rhyme.

Rhyme provides the reader with a paradigm of pronunciation. Every end word in a line of an *ottava rima* stanza has at least one and more frequently two available paradigms for pronunciation in the other words with which it is rhymed. Even skewed or imperfect rhymes call attention to a common sound quality which may not exist purely in either word but which one imagines nevertheless as somewhere between the two, a compromise formation. This compromise formation takes on a special significance in sight rhymes, where it stands for the tension between the signifier as sound and the signifier as inscription. Imagine a Spanish reader of Byron's *Don Juan*. For an actual, historical 'Juan' the rhyme must either remain a sight rhyme or violate his name. Repronunciation in this instance takes on the aspect of force, wresting from the reading subject control over the phonetic signifier in which he locates his identity.

In his book *Poetry as Discourse* Anthony Easthope offers a useful broad account of the two main modes of rhyming in English verse. The modern tradition inaugurated by Renaissance lyric renders rhyme subordinate to or coincidental with meaning, denying the equality of the signifier and the signified. Characteristic of poetry in the sixteenth century and after, this attitude comes to define the status of rhyme in prose.

> If rhyme occurs in non-poetic discourses, it is treated as an irrel-evant accident, as when someone out for a walk happens to say something like 'Put the dog on the log'. Because it is an effect of the signifier and so always risks showing the precedence of the signifier, rhyme is acknowledged in prose by the care taken to avoid it, precisely to treat it as incidental.[22]

Rhyme, as the prototypical enunciative marker, teaches us to say Juan, prescribing the material process by which inscription becomes sound pattern. In most realism, as in the attitude of non-poetic discourses towards rhyme described above, the markers of the enun-ciation are all turned away from the process of selection that creates meaning. Narrators do not express tastes or opinions in such a way as to subordinate the action to narrative desire. The underlying logic of avoidance is that such expressions threaten the reader's faith in mimesis, that if we know her eyes could just as well have been green, or blue, we won't believe so much any more that they 'were' brown, or any other colour for that matter.

This simple rule of fiction-making – don't call attention to your own preferences – amounts to a kind of 'all quiet on the set', an injunction that allows the illusion of having witnessed what you have read. The plot forms along the syntagmatic chain of discourse, that which carries the hero ahead, the telling of the story. Its ele-ments take on meaning in relation to one another as links in a chain. Like feet in a pentameter line, lines in a stanza, stanzas in a canto, or cantos in a poem, plot is essentially syntagmatic, the result of the way what has preceded and what will follow in it determines the significance of any isolated moment or element. Rhyme on the other hand, which repeats phonic elements accord-ing to an abstract schema, is asyntagmatic in function. Rather than reinforcing the syntagmatic axis, as does metre, rhyme reinforces the paradigmatic axis, calling to mind all the other words or sounds that could have been in the same place without breaking the rhyme. This is also what the foregrounding of narrative choice achieves at the level of the enunciation. By deliberately expressing the thoughts and feelings of the process of selection as part of the enunciation, the narrator opens up the ordinarily heavily syntagmatic axis of enunciation to the paradigmatic. The reader is invited to consider what else might have happened and who else might have appeared if the circumstances of the initial enunciation were different.

Easthope describes the consequences of a poetics that 'exhibits rather than tries to conceal the dependence of the signified on the signifier' in his chapter on the feudal ballad. The method of the ballad 'Three Ravens' is seen as essentially different from that of later discourses. In 'Three Ravens',

> . . . a place for the subject of the enounced is produced but it is exhibited as product of the process of enunciation on which it depends. 'Three Ravens' exemplifies a poetic discourse that offers a relative position for the ego, a position produced in acknowledged relationship to a field of forces, social, subjective, linguistic. The poem is openly presented to the reader in the first place as a poem, as an act of pleasurable speaking. In contrast the discourse founded at the Renaissance aims first of all to represent an individual speaking.[23]

Although Easthope's formulation of poetic discourses as essentially characterized by either relative or transcendental ego positions has helped me to understand Byron's method more fully, this very understanding has necessitated some revision of his historical account of the development of poetry as discourse in English. While it is true that some dominant modes of poetic discourse in the Renaissance and after have sought a stable and absolute ego position through the repression of the play of the signifier, the Romantic revival of the ballad runs directly counter to this mainstream. Easthope's choice of 'Tintern Abbey' as his example of Romanticism in English allows him to prosecute his case against egotistical pentameter in a way that the selection of almost any other poem in *Lyrical Ballads* would render impossible. It is the special interest of *Don Juan* to have brought the techniques of the discourse of relative ego position into the service of the project which Easthope identifies as primary for the absolute one, that is, the representation of 'an individual speaking'.

We begin with a title, *Don Juan*, which we have not yet learned to pronounce. The first stanza initiates the discourse by announcing in the first person the desire for, and lack of, a hero.

> I want a hero: an uncommon want,
>   When every year and month sends forth a new one,
> Till, after cloying the gazettes with cant,
>   The age discovers he is not the true one;

(I, st. 1)

The narrator's dilemma calls to mind all the heroes available – plenty of new ones, but no true ones. The material process of wishing out loud for a hero itself becomes the paradigmatic field that gives rise to the idea of using Don Juan. Dwelling for a moment on the transience of contemporary heroism, the narrative draws the poem's hero from out of the sound of its own desire. We learn to say 'Juan' to rhyme with 'new one' by wanting a hero in *ottava rima*. In blank verse a hero could have been named, but he would not have been materially determined by the phonetic properties of the lines in which he was desired.

Political philosophy, in so far as it recognizes the contingency of values and the possibility of competing systems of value, distinguishes between disagreements over meaning according to the following criteria. Some words or ideas (e.g. liberty, property, Utopia) attain a special status as essentially contested concepts. These ideas are by definition under dispute, and their meanings are understood to be points of confrontation between conflicting systems of value. Any dispute over terminology that results from an initial misapprehension is merely a radically confused debate, rather than a debate over an essentially contested concept. Essentially contested concepts originate in exemplars that are sufficiently internally complex, variously describable and 'open' in character to accommodate valid conflicting interpretations. Don Juan would appear to be such an exemplar and his character the literary or mythological equivalent of an essentially contested concept. In his initial manifestation in Spanish drama the Don registered anxiety about the way the abstract and mobile wealth of capitalism could render the aristocracy even more despotic and less responsible. As his myth grew and solidified into a contested character Don Juan became the locus for all kinds of anxieties about selfishness and responsibility in an age of commodity exchange.

Don Juan is a dialectically conceived sequence of romance transformations, dependent for its effect upon the historical consciousness of its audience. The structural roles of romance – hero, villain, object, donor – are shuffled and recombined by an encompassing narrative consciousness, a persona carrying on aesthetic and ethical quarrels throughout the course of the poem with historical figures living and dead. By crossbreeding the passive, 'mediocre' protagonist of the historical novel with a syndrome, Donjuanism, Byron opened the field of historical narrative to the analysis of ideological fantasy. Because the ideology of the Napoleonic era was romantic, the historicization of romance fantasies became a necessary part of any attempt to question the political convictions of a militarized audience. To penetrate the shell of habitual response separating the soldier male from his own actions and their effects, *Don Juan* alters the romance and thus destabilizes the fantasies that find satisfaction in it.

The necessary psychic attitude of the Christian soldier is one of denial, an attitude that says, 'I know very well (that this is killing, etc.), but all the same (I will do it anyway). Denial could be fairly characterized as the domestic policy of ideology, the internal aspect of a system in which people are required to behave in ways which they must disown emotionally. The detachment of the narrator in *Don Juan*, his aesthetic distance from the often bitter and sometimes grisly incidents he relates, is itself a species of denial, although the really exemplary instances of denial in the poem are those depicted as occurring within the romance formations of the individual episodes. Narrative denial runs counter to that which is evident within the episodes as Byron seeks to expose the inhibitions of his characters while opening his own and his reader's responses to new patterns of understanding.

The initial situation of *Don Juan*, involving Juan, his mother Donna Inez, and the married couple Donna Julia and Don Alfonso, testifies to an utter inhibition within the group about dealing with any of the traumatic aspects of their collective past. Inez, unable to forgive her husband, Don Jose, for his infidelities while he was alive, attempts to cope with the guilt precipitated by his sudden death and her continuing rage against him by seeking to dominate her son. Inez's stilted relationship with the younger Julia, deformed by the legacy of her old affair with Julia's husband Don Alfonso, intensifies when Don Jose's death thrusts Juan more fully into the adult group dynamic.

Julia's romantic interest in the young Juan elicits a response from him that he is not at first able to understand. The subterranean tensions of rivalry between his mother and Julia are invisible to him, and his apparent emotional confusion is still too tied in to Inez's own concerns and vanities for her to intervene.

> Those lonely walks, and lengthening reveries,
>   Could not escape the gentle Julia's eyes;
> She saw that Juan was not at his ease;
>   But that which chiefly may, and must surprise,
> Is, that the Donna Inez did not tease
>   Her only son with question or surmise;
> Whether it was she did not see, or would not,
> Or, like all very clever people, could not.
>
> (I, st. 97)

In the early stages of the romance, Inez is depicted as inhibited in her perceptions. As the infatuation between Juan and Julia intensifies, the narrator brings Inez's motivations more deeply into question and, in place of mere obliviousness, posits an unconscious wish:

> But Inez was so anxious, and so clear
>   Of sight, that I must think, on this occasion,
> She had some other motive much more near
>   For leaving Juan to this new temptation;
> But what that motive was, I sha'n't say here;
>   Perhaps to finish Juan's education,
> Perhaps to open Don Alfonso's eyes,
> In case he thought his wife too great a prize.
>
> (I, st. 101)

While stanza 101 offers a possible motivation for Inez to look the other way as Juan and Julia are drawn together, the analysis given in stanza 97, that clever people are blind to such things, is never entirely superseded. Nearly all such attitudes of denial in the first canto could be described as symptoms, with 'symptom' being defined as a formation whose consistency implies a certain blindness on the part of the subject. The subject can enjoy the symptom only in so far as its logic escapes him or her. A successful self-interpretation would dissolve it. Inez cannot consciously will the liaison between Julia and her son without destroying her enjoyment of Alfonso's cuckolding, so she at once turns a blind eye to them and, in so doing, encourages the affair.

Among the satirical targets of the canto are the symptoms that the lovers develop in lieu of consummation during the first stages of the affair. Juan's youthful romanticism and Julia's erotic Platonism are both systems the logic of which escapes those who employ them. The narrator himself uses the term symptom in describing the repressed resentment Julia may have felt towards Inez over her previous involvement with Alfonso.

> I can't tell whether Julia saw the affair
>   With other people's eyes, or if her own
> Discoveries made, but none could be aware
>   Of this, at least no *symptom* e'er was shown;
> Perhaps she did not know, or did not care,
>   Indifferent from the first, or callous grown:
> I'm really puzzled what to think or say,
> She kept her counsel in so close a way.

> (I, st. 68) (emphasis added)

When Julia's repression breaks down, the form it takes is that of 'confounded fantasy', a synonym for socialized symptoms/systems such as Wordsworth's poetry or Plato's metaphysics. The narrator utters this apostrophe to Plato in response to the fateful sixth of June, when Julia and Juan initiate the sexual phase of their romance.

> Oh Plato! Plato! you have paved the way,
>   With your confounded fantasies, to more
> Immoral conduct by the fancied sway
>   Your system feigns o'er the controlless core
> Of human hearts, than all the long array
>   Of poets and romancers: – You're a bore,
> A charlatan, a coxcomb – and have been,
> At best, no better than a go-between.

> (I, st. 116)

Julia's notion of Platonic love has allowed her to act on her lust for Juan without admitting to herself that that is what she is doing. For Julia this is the day when her Platonic system fails. For the narrator, as is evidenced by this stanza, this 'failure' is the end which such a system has been tending towards all along, and it is the function of 'Platonic love' as symptom to screen Julia's consciousness from that end in order that she may more pleasurably pursue it.

By far the most comic of the symptoms aroused by the repression of sexual attraction is Juan's pubescent romanticism, described in eleven stanzas. This, given the polemical dedication of *Don Juan* to Southey and Wordsworth, was most likely the satirical point around which the entire canto took shape. I quote only two of the stanzas, those that most directly raise the idea of the symptom.

> Young Juan wandered by the glassy brooks
>   Thinking unutterable things; he threw
> Himself at length within the leafy nooks
>   Where the wild branch of the cork forest grew;
> There poets find materials for their books,
>   And every now and then we read them through,
> So that their plan and prosody are eligible,
> Unless, like Wordsworth, they prove unintelligible.
>
> He, Juan (and not Wordsworth), so pursued
>   His self-communion with his own high soul,
> Until his mighty heart, in its great mood,
>   Had mitigated part, though not the whole
> Of its disease; he did the best he could
>   With things not very subject to control,
> And turn'd, without perceiving his condition,
> Like Coleridge, into a metaphysician.
>
>   (I, st. 90–1)

Once again the stress lies on the subject's blindness towards his symptom as the ground of its effectiveness – Juan 'turn'd, without perceiving his condition . . . into a metaphysician'. The rhyme enforces the judgement of Romanticism as pathology.

The narrative carries the logic of the symptom to another level as the story of Julia and Juan becomes complicated. When Don Alfonso stages his levée in his wife's bedroom Julia's speech succeeds in confusing the crowd and embarrassing her husband to such an extent that they leave without finding the hidden Juan. In this instance I would identify Juan himself as a symptom of the double standard, both within the marriage of Julia and Alfonso and as the double standard is employed in Spanish culture. Alfonso's *posse comitatus* is made up of men who, like Alfonso, benefit from the double standard concerning infidelity, including the lawyer, whose mercenary presence is a kind of metonymy for the male point of view. Julia's reproof restores the equilibrium of mutually tolerated deception in such a way as to make Juan, the young man who has come between her and her husband, actually disappear. For the duration of Julia's performance the hidden figure of Juan embodies the gap in their marital communication. Julia's harangue, with all its hilarious and gratuitous detail about opportunities virtuously forsaken, constructs the 'reality' which suffices them for everyday purposes, despite the fact that it does not 'tell the truth'. When Don Alfonso returns alone and the situation of accusation and rebuttal has lapsed, the Real (as opposed to reality as convention) appears in the traumatic form of Juan's shoes, shattering the illusion that is the marriage of Julia and Alfonso. One stanza in particular concerning Juan's mysterious hiding place brings out this new, more evolved use of the logic of the symptom:

> Of his position I can give no notion:
> 'Tis written in the Hebrew Chronicle,
> How the physicians, leaving pill and potion,
> Prescribed, by way of blister, a young belle,
> When old King David's blood grew dull in motion,
> And that the medicine answer'd very well;
> Perhaps was in a different way applied,
> For David lived, but Juan nearly died.

(I, st. 168)

The fascinating thing here is the way in which the comparison of Juan to David twists away from its initial referent and implies Julia instead, and then Alfonso. If we look at the situation from one perspective, it is Julia's blood that has grown dull in motion and Juan who plays the role of the young belle. If we turn to the allusion again and ask instead who in this scenario stands in the relation of king to the others it is old Alfonso who has, in marrying Julia, taken the physic of King David.

That Alfonso ever discovers Juan at all is presented as a matter of chance rather than the product of systematic investigation. It is only after he has given up all hope of proving his point and asked Julia for forgiveness that Alfonso stumbles over Juan's shoes. Hiding a pair of shoes should be easier than concealing an entire young man, and yet the unlikeliness of the whole situation leads one to consider just what Byron was after in presenting the discovery as accidental and prosaic in this way.

> Alfonso closed his speech, and begg'd her pardon,
>   Which Julia half withheld, and then half granted,
> And laid conditions, he thought, very hard on,
>   Denying several little things he wanted:
> He stood like Adam lingering near his garden,
>   With useless penitence perplex'd and haunted,
> Beseeching she no further would refuse,
> When lo! he stumbled over a pair of shoes.
>
> A pair of shoes! – what then? not much, if they
> Are such as fit with lady's feet, but these
> (No one can tell how much I grieve to say)
>   Were masculine; to see them, and to seize,
> Was but a moment's act. – Ah! Well-a-day!
>   My teeth begin to chatter, my veins freeze –
> Alfonso first examined well their fashion,
> And then flew out into another passion.

(I, st. 180–1)

Alfonso stands in a symbolic location Byron was very fond of, just outside the Gates of Eden, when his penitential reverie is broken by the explosive intrusion of the Thing, Juan's shoes, an unbearable materialization of the enjoyment his wife has been experiencing with someone else. Investing a common object with such overwhelming emotional power suggests the way in which reality, the system of conventions and mutually tolerated symptoms which passes for the truth of the everyday world, can be burst by the Real. The Real destroys the illusion of reality by tossing up an irreducible kernel of enjoyment in the form of an object or fetish. Juan's shoes are more horrifying than finding the couple *in flagrante* because they indicate that reality is permeated by such clues to another, possibly disturbing, existence going on just beyond our ability to piece such evidence together.

Having worked through the story of the first canto to a point at which the reality of the everyday has been seen to shatter upon the intrusion of the Real, we may return to and say a little more about the issue with which we began, the repronunciation of 'Juan'. Foregrounding the play of the signifier at the level of enunciation corresponds materially to recognizing the radical contingency of the Real within the narrative. Like Juan's obtrusive shoes, which awaken Alfonso from the reality constructed by his denial, a skewed rhyme or a forced repronunciation undermines the illusion of the transparency of language. If reality as a matter of course is dependent on the smoothness and consistency of the flow of its details, then the repronunciation of Juan works as a shock to the linguistic system, a traumatic moment in the otherwise seamless transfer of mythical 'material' between languages. Relative ego position thus comes to be understood as the repressed condition of absolute ego position, the internal contradiction that continues to exist as, for instance, the 'symptom' of unintentional rhyme in prose. Byron's narrative method of 'wanting' a hero, conjuring Juan out of the sound of the poem's own desire, undercuts the otherwise insuperable demands of convention for that consistency which guarantees 'reality' through denial.

Julia's farewell letter to Juan (I, st. 192–7) turns upon the traditional topos of woman's socially determined dependency. Julia writes from her convent-prison, wishing Juan well on his travels and declaring that, with little else to live for or look forward to, she will cherish all the more her memory of their love. The sentiment of this letter is, as has been previously remarked, somewhat undercut by its materiality – the gilt-edged paper and superfine wax of its seal suggesting a luxury and vanity which, as the vehicle for a message of resignation, hints at hypocrisy. Like the shoes that disclosed a hidden Juan to Don Alfonso, the object here defies the construction of the reality it conveys. Or better, as in the repronunciation of Juan, the material basis of linguistic communication becomes an integral part of its message. Yet the sentiment which Julia expresses is far from unimportant for the development of the poem. Fantasies of lasting romantic love continue to function as allegories of Utopia long after Julia has been abandoned by the poem and by Juan. But the qualification Julia interjects, the fact that opportunities for expression and achievement that are open to men are closed to women, also continues to operate in the poem. This qualification checks any impulse to idealize dependency and prods the narrative to own up to those material conditions that allow male fantasies to become coextensive with reality. The episode of Haidee reveals just such a dialectic and thereby realizes Julia's message in both its romantic and admonitory senses.

2
The Feminization of Male Fantasy: Reimagining Narrative Pleasure in Cantos II and III

All criticism, one may say, is annoying. A wise man should never read criticisms of his own work. It is invariably a painful process; for all blame is obviously unfair, and praise as certainly comes in the wrong place. Moreover, it is a bad habit to be always looking in a glass, and especially in a mirror apt to distort and magnify.

Leslie Stephen, 'Thoughts on Criticism, by a Critic'

Women have served all these centuries as looking glasses possessing the magic and delicious power of reflecting the figure of man at twice its natural size. Without that power probably the earth would still be swamp and jungle. The glories of all our wars would be unknown. We should still be scratching the outlines of deer on the remains of mutton bones and bartering flints for sheepskins or whatever simple ornament took our unsophisticated taste. Supermen and Fingers of Destiny would never have existed. The Czar and the Kaiser would never have worn their crowns or lost them. Whatever may be their use in civilized societies, mirrors are essential to all heroic and violent action.

Virginia Woolf, 'A Room of One's Own'

Masculine overestimation of the self by identification with the feminine is the subject of this chapter. It will describe the process of a fantasy, the stages of a male use of the figure of woman in a fantasy that constitutes one of the central myths of heterosexualization, the myth of woman as nature. In Woolf's scenario women stand for culture and nature, because as mirrors they are an artificial means of recognizing nature, not unrealistic so much as disproportionate in their representations of men. 'A Room of One's Own' indicates the ironic relationship between male fantasy and Progress. In it Virginia Woolf performs a comic dialectic of which this irony is the opening thesis: with masculine ideals so out of proportion that heroism demands violence, men must learn to appreciate the few healthy impulses towards self-ridicule which occasionally arise in an otherwise admittedly barbaric gender. *Don Juan* habitually expresses Utopian longings by means of erotic allegory, partaking in the male fantasy of an originary or absolute object of love as a way of imagining a perfected social order. At the end of *Childe Harold's Pilgrimage* Byron recognized that all such illusions were doomed to be 'the unreach'd Paradise of our despair', but in *Beppo* and then, more decisively, in *Don Juan* he displays the ruin of Utopian illusions as a proper object of laughter, if not a source of comic knowledge. Male fantasy has a well-deserved reputation for bloodshed and pomposity, but when men catch themselves looking in the mirror, as Byron does in *Don Juan*, they sometimes get a glimpse of something more worthy and humane. The peroration of 'A Room of One's Own' encourages women to prepare for the birth of Shakespeare's sister. *Don Juan*, an epic search for the woman evermore about to be, nevertheless repudiates conventional contemporary male Utopias. The urge to hold up sentimentality and self-pity for mockery which is so evident in *Don Juan* protests against the melancholy of straight, sincere fantasy.

As we have wanted a hero so our hero will in turn need women in whom to see himself as a hero. After a harrowing adventure at sea, in which the ship which carries him away from Spain and from Julia is wrecked, Juan washes up on the shore of a fantasy island. Here he becomes involved in what has become the most threadbare of erotic daydreams, 'The Return to the Blue Lagoon'. Near to death, miraculously delivered from the sea, he is reborn under the loving hands of a beautiful and unspoiled native girl. Stated thus baldly the prospects for the Haidee episode seem wretched indeed. Yet *Don Juan* approaches the clichéd material with several satirical points in mind, and makes of its very familiarity a virtue by carefully subverting the expectations that the pleasures it delivers arouse. The Haidee episode contains both the poem's most passionate female character and its most intense lyric of national liberation. Byron's experience of the Mediterranean and his reading of the *Odyssey* can be seen beneath the narrator's conjuring of a woman through whom he can dream of a free Greece, and a plot through which he can criticize his dream. The fantasy is elaborated, its constituent elements fragmented and set against one another, in the mode of narrative analysis to which male fantasies in *Don Juan* are subject. Readers have interpreted Haidee as the most natural of Juan's lovers, unspoiled by society and thus the young man's perfect looking glass. Precisely because Haidee can be natural and feel genuine love for Juan their involvement demands the poem's most sophisticated treatment. Like the term 'nature' itself, their first love is at once the sign of a genuine artlessness and the most artificial of constructs. The Haidee episode is as politicized by this idealization of romance as it is by the nationalist lyric it contains, 'The Isles of Greece'.

Haidee's island is Byron's fullest attempt in *Don Juan* at figuring the myth of a romantic paradise. But as soon as he has begun to do so, he sets about dismantling the reassurance the myth provides and provoking his reader to reconsider why, or if indeed, it is reassuring. The poet's consciousness in this sequence of mediating a collective experience of certain elemental tales (the expulsion from Eden, Odysseus' return) displays an understanding of the reception of literary tradition and its role in shaping social expectations. At the core of the social fantasies engendered by this particular literary archetype lies the character of the beloved. Penelope in particular serves to underwrite a sense of women's responsibility for the sanctity of the home. The contradiction *Don Juan* introduces into Haidee's identification with Penelope by conflating the Scherian and the Ithakan arrivals in the *Odyssey* heightens tensions in the reader's response evoked through a combination of allusion and dialogism. The narrator identifies Haidee by turns with Nausikaa (II, st. 129–30) and with Eve (II, st. 188; IV, st. 10), and indirectly with Penelope (III, st. 22–3) and even Clytemnestra (III, st. 38), confounding narrative expectations based on character and provoking a more complex, less reductive conception of her femininity. Byron's practice of characterization in *Don Juan* can be demonstrated by reading Haidee three ways: first as an icon of the strength men derive from seeing themselves reflected in women; then as an image of the limitations of this illusion; and finally as a metaphor for the poetry of *Don Juan* in its relation to the culture out of which it arose.

In his book on romanticism and imperialism, Nigel Leask theorizes Byron's response to colonialism as a questioning of the moral value of his own poetry in the face of the cultural illness that is colonialism.[1] The Haidee episode approaches the task of moral self-qualification in several ways.

In the 'Isles of Greece' lyric, which is sung at Juan and Haidee's banquet in canto III, the unnamed trimmer poet modulates the desire for a hero expressed at the outset of canto I by the narrator. This poet within the poem yearns for a leader to unite the Greeks and help them regain their freedom. Where the narrator of *Don Juan* wants a hero for an *epic poem*, the 'Isles of Greece' poet at least feigns to desire one for *immediate political purposes*. The contrast is interesting in itself, but more so when one considers how this patriotic song relates to the idyll of Juan and Haidee within which it appears. First, these rousing verses come from someone whose own political commitment is in doubt:

> And where are they? and where art thou,
>   My country? On thy voiceless shore
> The heroic lay is tuneless now –
>   The heroic bosom beats no more!
> And must thy lyre, so long divine,
> Degenerate into hands like mine?
>
> (III, ll. 713–18)

At the beginning of *Don Juan* the narrator wanted a hero to fulfil generic convention. He needed a protagonist in order to write his poem. The poet of the 'Isles of Greece' stanzas appears to want a flesh and blood hero to liberate Lambro's enslaved homeland and redeem his own degenerate verse. He imagines that the voices of the dead of ancient Greece are requesting such a leader:

> What, silent still? and silent all?
>   Ah! no; – the voices of the dead
> Sound like a distant torrent's fall,
>   And answer, 'Let one living head,
> But one arise, – we come, we come!'
> 'Tis but the living who are dumb.
>
> (III, ll. 731–6)

The lyric expresses the Philhellenic sentiments Byron was later to epitomize in his actions at Missolonghi. The tension in the author's life between active and literary responses to colonialism informs the relation between this political lyric and the narrative in which it arises. The extraordinarily complex irony of this lyric's digressive frame presents it simultaneously as an attack on Southey and a Byronic self-parody. It is performed as an entertainment for Juan, Haidee and their guests, who appear to be neither aware of the enslavement nor interested in the liberation of Greece. Lambro is a nationalist, but he has not returned in time to hear 'The Isles of Greece' and would in any event break up the party if he had. The narrator doubts that the cause being sung matters to either the singer or his audience:

> But now being lifted into high society,
>   And having pick'd up several odds and ends
> Of free thoughts in his travels, for variety,
>   He deem'd, being in a lone isle, among friends,
> That without any danger of a riot, he
>   Might for long lying make himself amends;
> And singing as he sung in his warm youth,
> Agree to a short armistice with truth.
>
> He had travell'd 'mongst the Arabs, Turks, and Franks,
>   And knew the self-loves of the different nations;
> And having lived with people of all ranks,
>   Had something ready upon most occasions –
> Which got him a few presents and some thanks.
>   He varied with some skill his adulations;
> To 'do in Rome as Romans do', a piece
> Of conduct was which he observed in Greece.
>
> Thus, usually, when he was ask'd to sing,
>   He gave the different nations something national;
> 'Twas all the same to him – . . .

                                                    (III, st. 83–5)

The poet attempts his song, then, not so much out of a desire to please as from a security in his freedom from censure. 'The Isles of Greece' renders nationalism alien by dislocating it from history and asserting its arbitrariness. Instead of adding social context to this poem within the poem, *Don Juan* subtracts it, depriving the lyric of a reception and rendering it a fantasy, a kernel of abstracted enjoyment. 'Nationalisms – they're all the same, and what does it matter, no one's listening carefully anyway' is the counter-message of narrative context to the lyric insistence on Greek pride. For the poet of the 'Isles of Greece', there is no active audience in the poem.

Fantasy structures the way the 'Isles of Greece' attempts to arouse nationalism by organizing male emotions around a political cause. The poem shapes Greek shame out of masculine anxieties. Here the poem employs an image of Greek womanhood as a motivation to heroism:

> Fill high the bowl with Samian wine!
>   Our virgins dance beneath the shade –
> I see the glorious black eyes shine;
>   But gazing on each glowing maid,
> My own the burning tear-drop laves
>   To think such breasts should suckle slaves.

(III, ll. 773–8)

The series of images clustered here amount to an obsessive formula. The bowl of wine offers Lethean forgetting; the reproachful gaze implies a self-consciousness of dependence; the teary eye and the suckling slave form the central tableau of an imprisoning fantasy of infantile regression.

Byron habitually imaged the dependence of male fantasy upon its feminine objects as an act of nursing. In their initial encounter Juan first becomes Haidee's patient and then, as she feeds him and restores his strength and health, her lover. For the first part of the Haidee episode Juan is involved in a phantasmagoria on the beach compounded of maternal, erotic and cultural idealisms. As Haidee brings him back to life and into the Greek language through her loving attention, Juan moves from the exigencies of survival to the passive dependency of regressive fantasy.

With the exception of the short-lived ministrations of the unfortunate Pedrillo, women educate Juan. As his mother once dictated his curriculum in Spain, so Haidee teaches him to speak Romaic Greek:

> And then fair Haidee tried her tongue at speaking,
>   But not a word could Juan comprehend,
> Although he listen'd so that the young Greek in
>   Her earnestness would ne'er have made an end;
> And, as he interrupted not, went eking
>   Her speech out to her protégé and friend,
> Till pausing at the last her breath to take,
> She saw he did not understand Romaic.
>
> And then she had recourse to nods, and signs,
>   And smiles, and sparkles of the speaking eye,
> And read (the only book she could) the lines
>   Of his fair face, and found, by sympathy,
> The answer eloquent, where the soul shines
>   And darts in one quick glance a long reply;
> And thus in every look she saw exprest
> A world of words, and things at which she guess'd
>
> And now, by dint of fingers and of eyes,
>   And words repeated after her, he took
> A lesson in her tongue; but by surmise,
>   No doubt, less of her language than her look:
> As he who studies fervently the skies
>   Turns oftener to the stars than to his book,
> Thus Juan learn'd his alpha beta better
> From Haidee's glance than any graven letter.
>
>   (II, st. 161–3)

These stanzas conflate three separate, but analogous fantasies of self-fashioning through relationship. The first is the fantasy of a man transfigured by a woman's unqualified adoration – the exploitation of woman as aggrandizing reflection identified by Virginia Woolf. The second fantasy involves the study of ancient Greek, another important looking glass that reflected a flattering image of Western European men in the early nineteenth century. The study of ancient Greek was one of the most exclusive means by which cultured men of Lord Byron's era rendered themselves legible and lovable to one another. If mirrors are necessary for violent and heroic action, then Greece has been perhaps the single greatest cultural looking glass in history. Lastly, this is an eroticized maternal fantasy. In this satirical moment the regressive aspects of the other fantasies show. Even as an exercise in the assertion of cultural identity, learning Greek finds some of its power in the phatic function of language, a childlike pleasure in making sounds.

Locating the initial encounter of Juan and Haidee within an idea of phatic communion reduces considerably the degree to which we may see the story as idealizing the other two aspects of the fantasy. The infant's mental situation is one in which fantasy is all one has. *Don Juan* anticipates object-relations psychology in seeing the fantastic as a mode that not only survives individuation but also persists as behaviour throughout life. Artists and writers cultivate their capacity for irrationality, yet culture cannot always recognize this about itself. Woolf's looking glass analogy identifies the mirror-stage of development with the woman as object as an indication of the persistence of the pre-Oedipal in a civilized world.

In contrast to this period early in the Haidee episode representing pure and natural love, Juan's other affairs seem compromised. The pure quality of the couple's time together before Lambro's return looks like regression – Haidee and her maid Zoë clothing and feeding Juan; his learning to speak Romaic. This scenario of isolated nurture resembles descriptions of the 'holding environment' of early childhood offered by object relations psychiatrist D.W. Winnicott. Due to the absence of Lambro, Juan has yet to enter the adult symbolic order of the island, and thus remains passive and dependent throughout the Haidee story. The location on the beach of this sequence may itself connote childhood, as in Wordsworth's 'Ode: Intimations of Immortality'. Winnicott often quoted a Wordsworthian line from Tagore, 'on the seashore of endless worlds children play', in order to 'aid in speculation upon the question, If play is neither inside, nor outside, where is it?'[2] Byron is likely to have associated learning Greek at Harrow with a childish freedom from constraint, particularly on sexual behaviour. Yet the overall effect of the Haidee story at its most ludicrous is far from dismissive. The tone is laughing, but also elegiac. In the following stanzas the narrator considers the modulations of his manner in *Don Juan*:

> As boy, I thought myself a clever fellow,
>   And wish'd that others held the same opinion;
> They took it up when my days grew more mellow,
>   And other minds acknowledged my dominion:
> Now my sere fancy 'falls into the yellow

> Leaf', and imagination droops her pinion,
> And the sad truth which hovers o'er my desk
> Turns what was once romantic to burlesque.
>
> And if I laugh at any mortal thing,
>   'Tis that I may not weep; and if I weep,
> 'Tis that our nature cannot always bring
>   Itself to apathy, for we must steep
> Our hearts first in the depths of Lethe's spring
>   Ere what we least wish to behold will sleep:
> Thetis baptized her mortal son in Styx;
> A mortal mother would on Lethe fix.

> (IV, st. 3–4)

Achilles' baptism into apparent invulnerability is a male fantasy of omnipotence and immortality. By turning what was romantic into burlesque, and laughing at his own pre-Oedipal impulses, the narrator avoids the self-pity engendered by the evanescence of romantic illusions. These stanzas say that one cannot simply 'get over' childhood fantasies. Other myths are necessary, burlesque myths, such as the one in which a mortal mother dips one in Lethe. It is not enough for the narrator simply to repudiate identification with Achilles, for if Achilles is undone by his heel, the symbol of the internal contradiction of his ambiguous status as half-man, half-god, so much the more is any mortal's enlightened disillusionment vulnerable to taking itself for invulnerable fact. Both the myth of Achilles' heel and *Don Juan's* revision of it involve defensive collaborations with the mother, imaginary symbioses with more than natural significance.

The poem's fascination with the pre-Oedipal as more than natural is especially significant for critics of Romanticism. As inheritors of a post-Enlightenment Freudian bias towards identification with the symbolic order, Romantic critics must make an effort to recover and understand modes of action that evade Oedipal symbolization. Jerome Christensen has attempted this difficult interpretive project in his explication of Byron's performance of Lordship.[3] Christensen points out the difficulty presented to a post-Enlightenment culture by literary works which 'side' with the imaginary:

Despite the ability of Freudian psychoanalysis to comprehend in general the passage from the imaginary to the symbolic, the dis-

cipline takes its place on the side of the symbolic. Psychoanaly-
sis is a partisan of the symbolic for other than ethical reasons; it
coalesced historically as a discipline after the passage *in theory*
to the symbolic (to the truly theoretical) – after, that is, the
discovery and determination of the oedipus complex. Psycho-
analytic grammar cannot command the pre-oedipal any more
than sociology can command aristocratic performance. The per-
sistence of the pre-oedipal in the world of adults (some of them
psychoanalytic critics) correlates with the persistence of a per-
formative aristocracy in an age of gentrification and reminds us
of the inadequacy of the enlightenment to master the differences
it perceives.[4]

For Christensen, Byron's strength is an effect of his symbolic mobil-
ity, the fascination exerted by his interstitial career. A movement
that evades the self-imprisoning categories of enlightenment dis-
course suspends the logic of the symbolic order.

One way to view the evasions of the interstitial Byron is as they
are reflected in his adaptations of contemporary revolutionary ico-
nography. *Childe Harold's Pilgrimage IV* deploys the revolutionary
icon of Roman Charity in a scene of a man and his daughter to-
gether in a prison:

> There is a dungeon, in whose dim, drear light
> What do I gaze on? Nothing: Look again!
> Two forms are slowly shadowed on my sight –
> Two insulated phantoms of the brain:
> It is not so; I see them full and plain –
> An old man, and a female young and fair,
> Fresh as a nursing mother, in whose vein
> The blood is nectar: – but what doth she there,
> With her unmantled neck, and bosom white and bare?

> Full swells the deep pure fountain of young life,
> Where *on* the heart and *from* the heart we took
> Our first and sweetest nurture, when the wife,
> Blest into mother, in the innocent look,
> Or even the piping cry of lips that brook
> No pain and small suspense, a joy perceives
> Man knows not, when from out its cradled nook
> She sees her little bud put forth its leaves –
> What may the fruit be yet? – I know not – Cain was Eve's.

But here youth offers to old age the food,
The milk of his own gift: – it is her sire
To whom she renders back the debt of blood
Born with her birth. No; he shall not expire
While in those warm and lovely veins the fire
Of health and holy feeling can provide
Great Nature's Nile, whose deep stream rises higher
Than Egypt's river: – from that gentle side
Drink, drink and live old man! Heaven's realm holds no
    such tide.

(*Childe Harold IV*, st. 148–50)

Two important pre-feminist articles deal comprehensively with Roman Charity as a cultural icon. Martin Meisel takes an interdisciplinary approach in his chapter on 'Dickens' Roman Daughter' in *Realizations*, while Robert Rosenblum offers an account of the many visual presentations of the subject in 'Caritas Romana after 1760: Some Romantic Lactations'.[5] Meisel does the better job of handling the subject without introducing an anachronistic, post-Freudian embarrassment:

'Roman Charity' was so named with reference to Christian Charity, and implied, in a Renaissance context, a secular, humanistic cognate of the supreme Christian virtue whose ultimate source and example was divine. 'Roman Charity' thus became the material counterpart within the limits of an admired 'natural' ethic and 'natural' feeling of a sacred, transcendental ideal. The image itself was the secular cognate of that sacred image of loving kindness, the Virgin and Child, and a literalization of the allegorical emblems of divine Charity in post-Renaissance iconography.[6]

Roman Charity was a preferred image of the print culture of the French Revolution because in that context it played off a raging public debate over the relative merits of maternal and wet-nursing. In pre-Revolutionary France, particularly among the literary elite, lactation became a political fetish, enjoyed partly as an erotic spectacle, but consciously understood and debated only as a social cause. The playwright Beaumarchais went so far as to turn his *Marriage of Figaro* into a perpetual benefit for the amelioration of working-class childcare. Appalled by the conditions he found among wet-nurses and their charges, he gave the profits from his show to establish the first welfare board for nursing mothers. Like Rousseau, Beaumarchais became obsessed with the purification of French milk, which they both believed must come from the child's natural mother. The aim of their programme of social reform was to free young, urban women from the economic pressures that forced them to send their infants to the overburdened wet-nurses, themselves destitute, in whose care approximately half of the children died.[7]

The debate over maternal nursing inevitably raised questions for the French public which transcended health and impinged on morality. Popular campaigns to eradicate nursing-for-hire depicted wet-nurses as an expedient resorted to by oversexed couples impatient to resume relations uninterrupted by screaming children, even their own. Beaumarchais, like other reformers who adopted the cause, asserted that parental desire, especially paternal desire, should be subordinated to the child's needs during infancy. Thus in France the Oedipal struggle became for a time a matter of public policy, and the holding environment of object-relations, including its 'good-enough mother', was founded in social legislation.

Recent feminist scholarship on the interaction between visual and political argumentation in the Revolutionary period has significantly changed the way we understand the graphic politics of such icons as Roman Charity.[8] In her article 'Incorruptible Milk: Breastfeeding and the French Revolution', Mary Jacobus catalogues 'representations of the Republic as a nursing mother', but cautions readers against literalizing 'the relations of specific historical practices and cultural formations to seemingly transhistorical psychic mechanisms'.[9] For Jacobus, the French fascination with Roman Charity is a place where 'anxieties about controlling women intersect with anxieties about purifying – about revolutionizing – signs themselves.' The wet-nurse 'serves as a fantasized conduit for all that is illegitimate or arbitrary in the social order'. The breast-feeding mother, on the other hand, 'figures the purification of Liberty's signs'. From a psychoanalytic perspective, the breast-as-signifier is the object of a primal hallucination, a fantasy that props itself on the vital order. Jacobus argues that:

> The same hallucination attends any reading of history that treats its discourses and representations as a merely mystified or displaced expression of (for instance) institutionalized wet-nursing or actual hunger – treats them as ultimately referential (as distinct

from material in their effects, as such discourses and representa-
tions on some level certainly were). If psychoanalysis and social
history neither signify nor explain each other, a psychoanalytic
reading of the meaning of breast-feeding during the French Revolu-
tion . . . would be one that draws attention to the persistence of
our wish to take the shortcut from hunger to hallucinating the
breast; or from material conditions and social practices to the
revolutionary allegories and symbolic systems propped on them
at a crucial remove.[10]

Byron criticism has long recognized the conflation in the Haidee
story of two episodes from the *Odyssey*: the Scherian sojourn and
the Ithakan homecoming. In this chapter I propose a second set of
conflated figures, related to Nausikaa and Penelope, but propped
against them at a crucial remove. The narrator's description of Haidee
follows conventions established in both French revolutionary cul-
ture and in the feminist culture of romantic era women writers for
the figure of woman as Liberty. This figure of the rebel daughter,
freed from the constraints of patriarchy, is in the Haidee story
conflated with the figure of the natural, nurturing mother of the
Republic. Beneath this conflation the shadow of Roman Charity
can be discerned, a shadow foreshadowing the contradictions in-
herent in the conflation of rebel daughter and natural mother.

The degree to which the Haidee episode can be correlated to images
from the French Revolution nearly defies systematization. Marie-
Antoinette and her favourites (many of whom were, like Juan in
the later cantos, foreign diplomats) embraced a cult of the natural,
wearing simple white muslin gowns and laurel wreaths rather than
the traditional stiff corsets and powdered wigs. Haidee, the natural
Greek maiden, renowned for her beauty and persecuted for her
unlawful love, would have had an instantly recognizable appeal
for Marie's sentimental and classically minded coterie. In the pub-
lic celebrations and unrest that followed the revolution, this fashion
for the natural was recoded as revolutionary.

Byron came of age during the 'paper war' debate over the French
Revolution in the British press. *Don Juan* is set in the revolutionary
era and revives many of its cultural assumptions. The lot of women
was often associated by the writers of the 1790s with that of other
oppressed groups, and the Revolution was seen as promising eman-
cipation for all. The British writer Helen Maria Williams participated

in French revolutionary festivals and reported back to England on her performance as Liberty in her *Letters from France* (1790). Williams moved easily from a sentimental critique of imperialism in her poem *Peru*, through exploring the sensibility of a woman tempted by illicit love in *Julia: A Novel*, into outspoken support for the Revolution in *Letters from France*. Sensibility extended the domestic role of women into a natural sympathy with the disadvantaged, and the Bluestockings exploited sensibility in their literary careers.

References to nursing (in 'The Isles of Greece') and to maternal situations (Juan cared for by Haidee) establish the breast/transitional object as the core male fantasy of the Haidee episode. From Haidee's point of view the image is a prospective one – she is pregnant at the end of the episode, and she and Juan can for a time expect to become parents themselves. From Lambro's admittedly extreme but nevertheless believable patriarchal perspective, the apparent estrangement of his daughter, her (im)maturity and desire to have a life of her own (ironically at his expense), must represent an end and not a beginning.

It is as this repressed aspect of the idyll that Lambro returns. From the moment the narrator switches from the point of view of the lovers to that of the father, their love, first depicted as fragile, pure and refreshing, takes on menacing and unnatural overtones. The excesses of their life together mount as the narrator repeatedly asserts that the liaison, however innocent in its initial, fantastic context, is an adulterous one in the eyes of society, and will not be tolerated for long. The island-wide *fête* to which Lambro returns celebrates the overthrow of his *ancien régime*. Revolution, like adultery an inherently unstable condition, calls forth new forms of repression, and Lambro's restraint upon encountering the unruly scene recalls that of Odysseus ducking flying footstools and plotting massacre. Lambro is 'the mildest manner'd man / That ever scuttled ship or cut a throat' (III, st. 41), and ordinarily behaves as politely as the most genteel of French aristocrats.[11]

In a lovely parody sequence (III, st. 32–3), a horned *ancien* ram is surrounded by diminutive *sans-culottes* engaging in a dance celebrating immaturity and impotence. Yet Lambro is neither (strictly speaking) cuckolded nor impotent. Repressed, sentimental and at times vicious, his love for his daughter's innocence is the last link between his hardened professional shell and the inevitably mushy interior it maintains:

> There his worn bosom and keen eye would melt
> Over the innocence of that sweet child,
> His only shrine of feelings undefiled.

(III, st. 52)

In the stanzas which follow Lambro is established as a late example of the Byronic hero and an exemplary family man of the pirate class. He is 'a good friend, but bad acquaintance' (III, st. 54). He enjoys the picturesque and bears all the marks of civilization, yet the situation that he confronts threatens the equilibrium that separates his cut-throat business personality from his gentle paternity (III, st. 56). The underlying fantasy paradigm of nursing finally surfaces in a condensed and disruptive version of the image by means of deliberate cliché and mixed metaphor:

> But whatsoe'er he had of love reposed
>   On that beloved daughter; she had been
> The only thing which kept his heart unclosed
>   Amidst the savage deeds he had done and seen;
> A lonely pure affection unopposed:
>   There wanted but the loss of this to wean
> His feelings from all milk of human kindness,
> And turn him like the Cyclops mad with blindness.

(III, st. 57)

The cliché of the milk of human kindness (drawn from Lady Macbeth, that bad mother) inverts the parent–child relationship and signals the return of the repressed in this Oedipal triangle, now understood from the position of the father. The second half of the mixed allusion, to the *Odyssey*, casts Juan again as Odysseus, giving his identification with Lambro yet another turn. Lambro may be driven mad by weaning from his daughter's love and made blind like Polyphemus, but like Lambro, Polyphemus, even before his blinding, was a good friend and a bad acquaintance. Lambro is already something of a monster, albeit a methodical, socialized one. For any type of strong emotion to survive without his acceptance under his patriarchal regime, he will of necessity have to be blinded. Juan and Haidee have violated the space of Lambro's fantasy, not only when he returns to find them together without his permission, but from the outset. The island is Lambro's fantasy – any occupation of it other than according to his dictate risks the destruction that will be the fate of Haidee, or the expulsion and enslavement Lambro visits on Juan. The entire episode illustrates brilliantly the fundamental incompatibility of overlapping individual fantasies. The conflicts that develop, first between Haidee and her father, who share identical yet mutually exclusive claims to their island, and then between Lambro and Juan, who are both objectified in their relations with Haidee, cause all the central characters to miss apprehending each other as human beings.

Nuances introduced by allusion undermine considerably any sympathy one might have been developing for Lambro. Where depicting Juan as Haidee's child is part of a conventional male fantasy, imagining Lambro at her breast, as the weaning metaphor of the stanza quoted above demands, involves a considerably more daring and less comfortable imaginative leap for the reader. The weak allusion to 'Macbeth' in that stanza, caught up as it is with the stronger one of Lambro as Polyphemus, demonstrates the distance Byron had come in just a few short years from his brilliant but lurid and conventional *Childe Harold* style to the more mature and original manner of *Don Juan*. Yet the image of Roman Charity is still there, faintly conditioning Lambro's titanic rage.

Susan Winnett's article in narrative theory, 'Coming Unstrung: Women, Men, Narrative, and Principles of Pleasure', allowed me to see that the image of lactation, however much it may unsettle male expectations, can provide a very effective paradigm for narrative pleasure. After explaining how the model for narrative pleasure obtaining in virtually all modern narratology conforms to the structure of the male orgasm, Winnett offers an alternative which, as we shall see, has significance for these texts of Byron:

> I would like to explore what would happen if, having recognized the Masterplot's reliance on male morphology and male experience, we retained the general narrative pattern of tension and resolution and simply substituted for the male experience an analogously representable female one. . . . I want to explore the different narrative logic – and the very different possibilities of pleasure – that emerge when issues such as incipience, repetition, and closure are reconceived in terms of an experience of the female body.
>
> Female experience does indeed include two highly representable instances of 'tumescence and detumescence', of 'arousal and

significant discharge', whose very issue might suggest why they have been ignored in conceptualizations of narrative dynamics. Both birth and breast feeding manifest dynamic patterns not unlike those described in the various orgastic sequences I cite above. Yet because [birth and breast feeding] do not culminate in a quiescence that can bearably be conceptualized as a simulacrum of death, they neither need nor can confer on themselves the kind of retrospective significance attained by analogy with the pleasure principle. Indeed, as sense-making operations, both are radically *pro*spective, full of the incipience that the male model will see resolved in its images of detumescence and discharge. Their ends (in both senses of the word) are, quite literally, beginning itself.

... Most important for our narratological purposes, however, both childbirth and breast feeding force us to think forward rather than backward; whatever finality birth possesses as a physical experience pales in comparison with the exciting, frightening sense of the beginning of a new life.[12]

While Winnett goes on to apply her fascinating alternative model for narrative pleasure to the text of *Frankenstein*, I will stop here and employ what I can of this paradigm as a guide to the dynamics of *Don Juan*. In particular I would point out the way in which this narrative paradigm is thematized in the Haidee episode as the presence of Haidee's desire running in opposition to her father's. While Haidee, pregnant with Juan's child and preparing for a new era on the island, may be said to understand the situation which has arisen in Lambro's absence *prospectively*, her assumption that Lambro has not returned because he is dead represents an evidently hasty foreclosure. At no time does she make provisions for dealing with his absence in any but the most drastic way possible. In this she is like her father. The triumph of Lambro's equally swift and univocal patriarchal interpretation of events results in the devastation of the island following Juan's expulsion:

> That isle is now all desolate and bare,
>   Its dwellings down, its tenants past away;
> None but her own and her father's grave is there,
>   And nothing outward tells of human clay;
> Ye could not know where lies a thing so fair,
>   No stone is there to show, no tongue to say

What was; no dirge, except the hollow sea's,
Mourns o'er the beauty of the Cyclades.

But many a Greek maid in a loving song
  Sighs o'er her name; and many an islander
With her sire's story makes the night less long;

(IV, st. 72–3)

The legend of what happened on this now eerily deserted island
lives on, *in two gender-specific versions*, as if to confirm our contem-
porary critical sense that what we have been dealing with is the
clash of masculine and feminine modes of narrative pleasure. Juan
manages to survive the masculine-conditioned closure of the epi-
sode but does so only to turn up in his next love affair transformed
by dress into a woman, the 'Juanna' of the harem sequence.

Did Byron understand nursing the way Winnett does, and make
the connection between romantic lactation and the pleasure prin-
ciple of narrative? In his initial experiment with Roman Charity in
Childe Harold's Pilgrimage I would say not. This looks, as do the
many illustrations in Robert Rosenblum's article on the image in
the visual arts of the period, like male fantasy run amok. But one
of the most difficult problems *Don Juan* presents for the critic is
described precisely by the main distinction Winnett claims for the
feminine pleasure principle – it is resolutely prospective in its nar-
rative logic. Very little in the way of retrospective explanation,
whereby the tragedy could be blamed on a single disruption of an
otherwise pure past, can be satisfactorily accomplished because there
is simply too much that theoretically *could* be true about the poem.
At times I have felt that things are with *Don Juan* the way Freud
claimed they are in the unconscious – the poem knows no 'no'. In
the case of Roman Charity I would say that by the time he wrote
Don Juan, Byron was sufficiently attuned to the resonance of this
highly overdetermined, positively garish instance of male fantasy
to understand that fantasy is what he was dealing with in *Childe
Harold*. He merely hints at this element in Lambro's relationship
with Haidee because he is no longer so much interested in the
male and female fantasies or pleasure principles themselves as he
is in what happens when they collide. The Haidee episode, in so
far as it demonstrates an interest in the fantasies that arise out of
lactation and pays sufficient attention to the essential incompatibility

of those fantasies as paradigms or pleasure principles, evinces an implicit or tacit knowledge of the different perspectives possible. I will conclude by demonstrating more closely how I understand *Don Juan* to be both a product of male fantasy as a practice *and* self-identified with a feminine pleasure principle.

In a letter to Richard Belgrave Hoppner dated 29 October 1819, Byron makes one of his most frequently quoted and patently objectionable sexist remarks.[13] It occurs in the course of refuting a story circulating about him – apparently a charge of sexual harassment.

> My dear Hoppner – The Ferrara Story is of a piece with all the rest of the Venetian manufacture – you may judge. – I only changed horses there since I wrote to you after my visit in June last. – 'Convent' – and 'carry off' quotha! – and 'girl' – I should like to know *who* has been carried off – except poor dear *me* – I have been more ravished myself than anybody since the Trojan war – but as to the arrest and its causes – one is as true as the other – and I can account for the invention of neither. – I suppose it is some confusion of the tale of the For[narina] – and of M[adam]e Guiccioli – and half a dozen more – but it is useless to unravel the web – when one has only to brush it away. –[14]

The composition of the Haidee episode took place in one long stretch of writing beginning in mid-September of 1819 and ending on 30 November, which would put this letter in the thick of it.[15] The rhetorical strategy Byron employs to turn the tables on his accusers, in which he portrays himself as having been ravished, may seem rather mean and obvious, even if the accusations are unfounded, but in the context of the poem in progress I think it is nevertheless enlightening. Putting himself in the woman's place, as Sonia Hofkosh has pointed out, must have strained Byron's sense of self-possession, but there is also an element of this identification which would lead one to consider feminine self-identification empowering as well.

The narrator's portrait of Haidee as figure (III, st. 73–6) is marked by both intonational quotation marks and the poem's most fully dialogized and comic vision of character. Its focus is on the 'long auburn waves' of her hair, which are said to reach 'to her heel'. This 'torrent' of hair, which 'the sun / Dyes with his morning light . . . would conceal / Her person if allow'd at large to run.' Haidee's long hair is a metaphorical landscape reminiscent of the luxurious

vegetation of Eden, and Byron's rather prurient idea of her un-
clothed except for it is a sly reference to the fall. The fascination
exerted by the Godiva motif is in its identification of a secondary
sexual characteristic, hair, with a commodity, clothing.[16] Byron
continues with Eden and Eve in mind in the next stanza, where he
suggests that, 'Her overpowering presence made you feel / That it
would not be idolatry to kneel.' Attention to tone helps us see the
interest here, which is of course in the possibility that it *would* be
idolatry to kneel. Haidee is a kind of invitation to transgression in
these stanzas, a promise of something more, and more forbidden,
than sex. The description takes off as a dialogic image in the fol-
lowing stanza, where those 'glossy rebels', Haidee's eyes, are said
to mock their make-up.

> Her eyelashes, though dark as night, were tinged
>   (It is the country's custom), but in vain;
> For those large black eyes were so blackly fringed
>   The glossy rebels mock'd the jetty stain,
> And in their native beauty stood avenged:
>   Her nails were touch'd with henna; but again
> The power of art was turn'd to nothing, for
> They could not look more rosy than before.
>
> The henna should be deeply dyed to make
>   The skin relieved appear more fairly fair;
> She had no need of this, day ne'er will break
>   On mountain tops more heavenly white than her:
> The eye might doubt if it were well awake,
>   She was so like a vision; I might err,
> But Shakespeare also says 'tis very silly
> 'To gild refined gold, or paint the lily.'

> (III, st. 75–6)

A Satanic undersong plays beneath the familiar Spenserian topos
of a beauty that overwhelms its own adornment. The project of
enhancing Haidee's beauty becomes incomplete in principle, as her
adornment is only successful in offsetting her natural qualities by
its inadequacy.

This strange victory is at the core of Byron's conception of his
art in *Don Juan*. Haidee's happiness is commodified and aestheticized,

her consciousness made palpable and appropriated as property. The luxury with which she has been surrounded serves precisely 'to gild refined gold', as she has herself become a form of Mammon to the entranced narrator. The reference to *King John* caps a passage which proclaims Haidee's charms so as both to establish a real image of a beautiful woman and to make it clear that this description is itself motivated, that the appreciation expressed has ends of its own in view.

In his note to the stanza about Haidee's hair, Byron desires that we know Haidee's coiffure is *not* fantasy:

> This is no exaggeration; there were four women whom I remember to have seen, who possessed their hair in this profusion; of these three were English, the other was a Levantine. Their hair was of that length and quantity, that when let down, it almost entirely shaded the person, so as nearly to render dress a superfluity. Of these, only one had dark hair; the Oriental's had, perhaps, the lightest of the four.
>
> (note to line 580, p. 699)

As with the earlier remark about idolatry (III, st. 74), the operative term in this note is 'nearly', as in 'nearly to render dress a superfluity'. Surely the less than subtle hint of conquest serves further to frame the narrator as not without intentions towards his creation. Here is a new dimension of the foregrounding of narrative desire I described in Chapter 1. In these 'Godiva' stanzas Haidee has become an ultimately beguiling and extraordinarily powerful image of *Don Juan's* hedonistic, luxuriantly digressive poetry. In *Don Juan*, poetic form becomes identified with transgressive, sensational and quite often *feminine* experience. The creation of these complex, self-mocking male fantasies, with their recurrent catastrophes and mesmerizing repetitions, is for Byron a way of evading the cant of socialized displacement. His pleasure in excess, the excess of pleasure of the sensational style, is the only way for him to reach a reactionary audience in which the feelings have been sentimentalized and domesticated beyond recuperation. Shelley's remarks on the erotic poetry of the Hellenistic and late Roman periods are a guide to this concept of poetry's social function:

> For the end of social corruption is to destroy all sensibility to pleasure; and, therefore, it is corruption. It begins at the imagin-

ation and the intellect as at the core, and distributes itself thence as a paralysing venom, through the affections into the very appetites, until all become a torpid mass in which sense hardly survives. At the approach of such a period, Poetry ever addresses itself to those faculties which are the last to be destroyed, and its voice is heard, like the footsteps of Astraea, departing from the world.[17]

Of all *Don Juan*'s women characters, Haidee represents the special integrity of the poem itself best because she does not give way on her desire. When the narrator finally breaks off her story for good, after Lambro has destroyed the island and Haidee has gone mad, he can't help but register his authorial identification:

> But let me change this theme, which grows too sad,
>   And lay this sheet of sorrows on the shelf;
> I don't much like describing people mad,
>   For fear of seeming rather touch'd myself –
>
>   (IV, st. 74)

Confronted with the unbearable truth of a social system that destroys its most pure and valuable experiences, the poet bypasses sympathy and compassion, which may too easily be seen as complicit in the circumstances of the oppression which they claim to reject, and identifies directly with the situation of the victim. Here at last is the truth of Haidee's sexual politics, although it takes the form of a deliberate lie. The narrator directs the poem's laughter at the madness inherent in overlapping fantasies, even his own. As in Shelley's preface to *Hellas*, where he says very simply 'we are all Greeks', Byron passes into relation with the fate of women by total identification – turning his hero into a heroine. The most laughter-provoking aspect of Juan's next sexual encounter, with Dudu in the harem, is that in it he appears as Juanna, a woman.

3

The Fantasy of Superfluous Heads: from the Harem to the Hydra

Don Juan as a whole is structured by a complex series of shifts in mode and emphasis. Tracing Juan's progress from his affair with Donna Julia to his sojourn on Haidee's island thus required a complementary transition in my critical method. I could explain what happened in Seville in terms of the rhetorical methods of the narrator and the social dynamics of Juan's family and Julia's marriage. The adventure on Haidee's island needed a 'depth' approach, focusing more on the narrator's apparent psychology and the basis for his imagery in infantile fantasies and wish-fulfilment. The next major transition in *Don Juan* is even more dramatic, and will require another shift in critical emphasis. Cantos III and IV, originally one long canto, take Juan from the middle of his affair with Haidee to the place where Lambro sends him as a result: the slave market. The poem's tone in turn modulates from the passionate, Romantic language of the love story to the lighter, more comic one of adventure. The journey to the slave market is as exotic as it is uncomfortable, and Juan finds himself for a time chained to 'a Romagnole', one of the more comely members of an enslaved opera troupe. While Juan manages to resist this temptation, the narrator succumbs to his own weakness for ambiguous irony. In the face of describing the extraordinary inhumanity of the slave auction he offers the following observation:

> Twelve negresses from Nubia brought a price
>   Which the West Indian market scarce would bring;
> Though Wilberforce, at last, has made it twice

What 'twas ere Abolition; and the thing
Need not seem very wonderful, for vice
  Is always much more splendid than a king:
The virtues, even the most exalted, Charity,
Are saving – vice spares nothing for a rarity.

(IV, st. 115)

Juan is sold to a sultan and taken to a palace somewhere within the Ottoman Empire. He has been procured for the benefit of the Sultan's fourth wife, Gulbeyaz. She hides him from her husband by having him disguised as a woman. Byron stopped working on *Don Juan* for more than a year after putting Juan in this awkward and absurd position. When he resumed the poem in early 1822 his relationship with his publisher John Murray was at the breaking point. Murray was never entirely comfortable with the poem and did whatever he could to rein in Byron's exuberance, both sexual and political. The next eleven cantos were written in a little over a year, an extraordinary feat of composition that coincided with Byron's decision to leave Murray once and for all and publish the rest of *Don Juan* with John Hunt. The consequences of this change were far-reaching, amounting to something like a new beginning for the poem as of Canto VI. Byron wrote a new prose Preface in which he made the political aspects of his work more explicit and announced his intention to depict the horrors of an actual historical war, the siege of Turkish Ismail by the Russians in November and December 1790. While it was possible, as I demonstrated in Chapter 2, to read between the lines of the Haidee episode for evidence of its association with the French Revolution, in the Ismail sequence the poet takes his materials directly from the historical record. Jerome McGann sees the new preface as signalling a crucial shift in the poet's method of handling history.

> Before the Preface to Cantos VI–VIII, Byron had not forced his audience to read the events of Cantos I–VI within a specific historical frame of reference. After the Preface, however, those events are drawn into the poem's newly defined historical scheme.[1]

For my purposes what is important about this transition from publishing the poem with John Murray to publishing it with John Hunt are its effects within the poem on the fantasies and attitudes displayed there. Two obvious points of departure are the harem, which was always a privileged sign in the discourse of Orientalism, and cross-dressing, which is by now perhaps too obvious an indication of 'gender trouble' to bear much more critical attention.[2] Yet there are several other important and thus far neglected points to observe in Cantos VI–VIII.

The poem as it came to be published by Hunt is more concerned with public fantasy than before, and less sympathetic to its consequences. Whereas the private delusions of the earlier episodes were held by and took as their victims isolated individuals, the applied fantasies of the harem and the siege are socially sanctioned and involve the fates of many thousands of people. This is in keeping with Byron's stated intention to make his poem more political and take a more confrontational stance towards European leadership. What McGann recognizes as a concerted effort to enforce the poem's historical framework can also be read as a shift in the balance formerly obtaining between regressive fantasy and compulsive 'factualization'. The type of tongue-in-cheek authentication seen in the footnote to the description of Haidee's hair becomes an explicit principle of composition rather than an entertaining diversion. By taking up the epic task of portraying warfare, Byron abandons the more narcissistic and personal elements of his image-repertoire while still adhering to certain compositional principles derived from his experiences with the earlier cantos. The result is an unusual and innovative approach to the problem of writing effective political poetry. The strategies devised in analysing the tangled motives of individuals over the course of the first five cantos are redeployed in a different register as Byron attempts to take the measure of the European cultural imaginary of his period. The shift revivifies the motto from Horace offered at the outset of the entire work as an epigraph: 'Difficile est proprie communia dicere.' By taking up widespread political concerns and focusing on the problems of the subjects of monarchs, the poet turns from speaking about the things that all of us go through to the things that go through all of us, putting a different emphasis on the word 'communia'.

Thus in Canto VI *Don Juan* begins again aiming at what is most difficult: 'to speak sensibly of the things we all share.' The *sermo* or 'middle' rhetorical mode of Horace was the original basis for one aspect of *Don Juan*'s style because it combines rarely compatible aims: reaching the widest possible audience and reforming their taste and morals. John Hunt, unlike John Murray, had no qualms about printing *Don Juan* in such a way as to allow it to reach the broadest possible audience. The synthesis of the poem's new *sermo* is democratic; its objective is to move the majority on their own terms, and in their own interest. In this chapter I shall examine the vicissitudes of this democratic style as it is employed and thematized through paradox and figuration.

When he offers an account of his own poetic ambition in satire, Horace describes the originality of his style in terms of the pain it would cost one to imitate him:

> I shall aim at a style that employs no unfamiliar diction, one that any writer might hope to achieve, but would sweat tears of blood in his efforts and still not manage it – such is the power of words that are used in the right places and in the right relationships, and such the grace that they can add to the commonplace when so used.[3]

The *sermo*, or plain style, appears democratic but hides an underlying tyranny in which the author reigns over his rivals with an absolutism enforced by the pain of their composition. Like Plato, who fears the effect of poetic imitation upon the guardians in his *Republic* because the impersonation of inferior men may weaken their characters, Horace realizes that his easy style conceals a threatening individuality. The poet pleases everyone until they try to imitate him, then inflicts confusion and suffering on would-be rivals. The hidden sublimity of a style that appears easy and commonplace, that goes unnoticed, is registered in pain. The paradox of the *sermo* is that it is only successful and persuasive when the audience cannot recognize what is unique or individual about it.

In what, then, does the appeal of the *sermo* consist? The plain style succeeds precisely when it persuades the listener to think in terms of him- or herself as a *subject without prejudice*. As in theoretical democracy, the subject of the plain style is conceived as a radically abstract, voided *idea* of an individual. The theoretical man or woman without qualities is the hidden principle at work within the Horatian description of the pains of rivalry. The pain of imitating Horace is the difficulty of knowing oneself well enough to shed all particularity in the service of an argument. To achieve a perfectly plain style it is necessary not only to know one's audience but also to know oneself to an extent where all particular qualities of the individual may be suspended in the service of an abstract reasonableness. Nowhere is the demand of the *sermo* as high as it is in situations where the abstract individuality being represented is abstract with reference to gender.

In the last chapter we saw how the narrator of *Don Juan*, in his satirical masculinity, implied an identification of the poem itself with a feminine pleasure principle. The difficult balance achieved between male and female perspectives is further heightened and challenged in the poem's next sequence. The most explicitly fantastic and stereotypically 'racy' sequence in *Don Juan* concerns Juan's adventures in a harem. Sold as a slave to the Sultan, Juan is coveted as a lover by Gulbeyaz, the Sultan's fourth wife, who disguises him as a woman, 'Juanna'. A formidable woman in every way, Gulbeyaz nevertheless finds it difficult to reach an understanding with Juan. His erotic adventures only begin when he escapes her attentions and enters the harem proper, where he meets a harem girl named Dudù.

Reading the Haidee episode has provided us with a set of approaches to divining the concerns of the harem sequence by focusing on the dialogic character of its erotic heroine, Dudù. In an appendix to *Don Juan in Conflict* on the middle style McGann points out Dudù's importance with respect to the *sermo*:

> This passage (VI, st. 52–5) is particularly interesting because Byron is using Dudù as a *figura* of the middle style, as we see not only in the various epithets he applies to her, but in his very conception of her as a sort of landscape, and a creature almost created for descriptive treatment. Byron is even more explicit when he contrasts her to the 'mighty passions' of 'the sublime.' In this contrast, however, the alternative 'style' which Dudù represents is not the realism of reportorial factiveness or satire (the provinces of the low style, invoked elsewhere), but the 'Luxuriant' and 'cheerful' qualities of the middle style.... Dudù is a present epitome of the Age of Gold, and consequently, in Byron's poem, if she comes to us in the aspect of the middle style, she stands for certain values which are, at certain times and in several important ways, prized more highly by Byron than heroic values and 'mighty passions.'[4]

McGann projects Dudù's value onto her blankness; as neither sublime nor realist, she provides an opportunity for the demonstration of Byron's most highly prized values – those that can be brought out only by something awaiting description – the heroic values of art. This reading suggests that Dudù is for Juan what Haidee failed to be – a *figura* of art rather than of nature. But the relationship between Dudù and Juan proves, as will his role throughout the harem sequence, rather less fixed.

In the harem episode we encounter both male fantasy in its most anonymous and pervasive form and gender identity at its most fluid. Juan's cross-dressing provides a model for a sexual attractiveness that transcends gender boundaries. A sexual *sermo*, Juan is all things to all men and women. For Gulbeyaz, the Sultan's fourth wife, he is a man, for Dudù, the harem girl, he is a dream of a man in the guise of a woman, and for the Sultan (V, st. 155) he is a woman. The episode is structured so that Byron can continuously have it not just both but all ways. This assertion of the polysexuality of the male body, its availability outside the conventions of hetero-sexuality, links Byron with such twentieth-century writers as Roland Barthes.[5] In Seminar XX Jacques Lacan explores *jouissance* as the excess of sexual identity, and examines the implications of this, which, while wide-ranging, centre on the problems raised by a culture that asserts the indivisibility and uniformity of male sexual identity. While considering the harem sequence in *Don Juan* one does well to keep in mind both that Freud's central insight, that sexual difference is a symbolic construct, is as easy to state as it is hard to adhere to in an analysis, and that what is at stake within our intellectual tradition whenever this sense of symbolic construction is lost is any sense of an unsubordinated femininity. In Seminar XX Lacan says that:

> The act of love is the polymorphous perversion of the male, in the case of the speaking being. There is nothing more emphatic, more coherent or more strict as far as Freud is concerned.[6]

When we ask why the women in the harem covet Juanna, the answer seems to be both because none of them knows he is a man and because they all must sense it. The narrator adopts the self-con-sciously prurient pose of not himself knowing exactly what is going on in order to undermine all attempts to get at the truth of any-one's perceptions within the tale. This narrative withholding is another destabilizing tactic in the poem's repertoire of moves de-signed to undermine authorial and moral authority.

And yet they had their little jealousies
  Like all the rest; but upon this occasion,
Whether there are such things as sympathies
  Without our knowledge or our approbation,
Although they could not see through his disguise,
  All felt a soft kind of concatenation,
Like magnetism, or Devilism, or what
You please – we will not quarrel about that:

But certain 'tis they all felt for their new
  Companion something newer still, as 'twere
A sentimental friendship through and through,
  Extremely pure, which made them all concur
In wishing her their sister, save a few
  Who wished they had a brother, just like her,
Whom, if they were at home in sweet Circassia,
They would prefer to Padisha or Pacha.

(VI, st. 38–9)

Everywhere Juan goes he undoes the master–slave relationship.
For Julia and Haidee, for Gulbeyaz and for Dudù, Juan represents
freedom from an immediate restraint imposed by a man. The women,
however, represent different things for him and for the narrator. In
comparison to the pure and angelic Haidee and Dudù, the two
wives, Julia and Gulbeyaz, are less purely sympathetic and more
complex psychologically. Each displaces a pre-existing relationship
of dominance and submission into a new and tenuous role-reversal
transference with Juan. Gulbeyaz fails to gain Juan's love because
of the bluntness with which she proposes the situation Julia en-
joyed. She is a kind of fallen Julia, encountered by Juan after the
possibility of Platonic extenuation has elapsed.

Dudù and Haidee, by contrast, gain much of their sexual inter-
est, at least for the narrator, from the abstractions out of which
they arise – nature and art. Their constraints are in some ways less
specific and at first less ominous – neither of these women is married.
Rather than transferring already developed power relations into a
new subjugation of Juan, these women embody idealizations, no-
tions of possibility rather than notions of determinism. Haidee
maintained a perpetual state of possibility because she kept shift-
ing identities from rebel daughter to nurturing mother, never settling

into a single role. Dudù's attraction appears at first to be less inter-
active and more essential:

> She was not violently lively, but
>   Stole on your spirit like a May-day breaking;
> Her eyes were not too sparkling, yet, half-shut,
>   They put beholders in a tender taking;
> She looked (this simile's quite new) just cut
>   From marble, like Pygmalion's statue waking,
> The Mortal and the Marble still at strife
> And timidly expanding into life.
>
> (VI, st. 43)

The description which follows employs topoi of inexpressibility,
the rhetoric of the sublime, and finally the oxymoron 'silent thun-
der' to develop a conception of Dudù that challenges art on its
own rhetorical grounds with what is understood as the body itself,
as in the stanza above, in which the Mortal and the Marble are
said to be at strife. Belief in the superiority of the body to any of
its representations, its uncanniness in relation to art, becomes the
means by which the poem confronts its own artificiality in imagin-
ing women. A vignette told by the narrator but clearly meant to be
understood as Byron's own adventure from his Venetian period makes
this principle clear:

> And yet last night, being at a masquerade,
> I saw the prettiest creature, fresh from Milan,
> Which gave me some sensations like a villain.
>
> But soon Philosophy came to my aid,
>   And whisper'd 'think of every sacred tie!'
> 'I will, my dear Philosophy!' I said,
>   'But then her teeth, and then, Oh heaven! her eye!
> I'll just inquire if she be wife or maid,
>   Or neither – out of curiosity.'
> 'Stop!' cried Philosophy, with air so Grecian,
> (Though she was masked as a fair Venetian.)
>
> 'Stop!' so I stopped. – but to return: that which
>   Men call inconstancy is nothing more

> Than admiration due where nature's rich
>   Profusion with young beauty covers o'er
> Some favour'd object; and as in a niche
>   A lovely statue we almost adore,
> This sort of adoration of the real
> Is but a heightening of the 'beau ideal.'

(II, st. 209–11)

The claims of Philosophy are teasingly reduced to the charms of yet another masked reveller, while the fair young woman from Milan takes her place in the pantheon of the 'beau ideal'. Byron implies that abstractions are more like missed opportunities or envious counterclaims against experience than true generalizations upon which judgement can rely. The satirical personification of Philosophy prepares for and counterbalances the elevation of the carnal to the aesthetic. The entire sequence presupposes an audience with inhibitions in proportion to their pretensions, and treats them accordingly.

In order to reduce the claims of the rhetoric of the sublime, for instance, Dudù is opposed to the kind of pleasure-in-fear inspired by less passive bodies:

> Dudù, as has been said, was a sweet creature,
>   Not very dashing, but extremely winning,
> With the most regulated charms of feature,
>   Which painters cannot catch like faces sinning
> Against proportion – the wild strokes of nature
>   Which they hit off at once in the beginning,
> Full of expression, right or wrong, that strike,
> And pleasing or unpleasing, still are like.
>
> But she was a soft Landscape of mild Earth,
>   Where all was harmony and calm and quiet,
> Luxuriant, budding; cheerful without mirth,
>   Which if not happiness, is much more nigh it
> Than are your mighty passions and so forth,
>   Which some call 'the sublime:' I wish they'd try it:
> I've seen your stormy seas and stormy women,
> And pity lovers rather more than seamen.

(VI, st. 52–3)

Faces which sin against proportion, the expressive hand of the artist, and the sublime are all opposed to the beautiful landscape of Dudù, a marvel of curves and balance, an object that outdoes art in its ideality and calm. Dudù's regulated features are an echo of her personality and her approach to the complicated business of winning Juanna away from the competing women of the harem. Her power comes from her ability to keep a secret, to remain silent about her desire:

> 'You, Lolah, must continue still to lie
>   Alone, for reasons which don't matter; you
> The same, Katinka, until bye and bye;
>   And I shall place Juanna with Dudù,
> Who's quiet, inoffensive, silent, shy,
>   And will not toss and chatter the night through.
> What say you, child?' Dudù said nothing, as
> Her talents were of the more silent class;

(VI, st. 49)

Like her appearance, Dudù's social presence is defined by negation. She achieves what others attempt directly (Lolah, Katinka, Gulbeyaz) by an indirection that is just distinguishable from passivity. Yet the narrator insists that her silences are a stratagem, that these negatives have a positive existence, even if this cannot, finally, be proven:

> A kind of sleepy Venus seemed Dudù
>   Yet very fit to 'murder sleep' in those
> Who gazed upon her cheek's transcendant hue,
>   Her Attic forehead, and her Phidian nose:
> Few angles were there in her form 'tis true,
>   Thinner she might have been and yet scarce lose;
> Yet, after all, 'twould puzzle to say where
> It would not spoil some separate charm *to pare.*

(VI, st. 42)

Dudù is glorious in her excess in this stanza precisely because that excess has no positive identity. Her charm is a result of the abundance of her body, but paradoxically this abundance has no specific character or locale, and is thus itself disembodied. Her body distinguished by ineffable excess, Dudù acts through refraining from action. The climax of this oxymoronic way of imagining a woman comes in the stanzas that take up the procedure by which catachretic naming allows language to obscure an absence in the service of an ideal:

> And therefore was she kind and gentle as
>   The age of Gold (when Gold was yet unknown,
> By which its nomenclature came to pass;
>   Thus most appropriately has been shown
> 'Lucus a *non* Lucendo', *not* what *was*
>   But what *was not*; a sort of style that's grown
> Extremely common in this age, whose metal
> The Devil may decompose but never settle;
>
> I think it may be of 'Corinthian Brass',
>   Which was a Mixture of all Metals, but
> The Brazen uppermost.) Kind reader! pass
>   This long parenthesis: I could not shut
> It sooner for the soul of me, and class
>   My faults even with your own! which meaneth,
> Put a kind construction on them and me:
> But *that* you won't – then don't – I am not less free.
>
> 'Tis time we should return to plain narration,
>   And thus my narrative proceeds: – Dudù,
> With every kindness short of ostentation,
>   Shewed Juan, or Juanna, through and through
> This labyrinth of females, and each station
> Described – what's strange – in words extremely few:
> I have but one simile, and that's a blunder,
> For wordless woman, which is *silent* Thunder.

(VI, st. 57)

Dudù, a figure rooted in and explicitly identified with artistic creations (the Landscape, Marble) attains to the sublime in so far as she remains silent, subjugated certainly, both by the Sultan and by the fantasist, yet curiously also deliberate in her silence, intending her distance from language, exploiting quietness as tact so that it becomes a positive quality working to effect her aims. It may be difficult to imagine a comic Cordelia, but to some extent that seems to be what Byron was aiming for in Dudù, the sublimity of an understanding that disdains expression in language. Her portrait recalls the blissful early stages of Juan's involvement with Haidee, before he learned Romaic. The fantasy is suggestively grounded in a familiar topos – the unselfconsciousness that precedes entry into the symbolic order. In the stanza before the one about the age of gold Dudù's lack of awareness of herself is built up into a supposedly strange, but really more calculatedly seductive quality.

> The strangest thing was, beauteous, she was wholly
>   Unconscious, albeit turned of quick seventeen,
> That she was fair, or dark, or short, or tall;
> She never though about herself at all.
>
> (VI, st. 54)

This empowerment by negation finds its rhetorical counterpart in the parenthetical remark in the following stanza concerning the derivation of the age of Gold. As in the false etymology of *lucus* ('a grove') from *non lucendo* ('not admitting light), the age of Gold is known for something it conspicuously lacked.

Language, by naming that which is unknown through catachresis, frequently derives its authority from a 'blunder' like 'silent Thunder', a breakdown of meaning surpassing sense in order to preserve syntax. Language thus displaces or hides that which it cannot name directly because it remains radically extralinguistic. The use of a series of impossible figures in the description of Dudù, the thematization as well as the deployment of oxymoronic and paradoxical explanations for her, distinguishes her characterization from a naturalistic one. As lovely as he asserts she is, the narrator de-objectifies Dudù through paradox, rather than objectifying her through the categories of conventional description. In this canto and description the poem uses a new strategy for evading the symbolic and its consequences – anti-selfconsciousness. The narrator persists in this pattern until Dudù reaches the most elemental of all tests of vanity, the 'mirror-stage:'

> In perfect Innocence she then unmade
>   Her toilet, which cost little, for she was
> A Child of Nature, carelessly arrayed:
>   If fond of a chance ogle at her glass,
> 'Twas like the fawn which, in the lake displayed,

Beholds her own shy, shadowy image pass,
When first she starts, and then returns to peep,
Admiring this new native of the deep.

(VI, st. 60)

The circuits of lascivious irony are so overloaded in this stanza that the modest reader hardly knows where to look. Is this fawn to be the prey of a faun? Shall we too, having read this stanza once, 'return to peep'? The innuendoes fall more thickly as the ostensible protest of innocence and unselfconsciousness becomes more elaborate. Throughout the harem sequence the language of the poem is like a veil, revealing what it covers more coyly than if it were the 'nothing' it tries to pass itself off as.

Why is this rhetorical decision remarkable? The harem itself is an interesting screen – many things can be projected on it. Anne Mellor makes this point in reference to women writers.

> When Romantic-era women writers looked to the East, they saw a rather different space, equally imaginary and culturally constructed with imperial eyes, but differently mapped. The harem, for instance, following Lady Mary Wortley Montagu's *Turkish Embassy Letters* published in 1763 could be seen as an arena not of female subordination to male desire but rather of feminine liberation, a feminotopia of lesbian sexuality and gratified sensual desire. Or it could be seen as the condition of *all* women, in Europe as well as in the East.[7]

Like the male writers for whom the harem enabled other, more 'direct' fantasies of 'feminotopia', the women writers who projected their imaginations onto the harem took advantage of its inaccessibility in fact to build an 'available' harem in their fantasies. As for Byron's description in *Don Juan*, taste and even Byron's twisted standard of decorum would have rendered the explicit fetishism of an erotic realism in this episode unacceptable. Generic expectations in the romance would be disturbed by naturalism, and *topoi* of inexpressibility existed that were traditionally employed in such romantic circumstances. Yet there is more at stake here than the appeal to practicality might immediately disclose. As is common throughout *Don Juan*, the neighbouring allusions carry a concealed counterargument running at an oblique angle to the main one. 'Corinthian brass' refers to the discordant trumpets of Paul's first letter to the Corinthians, symbols of the failure to attain to prophesy. The narrator asserts that most contemporary poetry proceeds through catachreses, saying, '*not* what *was*, but what *was not*'. The last-quoted phrase mimics the chiasmus it describes, and identifies the predominant trope of 'Corinthian brass', a poetry written expressly to re-enchant a secularized audience. Whereas in Paul's epistle the point being made is that without charity or love the people will never transcend speaking in tongues and become truly prophetic, the counter-Enlightenment of the Romantic fantastic seeks the partial magic of the incoherent but nevertheless visionary tongues which occupy the stage prior to absolute vision.

> Though I speak with the tongues of men and of angels, and have not charity, I am become *as* sounding brass, or a tinkling cymbal. (1 Corinthians 13, 1 (KJ))

As we saw in the last chapter, part of what Byron is seeking to recover in *Don Juan* is the enchantment of youth. Youth and charity are the implicit watchwords of the entire poem – the proper attitude of age towards youth is charity. The narrator recognizes the formal contradictions inherent in the paradoxes that are Juan's experience of Dudù, but he also creates and inhabits them as fantasies. Unlike 1 Corinthians, *Don Juan* does not offer itself as an exhortation to perseverance and maturity in the face of the doubt and confusion rendered by oxymoron, but rather challenges us with paradox to re-experience the magic of naive, youthful ways of thinking and experiencing. The chapter from Paul concludes with the following vision, one with which many Romantics may be imagined to have struggled.

> When I was a child, I spake as a child, I understood as a child, I thought as a child: but when I became a man, I put away childish things. For now we see through a glass, darkly; but then face to face: now I know in part; but then I shall know even as also I am known. (1 Corinthians 13, 11–12 (KJ))

Unquestionably one of the great moments in Paul, verse 12 nevertheless betrays a rhetorical narcissism that may be read against the grain. 'I shall know even as I also am known' implies an access of self-consciousness that in turn may draw a secondary meaning from the very sublime 'glass'. The problem with coming 'face to face', as it were, is that the glass may not be a window but instead a mirror. If man unmakes God through the prophecy of Enlightenment, the problem for the Romantic era writer is not so much how to achieve prophecy as how to avoid it. He would like to see something *through* the glass again, rather than see himself in it, and he cannot do so without first self-consciously and artificially reviving his sense of wonder.

This contextualization would tend to complicate the interpretation of Goethe's oft-quoted remark about Byron, that 'when he reflects he is a child'. Whether or not Goethe understood this to have been Byron's intent, at least in *Don Juan*, we may say that as adepts of the Romantic discourse of re-enchantment, we do not have to read the observation as a negative judgement. The dialogism of Juan as a character depends on the degree to which the rhetoric of the poem succeeds in implicating the reader in a regressive fantasy, and the dialogism of the poem as a whole depends upon the credence which the narrator establishes in the historical world called up by the regression. Recall the expostulation with which the narrator interrupts the digression on the use of catachresis:

> . . . Kind reader! pass
> This long parenthesis: I could not shut
> It sooner for the soul of me, and class
> My faults even with your own! which meaneth,
> Put a kind construction upon them and me:
> But that you won't – then don't – I am not less free.
>
> (VI, st. 56)

The chiasmus extends outward through the reading contract, as the freedom of the reader to construe unkindly becomes the freedom of the writer to ignore his censure. Imagining an absent reader, an abstraction realized in every actual reading of the stanza, the narrator might class his faults even with the reader's own at no risk to himself. Such reflexive moments materialize the otherwise prospective content of the poem, whatever associations and specifics each reader supplies in order to complete its meaning. These moments redefine Christian charity in a sceptical and secular idiom. In Byron's hands the erotic middle style becomes a way of advancing a mode of secular tolerance derived from the Christian virtue

of forgiveness. What is highlighted by this admittedly odd juxta-
position is the imaginative nature of the act of forgiveness, the
way in which it requires one to step out of one's everyday system
of emotional response. Ordinarily held in abeyance by representa-
tional claims of discourse, readerly imagination is here foregrounded,
albeit in the guise of an affected and facetious shame. Once again
in *Don Juan* the precedence of the signifier has been exploited in
order to implicate the reader in the subject position of the enun-
ciation.[8] The power of Byron's middle style in this poem often derives
from this kind of strategic manipulation of enunciative effects.

Having established Dudù as the fantastic object of transference
and identification by describing her in terms of oxymoron and
paradox, the plot then takes her to the limits of narrative represen-
tation. Do she and Juan consummate their relationship? The answer
is never given. The narrator provides a prurient catalogue of the
charms of the sleeping harem girls, but is then interrupted by Dudù's
scream. All the others gather around her and Juanna to hear what
has happened. Dudù describes her dream, in which she walked alone
in the woods. She stops in the middle, fascinated by a golden apple
hanging out of her reach. After throwing stones at it to knock it
down, she gives up. She tells the huddled crowd of harem women:

> That on a sudden, when she least had hope,
>   It fell down of its own accord, before
> Her feet; that her first movement was to stoop
>   And pick it up, and bite it to the core;
> That just as her young lip began to ope
>   Upon the golden fruit the vision bore,
> A bee flew out and stung her to the heart,
> And so – she woke with a great scream and start.
>
> (VI, st. 77)

Her dream of an apple of knowledge that bites back is as close as
we are allowed to get:

> I can't tell why she blushed, nor can expound
>   The mystery of this rupture of their rest;
> All that I know is, that the facts I state
> Are true as truth has ever been of late.
>
> (VI, st. 85)

I have pointed out that the *Ars Poetica* middle style might conceal a painful core experience of individuality related to the difficulty of emptying out the self sufficiently to attain to a universality of appeal and application. The narrator seems to open a position for the reader by questioning his own biased position or omniscience, and in the process he must unfix Dudù as well. Alan Richardson, in 'Romanticism and the Colonization of the Feminine', suggests that Romantic representations of women must be read dialectically:

> The Romantic tradition did not simply objectify women. It also subjected them, in a dual sense, portraying woman as subject in order to appropriate the feminine for male subjectivity. The implications of this Romantic program – that questions of gender and subjectivity are more likely to involve a dialectical relation than a simple dichotomy – should be kept in mind as we, men and women, continue to criticize our own subject positions.[9]

In the harem episode, *Don Juan* takes another step, portraying woman as subject through a lack of subjectivity in order to place the feminine in the ambiguous space available to the narrator, the hero, and the reader alike. Dudù, as a feminized negation, may help reassert the poem's masculinity, or she may aid the narrator in questioning truth; suggesting that things are never as they seem, leaving the reader to impose upon the characters some gendered subjectivity. In the character and experience of Dudù, *Don Juan* images first the universality of the middle style, through description of her by oxymoron and paradox, and then the hidden kernel of enjoyment/ pain at the core of that style, as Dudù's dream.

Juan's experience in the harem uncovers the irreducible difference that thwarts any attempt to establish universal understanding and communication. Enjoyment remains contingent and evanescent even in retrospect. It's not just that the reader is not allowed to know, or that the narrator makes a show of dissembling what happens between Dudù and Juan. Dudù herself is not sure what she has felt – it was all a dream. The rupture or gap that holds the place of enjoyment in Dudù's dream is a playful troping of Juan's sexual identity, a troping upon which the reader's attempts to fill this caesura turn. She doesn't know what she felt, and Juan isn't telling, so we can only suppose what happened. What is phallic, or becomes phallic, about the cross-dressed hero in this episode is that he is in a position to know, he is the *subject supposed to know* what has taken place. Sexuality, reduced to what is hidden by Juan's attire and disclaimed by the disingenuous narrator, is then conflated with this position, that of the one who knows. A condition which is initially conceived in terms of a positive, the possession of the phallus, becomes negative in so far as the position of the subject supposed to know is dependent not on knowledge, but rather on one's relation to its lack. Juan is only able to render the exclusion of the reader from the truth on the condition that the truth is not disclosed. Thus the knowledge he is supposed to have – and this goes for the narrator as well – only establishes his difference from the reader so long as it remains undisclosed, so long as the reader feels its lack.

The playful strategy of the middle style takes on a more explicitly political significance in the cantos that follow Juanna's adventure in the harem. The emphasis on group rather than individual behaviour, and applied rather than private fantasy, continues even after the poem leaves the erotic fantasy space of the harem. As in the poem's first two major episodes, the indulgence of a pleasurable erotic fantasy – the older woman fantasy in the case of Julia, the mixture of rebellious daughter and nurturing mother presented by Haidee, most recently the polymorphic and voyeuristic sensuality of the harem sequence – gives way to a waking nightmare derived from the anxieties aroused by indulging in the original pleasurable daydream. In the cantos that follow, the poem converts anxieties about the harem into anxieties about the mob. The 'feminotopia' of the harem is revealed to be a political allegory, one just as important in its way as the idyll on Haidee's island, but (shockingly, given the historical context) more *democratic*. Dudù, representative of the 'people', wins out over the fourth queen. Recalling our parallel case of theoretical democracy the logic of this internal contradiction finds its expression in nationalism. The radically abstract citizen is structurally incompatible with the real human being, thick with associations, qualities and desires. Historically, democracy has always existed at the expense of excluded populations and in the form of limited national entities. Democracy is always embodied in some form of the State, and has never existed as a 'world-wide' situation, and this fact conditions the participation of every individual citizen. One might imagine a planetary democracy as easily as one might imagine the next Utopia, but historical experience points to the difficulty of actually generating any political enthusiasm for it. Canto VI recalls the treatment of 'The Isles of Greece' in Canto III, in which a singer who didn't care sang a patriotic song to an audience that wasn't listening. The nationalism of 'The Isles of Greece' depends upon the position of a subject supposed to know, but the very relation he or she must hold to the auditor necessarily brackets the convictions of the subject. The irony of this performance is that, while the poet is attempting to develop a rapport with his Greek audience, they lack the necessary anxiety about being Greek to hear it.

The mixed feelings with which the prospect of universal suffrage was contemplated in England in 1819 is embodied in the fantasy of the Hydra, an imaginary beast with many heads. The figure of the Hydra or Briareus from Greek mythology was a staple of the popular imagination of the consequences of democratic political reform. Reversing the logic of Hobbes's Leviathan, this is a beast that lives without a central, sovereign head. This motif of the Hydra plays itself out in *Don Juan* in a number of ways, forming a thematic paradigm for the harem and siege cantos, much as the breast did for the Haidee episode. Here is its first appearance, in the early stages of the harem scene, before the stanzas describing Dudù:

> Don Juan in his feminine disguise,
>   With all the damsels in their long array,
> Had bowed themselves before the imperial eyes,
>   And at the usual sign ta'en their way
> Back to their chambers, those long galleries
>   In the Seraglio, where the ladies lay
> Their delicate limbs; a thousand bosoms there
> Beating for love as the caged birds for air.

> I love the sex, and sometimes would reverse
>   The tyrant's wish, 'that mankind only had
> One neck, which he with one fell stroke might pierce:'
>   My wish is quite as wide, but not so bad,
> And much more tender on the whole than fierce;
>   It being (not now, but only while a lad)
> That Womankind had but one rosy mouth,
> To kiss them all at once from North to South.

> Oh enviable Briareus! with thy hands
>   And heads, if thou hadst all things multiplied

In such proportion! – But my Muse withstands
  The giant thought of being a Titan's bride,
Or travelling in Patagonian lands;
  So let us back to Lilliput, and guide
Our hero through the labyrinth of love
In which we left him several lines above.

(VI, st. 26–8)

Byron here picks up on the peculiar complementarity of the harem and the hydra. While harems are maintained for the benefit of single individuals, a being capable of entering into a truly reciprocal physical relationship with a harem would have to have 'all things multiplied / In such proportion'. Here we encounter a fantasy that will become more graphic and urgent as the canto continues, that of the corporate being of sex and death, the Briareus. The image would seem to confirm Freud's hypothesis, in the essay on the Medusa's Head, that the multiplication of phallic symbols signifies castration; but even more immediately suggestive is the martial analogy which will be confirmed in the second part of the sequence by General Suwarrow's tactics when he invades Ismail. The Russian forces Suwarrow commanded were renowned for their bayonetry, that being their weapon of choice in the siege of Ismail. A veritable Briareus of deadly penetration, the Imperial Russian army is the inverse equivalent of the harem. Maintained by a female monarch, this mercenary army duplicates the diversity of the harem in its demographic composition. Like the women gathered from all parts of the world for the Sultan's pleasure, Catherine's troops are a collection of French émigrés, English mercenaries, Russians, Cossacks and others (VII, st. 18).

The paradigm of the Hydra or Briareus calls the army forth symbolically, out of the existence of the harem: for both entities represent fantastic associations formed around degraded leaders, an imagining of democracy as doubled by tyranny. Catherine's army and the Sultan's harem are asserted to be, on at least one level, functionally equivalent:

Had Catherine and the Sultan understood
  Their own true interests, which kings rarely know,
Until 'tis taught by lessons rather rude,
  There was a way to end their strife, although

> Perhaps precarious, had they but thought good,
>   Without the aid of Prince or Plenipo:
> She to dismiss her guards and he his harem,
> And for their other matters, meet and share 'em.

(VI, st. 95)

Again the homology between these mirror-image male fantasies of indiscriminacy asserts itself. The Sultan and Catherine are equally tyrannical because they reverse their gender positions through asserting their power. Catherine is made phallic by the army, the Sultan is feminized by the harem, but is the harem made phallic? Men defined by their bayonets render their phalluses superfluous. What of women defined as sex-objects? Napoleon is reported to have said that the only thing one couldn't do with bayonets was sit on them.

Delving into Byron's past is often a good way to decode the shifting significations of his *Don Juan* manner. In my analysis of the significance of breast-feeding in the Haidee episode I identified the image as an allusion to Canto IV of *Childe Harold's Pilgrimage*. There is a precedent worth mentioning for the Briareus as well. In his maiden speech before Parliament on the frame-breakers, Byron evokes the popular image of the hydra in a rebuke to the 'capitally' minded Lords:

> You call these men a mob, desperate, dangerous, and ignorant; and seem to think that the only way to quiet the 'Bellua multorum capitum' is to lop off a few of its superfluous heads. But even a mob may be better reduced to reason by a mixture of conciliation and firmness than by additional irritation and redoubled penalties.[10]

This 'mixture of conciliation and firmness' was something which Byron continued to advocate in his exile and for which there remained a real need as Britain edged closer to becoming a police state in the years following the Peterloo massacre. There is a long-standing dispute regarding the significance of Byron's letters of 1820 to Hobhouse concerning these matters. In them he abuses Henry Hunt and William Cobbett, and with them Hobhouse and Sir Francis Burdett, for having succumbed to demagoguery and relinquished (or in the case of 'Orator Hunt', gained) control over the masses in

England. One group of partisans view Byron as a typical Regency Whig and use the letters to seal their case for a reactionary late Byron, more disgusted by than sympathetic to the cause of Reform, and permanently disillusioned with British politics by Hobhouse's involvement with the mob.[11] At last true to his aristocratic background, forsaking transient Republican ideals in the face of the reality of democratic reform, this Byron must comfort many who would like to imagine him ineffectual. But can this interpretation of his correspondence account for his simultaneous involvement with the Carbonari and his subsequent action on the behalf of Greece? Michael Foot would mitigate the apparent conservatism of Byron's letters to Hobhouse on the grounds that Hunt's role in Peterloo, indeed the whole incident, had been misrepresented not only to Byron but to the world, and that it would be some time before the facts of the matter were sufficiently known to make an accurate assessment possible, especially from such a distance.[12] Foot takes pains to demonstrate that the remarks which have been enlisted on the side of complacency should not preclude commitment. This position opposes that of Malcolm Kelsall, whose *Byron's Politics* contends that Byron's life was of no real political significance.

From Kelsall's point of view, Byron's involvements with the Italians and the Greeks are in the end inconsequential and fantastic, the results of mere caprice and ennui. Although the narrator of *Don Juan* is not an entirely reliable register of Byron's own beliefs, in the description of the siege he expresses an attitude towards revolution that affirms Foot's hypothesis of Byron's commitment to reform and provides another perspective from which to view these issues:

> But never mind; – 'God save the king!' and kings!
>   For if *he* don't, I doubt if *men* will longer –
> I think I hear a little bird, who sings
>   The people by and by will be the stronger:
> The veriest jade will wince whose harness wrings
>   So much into the raw as quite to wrong her
> Beyond the rules of posting, – and the Mob
> At last fall sick of imitating Job:
>
> At first it grumbles, then it swears, and then,
>   Like David, flings smooth pebbles 'gainst a giant;
> At last it takes to weapons such as men
>   Snatch when despair makes human hearts less pliant.

> Then comes 'the tug of war;' – 'twill come again,
>   I rather doubt; and I would fain say 'fie on't',
> If I had not perceived that Revolution
> Alone can save the Earth from Hell's pollution.

(VIII, st. 50–1)

In these stanzas on political matters Byron is less passionately involved than historically aware. His portrayal of the grumbling mob is only marginally positive, yet he sees the historical necessity of their revolt as part of a purging of the Earth. The word that Byron rhymes with revolution, 'pollution', is of special significance. With no contemporary ecological discourse within which to mean what it has come to signify today, the notion expressed is closer to that of the Greek tragedies in which the *polis* is seen as beset by pollution. In this perspective Revolution is the ritual scapegoating of a king who is understood to have contaminated men's ways of life. The opposition of 'Mob' to 'kings,' and especially the historical obsolescence and social inefficacy of monarchy, are themes which dominate the cantos of siege, in which the poem's most absolute ruler, the Sultan, is the victim of a new breed of the man of talent, the butcher Suwarrow. The entire sequence of the 'new' poem, Canto VI–VIII, can be read as a meditation on the challenges posed to traditional authority by those who rose out of the ranks. Even the dreadful jealousy of Gulbeyaz upon learning of Juanna's night with her 'common' rival Dudù fits this general pattern. And in Canto IX, when Juan becomes the lover of Catherine of Russia, he comes closest to breaking the spell of narratorial and readerly sympathy simply by siding with and catering to the will of a tyrant.

The siege of Ismail provides vivid images of both disentanglement and dependence, iconic references to the complexes played out in more elaborate social forms elsewhere in the poem. The recurrent image of the mob as a human Hydra appears at the outset of the canto:

> All was prepared – the fire, the sword, the men
>   To wield them in their terrible array.
> The army, like a lion from his den,
>   Marched forth with nerve and sinews bent to slay, –
> A human Hydra, issuing from its fen
>   To breathe destruction on its winding way,

Whose heads were heroes, which cut off in vain
Immediately in others grew again.

(VIII, st. 2)

The immediate significance of the image in this stanza is that
war and the conventional means of recording its events are of little
use in establishing the independent existence of any particular human
being from out of the mass. When the narrator goes on to assert
that 'History can only take things in the gross', the association
established by the previous stanza locates History in the position
of the executioner, taking heads in the gross. Byron challenges the
mimetic authority of history and of the Gazettes in this canto on
war because war creates a radical doubt about the meaning of indi-
vidual life. The constant refrain of justification for life-endangering
heroism – that it will earn one a place in the Gazettes – deploys
two ironies. One is the simple one in which being in the newspaper
is hardly worth anything to someone who is dead, but the second
has to do with the question of what representational strategy might
be capable of rendering death in a suitable manner. How may mi-
mesis respond effectively to carnage?

Two images of individual differentiation from the hydra-like mass
are offered as positive and negative ways in which one might aspire
to individuality in such extreme circumstances. One comes when
a dying Moslem is momentarily lifted out of obscurity by biting a
Russian soldier on the heel. The other occurs when Juan saves a
child of ten from a heap of corpses. Both set parameters on the
individuation possible under wartime conditions.

The first gruesome event is a parody of distinction from the other-
wise anonymous pile of bodies.

> A Russian officer, in martial tread
> Over a heap of bodies, felt his heel
> Seized fast . . .
> In vain he kicked, and swore, and writhed, and bled,
> And howled for help as wolves do for a meal –
> The teeth still kept their gratifying hold,
> As do the subtle snakes described of old.
>
> A dying Moslem, who had felt the foot
> Of a foe o'er him, snatched at it, and bit

> The very tendon, which is most acute –
> . . .
>
> He made the teeth meet, nor relinquish'd it
> Even with his life – for (but they lie) 'tis said
> To the live leg still clung the severed head.
> . . .
> The regimental surgeon could not cure
>   His patient, and perhaps was to be blamed
> More than the head of the inveterate foe,
> Which was cut off, and scarce even then let go.
>
>   (VIII, st. 83–5 passim)

The dialogism of Byron's narrative technique renders this gro-
tesque anecdote dense with implications. There is an incredibly swift
multiplication of metaphors – serpent upon hydra upon cannibal
upon Achilles upon Jacob – topped off at the climax with a paren-
thetical general retraction – '(but they lie)'. The source of all the
description in the siege cantos is historical – Castelnau's 'Essai sur
L'histoire Ancienne et Moderne de la Nouvelle Russie' is a monar-
chist celebration of this imperial Russian victory. What, then, are
we to make of this feisty Moslem's post-mortem tenacity? It is as
vivid as the gory exploits of epic warriors, but lacks the dignity of
their purposiveness. Christian values take on Moslem form and nip
the heels of an outdated and degraded epic system. When the nar-
rator employs this particularly outlandish anecdote as the point of
departure for his praise of truth-telling and facts, his tone is al-
most impossible to pin down. Is this the truth about war because
war is a grotesquerie, or because it really happened? If the latter,
why the parenthetical disclaimer?

> But then the fact's a fact – and 'tis the part
>   Of a true poet to escape from fiction
> Whene'er he can; for there is little art
>   In leaving verse more free from the restriction
> Of truth than prose, unless to suit the mart
>   For what is sometimes called poetic diction,
> And that outrageous appetite for lies
> Which Satan angles with, for souls, like flies.
>
>   (VIII, st. 86)

The individuation of the Moslem soldier from out of the heap of bodies in which he lies entangled is bought at the price of his head, but he nevertheless strikes the Russian victor in a vulnerable, heroic spot and renders him lame. Striving with the oppressor and biting his heel brings the anonymous soldier into company with the serpent and with Jacob, two symbols of revolutionary individuation. Even when it is futile, revolution brings its heroes legitimate distinction. Subtly, iconographically, these horrific stanzas reinforce the poem's commitment to representing a world in which distinction, however tragic, may be achieved from out of the mass.

When Juan finds the young orphan Leila, just five stanzas later, she too is at risk of disappearing into the shapeless, identity-destroying heap of the dead:

> Upon a taken bastion where there lay
>   Thousands of slaughtered men, a yet warm group
> Of murdered women, who had found their way
>   To this vain refuge, made the good heart droop
> And shudder; – while, as beautiful as May,
>   A female child of ten years tried to stoop
> And hide her little palpitating breast
> Amidst the bodies lulled in bloody rest.
>
> Two villainous Cossaques pursued the child
>   With flashing eyes and weapons: matched with them
> The rudest brute that roams Siberia's wild
>   Has feelings pure and polished as a gem, –
> The bear is civilized, the wolf is mild:
>   And whom for this at last must we condemn?
> Their natures? or their sovereigns, who employ
> All arts to teach their subjects to destroy?
>
> Their sabres glittered o'er her little head,
>   Whence her fair hair rose twining with affright,
> Her hidden face was plunged amidst the dead:
>   When Juan caught a glimpse of this sad sight,
> I shall not say exactly what he *said*,
>   Because it might not solace 'ears polite;'
> But what he *did*, was to lay on their backs,
> The readiest way of reasoning with Cossaques.

(VIII, st. 91–3)

Little Leila emerges like the gory Moslem from a heap of corpses and turns Juan momentarily against his new comrades, the Cossacks. In seeking to explain the significance of Leila, the male fantasy of the dependent woman as a confirmation of one's individuality seems particularly apposite given the circumstances of her appearance in the poem. As disparate as these scenes may be, they acquire a unity through the application of the 'fantasy principle', in which tragic male rivalry interchanges with feminine dependence in a continuous process of imaginary self-fashioning.

The hydra finally may be said to have, as did the image of breast-feeding, a prospective and a retrospective significance. In its retrospective significance, the Hydra of universal suffrage or democracy will end in the madness of national rivalry and armed conflict. The Moslem biting the heel of the Cossack is an image of the madness (and moral rigor mortis) of revolutionary violence. Prospectively, the beast with many heads of a democratic future may be imagined as the home of Leila, a child separated from her Moslem background by a Russian invasion, saved from death by a Spaniard, eventually to be raised by a British nanny. But the war cantos have precious little of the prospective, as is evidenced by the position in which we next find Juan – his first truly mercenary affair, with the Empress Catherine, is a result of the degradation and regression he undergoes in battle.

Juan is lost for the duration of cantos VII–X in so far as in them he loses contact with the poem's life principle of the feminine ideal. The coarseness of the sexual humour in the Catherine stanzas invalidates the premise of erotic experience as liberation upon which his encounters with Haidee, Dudù and even Julia are based. Because Juan lapses into the unthinking, mimetic behaviour of slaughter and sexual servitude in these episodes, the narrator cannot return to presenting him as an ideal lover. This inhibition will have real consequences for the hero in his adventure as a foreign consul in England. In the meantime, the Russian sequence that begins with the siege leaves the realm of experimental, literary male fantasy, and descends into the poem's equivalent of the underworld, the frightening realm of applied fantasy.

The emerging conflict in Juan's character between fantasy as such and the applied fantasy of regressive social behaviour opens when he first responds to the battle by identifying with and imitating the imperial soldiers. Juan responds heartily to warfare, taking up arms against his Moslem captors and aiding the conquering Russian army under Suwarrow:

But Juan was quite 'a broth of a boy',
  A thing of impulse and a child of song;
Now swimming in the sentiment of joy,
  Or the *sensation* (if that phrase seems wrong)
And afterwards, if he must needs destroy,
  In such good company as always throng
To battles, sieges, and that kind of pleasure,
No less delighted to employ his leisure;

(VIII, st. 24)

The stanza is enjambed with the one following – 'No less delighted to employ his leisure;// But always without malice.' This makes the reader wait for Juan's good intentions with the uncomfortable idea of destruction as leisure. The most decisive possible departure from earlier heroic and mock-heroic poetry is happening here. Never before Byron and Shelley do we find a real, final and absolute disengagement from martial epic values in English poetry. The narrator then develops the idea of 'good intentions', as the canting term for participation with neither malice nor commitment. Juan has raised his sword partly in anger, but mainly in mimicry:

But always without malice; if he warr'd
  Or loved, it was with what we call 'the best
Intentions', which form all mankind's *trump card*,
  To be produced when brought up to the test,
The statesman, hero, harlot, lawyer – ward
  Off each attack, when people are in quest
Of their designs, by saying they *meant well*;
'Tis pity 'that such meaning should pave Hell.'

I almost lately have begun to doubt
  Whether Hell's pavement – if it be *so paved* –
Must not have latterly been quite worn out,
  Not by the numbers Good Intent hath saved,
But by the mass who go below without
  Those ancient good intentions, which once shaved
And smoothed the brimstone of that street of Hell
Which bears the greatest likeness to Pall Mall.

(VIII, st. 25–6)

This last line looks forward to the description of London as the 'Devil's drawing room' at the end of Canto X, and back to Byron's earlier satire, 'The Devil's Drive'. The conventions that have allowed poets to describe hell by comparing it to a city (see *Paradise Lost* in particular) are here inverted, with hell allowing the poet to describe the real world. The narrator sees this inversion as the only legitimate way available to him to compete with Homer.

> Oh, thou eternal Homer! . . .
> To vie with thee would be about as vain
> As for a brook to cope with Ocean's flood;
> But still we Moderns equal you in blood;
>
> (VII, st. 80)

Good intentions are the social lie that mask Juan's mimetic behaviour, which may appear – and sometimes even be – unselfish, although not in a positive sense. Though Juan is not acting out of altruism, he is not acting for himself either: his action arises in imitation of another's desire. The self-possession required for selfishness is lacking. As in the distinction between a sentiment and a sensation, mimetic desire is physiological more than psychological or social. When John Johnson, Juan's friend from the slave market and Byron's countryman, rallies some stragglers to the battle his exertions are described as perversely inhuman:

> His soul (like Galvanism upon the dead)
> Acted upon the living as on wire,
> And led them back into the heaviest fire.
>
> (VIII, st. 41)

Johnson appears as an ironic Dr Frankenstein, zapping the living towards death. His desire is communicated no more socially or personally than an electric current, activating men as if they were appliances. The question of political commitment in *Don Juan* is generally most interesting for the way in which it obscures more threatening questions of agency. When Byron responds to the poetry of the Lakers or the policies of the Holy Alliance, it is as someone who has pondered and suffered the mechanisms by which human activities that exist outside the realm of individual agency are recovered for passive consumption in the form of military heroes and poetic tales. Byron's Juan is a new one, at times more passive and sympathetic than the original Don, but compounded out of the same observation that drives the pantomime – that a portion of human behaviour, and an important portion at that, passes beyond the range of intention. Neither entirely free nor completely enslaved and determined, individual existence must learn to see itself as typically ambivalent. Commitment and its alternatives, insincerity and pragmatism, merge in a new category: the complacent. Juan distills the banality of evil from the virulence of its agents in the world, providing us with an image of human agency circumstantially stripped of any particular guilt, yet derived from the type of the mechanical destroyer, the desiring machine.

We may find a useful analogy in twentieth-century iconography by turning to a popular trope of the Frankfurt School, the 'angel of history'. In the conclusion to his 1962 essay 'Commitment', Theodor Adorno calls attention to a transfiguration in the art of Paul Klee:

> During the First World War or shortly after, Klee drew cartoons of Kaiser Wilhelm as an inhuman iron eater. Later, in 1920, these became – the development can be shown quite clearly – the *Angelus Novus*, the machine angel, who, though he no longer bears any emblem of caricature or commitment, flies far beyond both. The machine angel's enigmatic eyes force the onlooker to try to decide whether he is announcing the culmination of disaster or salvation hidden within it. But, as Walter Benjamin, who owned the drawing, said, he is the angel who does not give but takes.[13]

The origin of Klee's angel comes as something of a shock. Kaiser Wilhelm is at once nastier and more real than anything we might have expected to stand behind the radiant 'Angelus Novus'. Yet this type of transformation is also at work in *Don Juan*. Juan is a kind of Napoleonic monster himself, leaving behind broken families, smoking islands and decimated Seraglios. The fact that he does not intend the destruction that inevitably overtakes his arrival advances the theory that this 'angel' is a cancelled Kaiser, the product of an artistic transformation in which all that is allowed to remain of 'inhuman' evil is a basic lack of satisfaction with the world and a concomitant urge to exert oneself in it. Juan exemplifies a kind of emptied out imperialism: desire without the ideological baggage that allows it to be mistaken for and judged by the standards of the real.

The language of paradox or 'Corinthian brass' uses words to describe and discuss things that are not. This is one of the most important and least appreciated functions of discourse – the investigation of alternative states without regard to the possibility of their being realized. The temptation of prophecy is to insist on the application of fantasies or the concrete realization of ideals; but when realized as history, the positive effects of ideals as discourse can become very negative. In *Don Juan* the primary distinction between useful or harmless male fantasy and its regressive application in the world as misogyny, racism and warfare remains the divide between that which gives life to the poet and his protagonist and that which takes it away. Social institutions structured by applied fantasies, such as the harem or the hydra, cannot offer the individual a stable enough context for acquiring a lasting identity. In recognizing this divide as more important to the creative mind than the Enlightenment dichotomies that dominated contemporary public discourse, *Don Juan* takes a unique position in the intellectual life of its era.

4
Mortal Fantasies: the Politics of Scepticism

Don Juan's variations on the conventions of popular fiction allow its readers to evaluate the consequences of nineteenth-century narrative expectations for their cultural imaginary, and to compare the differing responses to these conventions among the poem's readers at various points in history. Thus it is possible to read the poem's reception as a differential clock, marking the incremental variations within otherwise indistinguishable critical positions assumed by readers this side of modernity towards the early nineteenth-century cultural situation. For example, two kinds of feminist theory about the pervasive shift in early nineteenth-century cultural relations to narrative intersect in the issues raised by the figure of Donna Julia. As a late instance of the epistolary heroine of sensibility, Julia's character bears on the grand narrative of containment that ascribes disciplinary power to the discourse of the nineteenth-century novel. In this model of the epistemic shift in cultural relations to narrative, the nineteenth-century novel, the literary reviews and the postal system act as a police force, coercing the revolutionary energy of a feminine-identified epistolarity into structural conformity with an ethos of heterosexuality, marriage, private property and narrative closure.[1] This literary-theoretical account of nineteenth-century discursive practices emphasizes the fate of the letter's revolutionary feminist instrumentality, and reads *Don Juan* as 'a fundamental undoing of radical genres', rather than as a radical text in itself.[2] In examining the power politics of genre played out among romantic texts in relation to the feminized legacy of Rousseau, Nicola Watson identifies *Don Juan* as an imposition of masculine romantic form on more liberatory feminine expressions of subjectivity. *Don Juan* 'enforces' the 'obsolescence' of sentimental epistolary discourse in a literary exorcism, defined as

> a deliberate attempt to supersede a narrative of revolution founded within the novel and upon the female body to refocus such a narrative as poetic, autobiographical, and of the male body.... Romantic subjectivity would therefore appear to be not merely based upon the model of subjectivity extrapolated from Rousseau's autobiographical project, but . . . upon a concomitant suppression of a model of revolutionary subjectivity offered by *La Nouvelle Heloïse.*[3]

Caroline Franklin's cultural theory offers another feminist reading of the poem's relation to the changing cultural fate of narrative.[4] Her less exclusive focus on the instrumentality of women's writing yields a different account of the conflict between *Don Juan* and the sentimental epistolary novel. Franklin takes her cue from Foucault's argument in the *History of Sexuality* that an improvement in life expectancy in the eighteenth century precipitated a sense of the life of the species in the political sphere. The eighteenth-century conduct novel thus responds to the displacement in social discourse of nobility, the prestige of blood, by bourgeois legitimacy and the heredity of race and class, with a heightened cultural regard for the chastity of women. As the prestige of the nobility was gradually replaced in the novel's hierarchy of values by the propriety of the bourgeoisie, a different and perhaps greater stress was put on legitimacy. A cultural theory of the debate in the sentimental epistolary novel over the role of women is thus less concerned with the fate of the passionate letter than with the social status of women's desire. Where Watson sees a duel between literary superpowers for a market share, Franklin reads the cultural consequences of *Don Juan* in the effect of its reception on society rather than in (hypothetical) literary production:

> Women formed a large part of Byron's readership. Women and the working class were both characterized as so susceptible to subjectivity and irrationality that they would be more easily corrupted by the dangerous individualism of the poem into subversive lawlessness. It is a historical irony that it was a libertine who was in a position to challenge the consensus on the necessity for female chastity, and an aristocrat who could discern the

bourgeois nature of contemporary liberal thought. [*Don Juan* is] an attack on the hagiography of the family. . . . Freedom over his/her sexuality is the measure of the individual's degree of autonomy.[5]

In this cultural reading of *Don Juan*, the poem's disciplinary role in trumping the revolutionary bid of a feminized epistolarity is superseded by its liberating effect on attitudes towards the consensus on chastity. By foregrounding questions of sexual autonomy and social agency, Franklin's feminist cultural approach to *Don Juan* differentiates among Romantic texts at the precise moment that Watson's feminist literary theoretical approach binds disparate phenomena into a single, monolithic moment of masculinization. In a theory focused exclusively on style, *Don Juan* ought to differ significantly enough from the *Prelude* to make a difference, yet both texts are understood by feminists such as Watson to recentre literary production within a relatively homogeneous masculine, literary cultural space. Franklin's cultural theory produces a more nuanced, less oppositional reading of the politicization of genre than feminist literary theory because it reads and evaluates aestheticizations of politics as well.

How, then, did the gendered aesthetics of late eighteenth-century novels shape politics? The figure of woman in the cultural imaginary of conduct and courtship came, in the wake of the Revolution debate, to mediate the claims of a larger set of subjects seeking social recognition:

The late eighteenth-century novel concentrated to an extraordinary extent on the theme of the education and courtship of an individual young girl: her successful socialization could result in a possible rise through the ranks through a wealthy marriage; her transgression, however, meant social ostracism. It seems possible that these novels displaced and expressed metaphorically the universal preoccupation of the age with the possibility of the socialization of the individual subject in general.[6]

The heroines of *Don Juan*'s early cantos thus index the relative degrees of individual liberty, potential and actual, available in their societies. In the English cantos of *Don Juan*, the basis both for personal autonomy and for the possibility of the socialization of the subject changes: it becomes more economic. In the later cantos, the poem's emphasis on the differentiation of gender roles as a metaphor for the process of achieving individuation and composure through social recognition becomes explicitly subject to the stops and seizures of a commercial society. In the Haidee episode, for example, conflicting gendered accounts of the significance of Haidee's involvement with Juan played out along lines that could be identified with psychic agencies. Lambro's return reasserted patriarchal authority and embodied the perspective of the punitive superego towards the ego's quest for social recognition and fulfilment in love. While the superimposition in the Haidee episode of fantasies drawn from different moments of masculine self-identification caused a conflict, that conflict remained legible.

In the commercial society of the English cantos, conflicts of ego with superego are either sublimated through economics into questions of status and privilege, or desublimated in acts of violence. In this chapter I want to investigate some narrative fantasies that endorse violence, socially sanctioned and unsanctioned, and comment on the relation that the narrator's increasing presence in the poem bears to its representation of psychic conflict.

Juan's first act on British soil is to kill a man. He makes a rare and ironic speech in the moments leading up to this act and his words are a perversely significant prelude to the encounter that follows:

> I say, Don Juan, wrapt in contemplation,
> Walked on behind his carriage, o'er the summit,
> And lost in wonder of so great a nation,
> Gave way to't, since he could not overcome it.
> 'And here', he cried, 'is Freedom's chosen station;
> Here peals the people's voice, nor can entomb it
> Racks, prisons, inquisitions; resurrection
> Awaits it, each new meeting or election.
>
> 'Here are chaste wives, pure lives; here people pay
> But what they please; and if that things be dear,
> 'Tis only that they love to throw away
> Their cash, to show how much they have a-year.
> Here laws are all inviolate; none lay
> Traps for the traveller; every highway's clear:
> Here' – he was interrupted by a knife,
> With, 'Damn your eyes! your money or your life!'
>
> (XI, st. 9–10)

While it is ironic that Juan is talking about how safe he is when he is assaulted, it is plainly too coincidental not to be a narrative ploy. The falsity of the last statements in his anaphoric sequence – 'none lay / Traps for the traveller; every highway's clear' – sheds a retrospective doubt on the items that have come before. The narrative ploy is one in which the truth of a statement, or in this case a whole series of statements, is subjected to immediate contradiction through experience. It is as though Juan, with no personal knowledge of England, was trying out a few things that might or might not be true about the place. When he finally hits on one that is ready to be contradicted, up steps Tom to act out what Juan's speech has anticipated, albeit in the negative form of a conjecture that it 'couldn't happen here'.

The narrative logic is that of the unfortunate, perhaps familiar, moment in which one becomes aware of one's good health. 'How long it has been since I have been ill!' or 'How extraordinarily fit I am feeling!' one says, in an expression of health that is tantamount to a symptom in so far as it would appear to announce the onset of an illness on the verge of manifesting itself as such. This logic is also common in historical developments. The assassination of Julius Caesar was undertaken in the hopes of heading off the historical inevitability of dictatorship. Julius was eliminated, but the event his murder was intended to forestall was in the process effected, as Augustus became the first caesar.[7] According to Lévi-Strauss, repetition in inversion also patterns the transmission of myth, particularly between languages:

> When a mythical schema is transmitted from one population to another, and there exist differences of language, social organization, or way of life that make the myth difficult to communicate, it begins to become impoverished and confused. But one can find a limiting situation in which, instead of finally being obliterated by losing all its outlines, the myth is *inverted* and regains part of its precision.[8]

The myth of Don Juan is inverted in Byron's *Don Juan*, relinquishing its original (exhausted) cultural function of ritually re-enacting the repression that founds monogamy, and signifying instead its inverse, the decathexis of a hypocritical, commercialized monogamy fetishizing female chastity.

To return to Canto XI and the poem's action, according to the logic of repetition in inversion, Juan is in some way on his guard against assailants because he is ostensibly thinking about how he need not be. The objective condition of fearfulness and caution has set in before it can become conscious in another form than denial. When the imaginable impossible robbery occurs Juan is ready because, by going through with denying his anxiety, he has prepared to act it out without having to think it through.

When Tom the highwayman and three other 'pads' ambush Juan with the threat, '"Damn your eyes! your money or your life!"' (XI, st. 10), the line is, significantly, unassigned. The episode that follows is one of the freshest and most remarkable in the poem. It captures, in eleven stanzas of violent summary justice, a male fantasy akin to cursing in its exploitation of righteousness: the fantasy of murder committed in self-defence.

The story of Tom the highwayman turns cross-cultural misunderstanding into nihilistic slapstick. Language barriers are particularly productive points of departure for fantasies because they allow the participants to react selectively to the provocations they encounter, elaborating those elements they understand and ignoring those they cannot (or choose not to) decipher. Thus Juan, confused by the English command to stand and deliver, is nevertheless quite aware of the highwaymen's intentions towards him:

> Juan yet quickly understood their gesture,
>   And being somewhat choleric and sudden,
> Drew forth a pocket-pistol from his vesture,
>   And fired it into one assailant's pudding –
> Who fell, as rolls an ox o'er in his pasture,
>   And roared out, as he writhed his native mud in,
> Unto his nearest follower or henchman,
> 'Oh Jack! I'm floored by that here bloody Frenchman!'
>
> (XI, st. 13)

The entire scene is a riot of slurs and mistaken nationalisms, Tom the highwayman displaying the principle of national rivalry at work in the British cultural imaginary when he mistakes Juan for a hostile Frenchman.

Tom is one of the poem's most intensely realized incidental characters. The narrator's eulogy of him achieves a startling heteroglossia.

He from the world had cut off a great man,
  Who in his time had made heroic bustle.
Who in a row like Tom could lead the van,
  Booze in the ken, or at the spellken hustle?
Who queer a flat? Who (spite of Bow-street's ban)
  On the high toby-spice so flash the muzzle?
Who on a lark, with black-eyed Sal (his blowing)
So prime, so swell, so nutty, and so knowing?

(XI, st. 18–19)

The concluding question, 'Who ... so prime, so swell, so nutty, and so knowing?' could as well be asked of the narrator as of Tom. He handles 'flash' jargon as if it were a part of the poetic inheritance, easily incorporating it into the *ottava rima*. Although it is hardly the kind of thing Wordsworth had in mind, this is nevertheless unquestionably 'a man speaking to men'. In some ways the stanza delivers a more distinctly masculine idiom than anything in Wordsworth.[9]

The virtuosic incorporation of Tom's flash jargon within the verse form gives a pleasure perhaps not unrelated to the one it gave those who used the flash idiom more in earnest. Byron and his friend Charles Matthews used the French 'e' at the end of the word *methodiste* in their correspondence to encode references to sexual encounters with other men.[10] The flash language of the highwaymen, like the *methodisme* Byron practised, encodes their desire to create and define secret male associations. By bringing this special vocabulary into the poem in his own voice, rather than as a quotation, the narrator calls attention to his own act of incorporation.

It falls to the narrator to tell Tom's story in flash slang because Tom is dead. In *Don Juan* the drive to represent a consciousness in appropriate language often outlives the bearer of the consciousness. The murder, and the poetic representation of the linguistic consciousness of the man murdered, are integral parts of a continuous process of appropriation in which an example of idiolect is first killed, and then fixed in a medium, verse. Poetic form preserves the otherwise organic and ephemeral slang of the robber Tom as if it were a specimen of tissue in a jar of formaldehyde. This function of poetry is acknowledged explicitly in Byron's *The Prophecy of Dante*:

> I am not of this people nor this age,
> And yet my harpings will unfold a tale
> Which shall preserve these times when not a page
> Of their perturbed annals could attract
> An eye to gaze upon their civil rage,
> Did not my verse embalm full many an act
> Worthless as they who wrought it.

('Prophecy of Dante', Canto I, ll. 143–9)

Readerly affect in the instance of Tom is, however, different from what the character Dante suggests. Both the narrator and the reader of the eulogy, likewise 'not of this people nor this age' (probably not highwaymen, for example), are nevertheless thrilled by the worthless jargon of Jack and Tom. The narrator bids farewell to Tom with the observation that:

> Heroes must die; and by God's blessing 'tis
> Not long before the most of them go home.

(XI, st. 20)

Jerome Christensen reads the Tom episode as an illustration of an aphorism from the Ismail cantos, 'Short speeches pass between two men who speak / No Common language' (VIII, st. 58). For Christensen: 'Tom's inability to converse is bound up with his endeavor to acquire by force what by law of this economy can be gained only by exchange.'[11] A distinctive idiom, ordinarily a marker of distance from the metropolis and from privilege, identifies Tom as a boulevard gangster, far from the elite but close to the action. Christensen calls Tom 'Byron's last hero' because Tom resists the pathology of consensus in his commercial society. Tom's unintelligibility indexes his exclusion, not only from polite society, but also from the legitimate economy. In Christensen's reading of Canto XI, Tom represents the dispossession of the working class at the beginning of the nineteenth century, and his assault on Juan is thus an inarticulate reprisal against the inadequacies of the ideology of political economy.

While I sympathize with Christensen's critique, I cannot agree that the killing of Tom is exempt from the moral judgement of the poem.[12] The poem does make a sacrifice of Tom, but the Tom stanzas invite an inadvertent, nearly undetectable identification. Tom's flash talk is amusing and exotic from the point of view of the reader only in so far as the reader is able to feel superior to him. This perception of Tom's dialect as deficient is a mistake, not the 'truth' of the situation but rather a function of the subjective position of the perceiver. Juan doesn't need to understand his language to interpret his alienating demand and know that he must shoot him. Presumably the reader gets more of what Tom is saying, but not enough for him to live on.

The necessity of policing the kind of internal economic tensions that issue in robbery is one aspect of the demand for the fusion of military and judiciary functions that accompanied the rise of the modern nation-states at the beginning of the nineteenth century. While some recent critics have been satisfied with an understanding of Romanticism as coercive ideology acting in concert with an ensemble of repressive social institutions, Christensen has posed *Don Juan* as exemplary of an anti-ideological Romantic textual politics. In an intriguing literalization of the poem's suggestive relation to psychosocial concepts and categories, he terms *Don Juan* a 'psychotic text'.[13] For Juan, the narrator's voice remains inaudible, just as the entire text 'will, for better or worse, never overcome its incapacity to hear the paternal command and achieve thereby symbolic reconciliation'.[14]

There is unquestionably something grand and compelling about a psychotic text. Yet going back to the first step in reading the poem that I described in chapter 1, 'learning to say Juan', I would explain the psychotic split between the narrator and the protagonist differently. While it is true that Juan can never hear the narrator, the same is not true for the reader. The reader not only can hear the narrator, she can hear that Juan can't hear him, every time she reads the word 'Juan'. The repronunciation of Juan renders the psychotic split between the narrator and Juan available to the reader as her own performance of the text, the enunciation that 'produces' both Juan's story and the narrator's voice. By focusing exclusively on the avoidance of Oedipal conflict within the text, Christensen overlooks the poem's locus of symbolic reconciliation, the relation of the narrator to his readers. In contrast to more conventional structures of narrative closure, the arc of Juan's consciousness never threatens to coincide with that of his narrator. Instead, as the poem progresses the narrator's digressions become less explicitly linked to the plot and more dependent on the anticipation of a counter-plot of readerly response. The narrator's interruptions of the plot can create continuity for his audience on the level of the telling.

Sometimes the associative logic of *Don Juan*'s telling must be brought to bear as context on enigmatic episodes such as this one. As soon as the narrator drops Tom's story he brings up capital punishment. A fantasy of self-defence animates the logic of deterrence used to justify the death penalty. Capital punishment is predicated on the denial of agency that founds abstract justice and separates it in the citizens' minds from simple revenge. If society makes it clear that those who violate certain laws will be punished by death, then punishment ceases to be the responsibility of the society, in that a criminal presumed to have known about the consequences of his act brings those consequences upon himself. Lining up these three principles in the logic of deterrence, one becomes aware of an excessive faith in the power of identification. The assumption is that once everyone knows that someone else has been executed they will understand execution as something that could happen to them. Of course, the lesson of the Terror was that public reaction to executions rarely follows the logic of deterrence. Byron made this point about the inefficacy of capital punishment as deterrence in his maiden speech in the House of Lords.[15] Opposition to capital punishment was one of his longest standing and most deeply held political convictions. In a subtle reprise of the considerations occasioned by Juan's shooting of Tom he conjures the twin *ignis fatui* of capital punishment and mob violence. After describing 'The line of lights too up to Charing Cross, / Pall Mall, and so forth' as part of Juan's first impressions of a London evening, the narrator contrasts these much discussed public improvements with 'the Continent's illumination'. At the time England prided itself on having streetlights before France did. The narrator observes that, while the British illuminated their cities first, the French did not follow this 'old way' of lighting the streets –

> The French were not yet a lamp-lighting nation,
>   And when they grew so – on their new-found lanthorn,
> Instead of wicks, they made a wicked man turn.
>
> A row of gentlemen along the streets
>   Suspended, may illuminate mankind,
> As also bonfires made of country seats;
>   But the old way is best for the purblind:

The other looks like phosphorus on sheets,
  A sort of Ignis-fatuus to the mind,
Which, though 'tis certain to perplex and frighten,
Must burn more mildly ere it can enlighten.

(XI, st. 26–7)

Like the catharsis Aristotle postulated as an effect of tragedy, the public execution of criminals and revolutionaries can be understood as having a stabilizing influence on the audience. They are purged with pity and fear, identifying with the sacrificial victims and thus coerced by the fate they suffer vicariously to abide by the law. Tragedy is the dramatic representation of a more ancient rite of sacrifice, the scapegoating of an individual in order to cure the *polis* of a curse. Thus the rite of capital punishment revives a pre-tragic method of restoring society's equilibrium. In remarking that such practices 'Must burn more mildly ere [they] can enlighten', the narrator suggests what society may confirm by valuing art over the violence it represents – that the sacrifice of the *pharmakon* must be dimmed and shaped as representation before it can enlighten, rather than simply frighten.[16]

The dichotomy that arose at the conclusion to the last chapter between the mostly benign fantasies of art and the savagery of applied fantasy is nowhere more apparent than in the instance of capital punishment. The death penalty is ur-tragedy for those unable to respond to representation and who have no use for the hard-won cultural distance that separates justice from revenge. In spinning out a fantasy of killing in self-defence the narrator of *Don Juan* becomes ambivalent. The fantasy of self-defence is one of the ways in which civilized people think about the feelings occasioned by such things as armed robbery. But begin to string up real men and they will fight for their rights as if they were their own, because, of course, in a sense they are, just as all of us are subject to the same laws as those upon whom sanctioned penalties are visited. London, however, was not lit by lamplight alone. Byron lived at the end of an era that the historian Peter Linebaugh has usefully termed a 'thanatocracy', which he defines as a society in which the government rules by frequent exercise of the death penalty. Linebaugh quotes John Locke as the theorist of British thanatocracy:

Political power, then, I take to be a right of making laws with penalties of death, and, consequently, all less penalties for the regulating and preserving of property, and of employing the force of the community in the execution of such laws ... and all this only for the public good.[17]

The discussion of scepticism in contemporary metaphysics which precedes the Tom episode in the introduction to Canto XI also belongs with the story, because in it the narrator explores the relationship between death and representation, conditioning readerly response to the events that follow. After doubting if doubt itself be what people take it to be, the narrator begs our leave to dismiss further 'metaphysical discussion' as 'neither here nor there'.

> ... our days are too brief for affording
>   Space to dispute what *no one* ever could
> Decide, and *every body one day* will
>   Know very clearly – or at least lie still.
>
>   (XI, st. 5)

The pun in the final line on the word 'lie' enacts the undecidability the stanza recommends. Metaphysical sceptics who question our ability to know the truth about ourselves or the world we live in are right in so far as they indicate that representation has its limits, but wrong to assume that in the act of indicating those limits the limits themselves are known. If one's own death is at once unrepresentable, and the only perspective from which one may judge the felicity of all representation, then sceptics are correct to deny the metaphysical grounding of representation in the subject. Any future state that will admit of continued individual acts of judgement is one in which representations may continue to misrepresent. An afterlife in which we are not absolutely deprived of consciousness, simply 'still', is an afterlife in which we may continue to lie and be deceived.[18]

The 'sublime discovery' that Byron ascribes to Bishop Berkeley, 'That all's ideal – *all ourselves*', corresponds to what *Don Juan* has been demonstrating, albeit in a different register and with a greater degree of sophistication. The individual consciousness that underlies even the most self-effacing Horatian persona or abstract democratic citizen is at the base of any idea of universality, whether sceptical or positivist.

What a sublime discovery 'twas to make the
    Universe universal Egotism!
That all's ideal – *all ourselves*: I'll stake the
    World (be it what you will) that *that's* no Schism.
Oh, Doubt! if thou be'st Doubt, for which some take thee,
    But which I doubt extremely – thou sole prism
Of the Truth's rays, spoil not my draft of spirit!
Heaven's brandy, – though our brain can hardly bear it.

For ever and anon comes Indigestion,
    (Not the most 'dainty Ariel') and perplexes
Our soarings with another sort of question:
    And that which after all my spirit vexes,
Is, that I find no spot where man can rest eye on,
    Without confusion of the sorts and sexes,
Of being, stars, and this unriddled wonder,
The World, which at the worst's a glorious blunder –

                      (XI, st. 2–3)

The limitation of scepticism as a system rather than as a specula-
tion is that there is always a spot in the sceptic's picture, a place
from which the view itself can be doubted. Lacan liked to say,
'You never look at me from the place from which I see you.'[19]
When Byron says that he can 'find no spot where man can rest eye
on', he means that there is no rest for the sceptical eye, which
must go on turning the picture, looking for the anamorphoses that
constitute the perspectives from which others see us. The sugges-
tion that the world itself is a 'glorious blunder' employs the logic
of a truly sceptical stance, which is different from that of a scepti-
cal system. In Byronic scepticism one must be able to be wrong in
order to ever be right about anything important. The world as blunder
is a way of characterizing this approach, in which the systemati-
cally non-duped err and the mistaken are at least on their way to
knowledge.

Similarly, when Juan is said to mistake 'God Damn' for the 'Salam'
of the English-speaking world, this is not the simply ironic and
relativizing remark it appears:

Juan, who did not understand a word
    Of English, save their shibboleth, 'God damn!'

And even that he had so rarely heard,
  He sometimes thought 'twas only their 'Salam',
Or 'God be with you!' – and 'tis not so absurd
  To think so; for half English as I am
(To my misfortune) never can I say
I heard them wish 'God with you', save that way; –

(XI, st. 12)

'God damn', like 'Salam', reflects a desire to pronounce on something that remains undecidable. Whether we exploit God's name in cursing our rivals or praise him in the course of living in his world, by pronouncing such epithets we invest them with some more or less vague presumption of their efficacy. That the ubiquity of 'God damn' degrades belief beyond recognition only corroborates the narrator's point that such verbal behaviour serves a purpose other than that which it supposes. Although he does not define that purpose, we can speculate: cursing is nearly emblematic of men in groups. Cursing, as Shakespeare demonstrates with the drunken Caliban and his comrades Stephano and Trinculo in the *Tempest*, is among the first steps in forming many masculine associations.

In order to focus what I see as the most significant and central area of concern within this constellation of narrative digressions, I now move backwards in the poem to the story of the death of the Commandant at Ravenna. This remarkable episode was drawn very directly from the poet's life, and had its genesis in a series of accounts Byron wrote first in his personal letters. The incident occurred while Byron was the *cavalier servente* of a young Italian noblewoman, Teresa Guiccioli. Her family, the Gambas, were deeply involved in the Italian resistance to the imperial Austrian forces which occupied Italy at the time. Byron became a close associate and fellow traveller of the Gambas' secret society, the Carbonari. The assassination of Del Pinto, the Commandant of the Imperial Austrian occupying forces in Ravenna, must have affected Byron strongly, as he was at the time storing munitions for the Carbonari at his residence. To an outsider who yearned to be part of an heroic uprising, the murder of the Commandant was both a sign that the time for revolutionary action might be near and a warning of just how serious the consequences of involvement in Italian politics could be. The narrator's version, as distinct from those Byron sent home to England in his correspondence, is saturated with the poet's most sophisticated literary allusions and adopts his most public, theatrical voice. The sequence is a virtuosic performance, but the reader is left to puzzle out exactly of what. The closest analogy to what the speaker is doing offered in the poem comes in the Preface to Cantos VI–VIII, which was written when Byron resumed the poem sometime after the Ravenna incident. In the Preface Byron mocks the Tory eulogists of the suicidal Foreign Secretary Castlereagh:

> But the Minister was an elegant Lunatic – a sentimental Suicide – he merely cut the 'carotid artery' (blessings on their learning) and lo! the Pageant, and the Abbey! and 'the Syllables of Dolour yelled forth' by the Newspapers – and the harangue of the Coroner in an eulogy over the bleeding body of the deceased – (an Anthony worthy of such a Caesar) – and the nauseous and atrocious cant of a degraded Crew of Conspirators against all that is sincere and honourable.
>
> (*CPW* V, p. 296)

The pitch of hysteria that enters the poem whenever the subject is Castlereagh has tangled roots in a number of Byron's complexes. Louis Crompton has shown the degree to which the circumstances of Castlereagh's suicide (most likely fear of disgrace from exposure as a homosexual) set off Byron's anxieties. Another aspect of the extreme reaction Castlereagh always evoked for Byron would appear to be visible here in the painful questions his method and success as Foreign Secretary raised about the moral limitations of political leadership. Byron desired a more direct and public role in European politics, yet he ceaselessly pursued his perception that political leadership ordinarily functions only within certain seemingly immutable limits. While he detested Castlereagh for betraying the trust of his own and other countries, he also feared that the Christian values that mattered to him, charity in particular, were simply incompatible with earthly authority. The following sequence represents some of Byron's most profound and least partial and reductive thinking about political leadership.

The incorporation of a bulletin from Ravenna into Canto V of *Don Juan* (stanzas 33–9) has been said to demonstrate the extreme flexibility of the form of the poem, its openness to digression and heterogeneous elements. T.G. Steffan describes it as a signal instance of the accretive method, in which the poet incorporated new stanzas within matrices of standing material.[20] The matrix of this digression on political assassination finds Juan a slave at auction, still pining for his last love, Haidee. The narrator breaks the story off in order to relate some news from occupied Italy.

The narrator tells us of an assassination that has just occurred outside Byron's Ravenna home. Del Pinto, leader of the occupying forces, has been murdered, presumably by a member of the Carbonari, the insurrectionary force with whom Byron has been collaborating. Byron's self-presentation here is crucial. The assassination calls into question as nothing else could the ethics of his involvement with the *turba*, or mob. The stanzas describing this event are overlaid with a pattern of allusion suggesting that Byron was aware of, and could anticipate, the kind of criticism his actions on behalf of the Carbonari might provoke. As the fictional characters of *Don Juan* are encoded with biographical and literary references, so the ostensibly autobiographical may also prove in some ways fictional.

One approach to reading this digression is through literary allusions. Looking at the body of the dead Commandant, the narrator muses:

> So as I gazed on him, I thought or said –
>
> 'Can this be death? then what is life or death?
>   'Speak!' but he spoke not: 'wake!' but still he slept: –
> *But yesterday and who had mightier breath?*
>   A thousand warriors by his word were kept
> In awe: *he said, as the centurion saith,*
>   *'Go', and he goeth; 'come' and forth he stepp'd.*
> The trump and bugle till he spake were dumb –
> And now nought left him but the muffled drum.'
>
> (V, st. 35–6)

'But yesterday and who had mightier breath?' is from Antony's speech to the crowd over the body of Caesar in *Julius Caesar*, III. ii. 119–20. The story of Jesus' encounter with the Roman centurion appears in Matthew 8. 5–13, Luke 7. 1–10, and John 4. 46–53. The two words 'No more' are seen by G. Wilson Knight as a reference to *Hamlet*, III. i. 61, the 'To be or not to be' speech.[21] Allusion only two words in length is tricky; Knight is notoriously excessive in his view of Byron as Shakespearean. In view of what appear to be numerous half-echoes of both *Hamlet* and *Measure for Measure*, I appeal to an observation of Jonathan Bate's in *Shakespeare and the English Romantic Imagination* for corroboration:

> The occurrence of two allusions in quick succession, the second usually quieter than the first, is very frequent in *Don Juan*; once the mind is sent to Shakespeare, it dwells there for a moment and picks up a second treasure.[22]

It would seem likely that this is an instance of the pattern Bate identifies, although it is not one of the examples he gives. In any event, I shall treat it as such.

The reference to *Julius Caesar* conjures a political context that is elsewhere assiduously suppressed. The narrator feigns ignorance of the Carbonari and their 'quarrels' with the occupying army and the Commandant, only to take up, in his oration over the dead body, the guise of an eminently dangerous and political man. Frederick Beaty sees this canto as the Roman or Stoic canto of *Don Juan*, finding in Juan's conversation with the English mercenary John Johnson in the slave market 'an authentic replica of the dialogue form in which both Horace and Persius treated Stoic doctrines'.[23] The question raised by Stoicism and *Julius Caesar* alike that concerns us here is the degree to which we can not only *have* but also *use* our emotions to stir others to action. Antony reveals his feelings at this moment with a particular end in view, and thus opens himself to the charge of insincerity. We are likely to assume that his speech is all show because it works as a show. But the assumption is not necessarily valid. A.D. Nuttall's *A New Mimesis: Shakespeare's Representation of Reality* argues this point:

> We may further ask, is Antony sincere? The question, oddly enough, can be answered with slightly more confidence when the reference is to a fictional person (where the clues are finite) than with reference to a real-life person (where they are indefinite and in any case liable to subversion). I think that Antony is sincere. He feels real grief for Caesar but is, so to speak, effortlessly separate from the grief even while he feels it. We therefore have something that is psychologically more disquieting than the ordinary machiavel, who pretends emotion while he coldly intrigues for power. Antony feels his emotions and then *rides* them, controls them, moderating their force as need arises.[24]

An unsettling allusion to a psychologically disquieting character and moment, the reference is both commonplace (few speeches in Shakespeare are better known), making it almost not a reference at all, and ironic. (In Canto IX, stanzas 14–6 Byron ridicules those who quote from obvious passages in Shakespeare.) The allusion is an historical observation in the form of an extremely self-conscious kind of play-acting ('So as I gazed at him, I thought or said –'). The passage reflects Byron's practice of Roman reference which suggests that the 'scars' of 'old wounds' are always near the new, and that the 'horrid contrast' of continuing strife in the countries of classical civilization was a Byronic obsession:

> But it was all a mystery. Here we are,
>   And there we go: – but *where*? five bits of lead,
> Or three, or two, or one, send very far!
>   And is this blood, then, form'd but to be shed?
> Can every element our elements mar?
>   And air – earth – water – fire live – and we dead?
> *We*, whose minds comprehend all things? *No more*;
> But let us to the story as before.
>
> (V, st. 39)

As difficult to pin down as Byron's Shakespearean references are, the one to the New Testament seems even more mystifying and ambivalent. The Centurion of Capernaum comes to Jesus and asks him to heal his slave, who is dying. Jesus prepares to return with the man to his home and the Centurion stops him. In Luke he uses the words familiar to Catholics as the prayer before Holy Communion:

> Lord, do not trouble yourself, for I am not worthy to have you come under my roof; therefore I did not presume to come to you. But say the word, and let my servant be healed. For I am a man set under authority, with soldiers under me: and I say to one, 'Go', and he goes; and to another 'Come', and he comes; and to my slave 'Do this', and he does it.
>
> (Luke 7.8, RSV)

Jesus is surprised by this demonstration on the part of a Roman soldier and holds him up as an example, saying, 'I tell you, not even in Israel have I found such faith' (7.9). The narrator thus casts himself as an unsuccessful Saviour ('Speak!' but he spoke not: 'wake!' but still he slept: –) and conflates, in the figure of the Commandant, the Centurion and his slave. We are in the presence here of the Jesus most doubted by the Enlightenment *philosophes* and some of the Romantics (see Shelley) – the worker of miracles, the raiser of the dead, the juggler whose artifice led a naive population into the Christian era.[25] An unsuccessful Jesus and an ironic Antony make strange companions in this shadow-play behind the stanzas. The poet's ambition to lead and his scepticism about authority have reached a deadlock. Unable to act decisively either to undo the murder of the man who lies in front of him or to capitalize on his death as a step towards throwing off the imperial Austrian yoke for Italy, Byron is left with blood on his hands and nothing to show for it. By storing arms and aiding the Carbonari financially he tacitly participates in the assassination, yet when this revolutionary violence occurs, the only role available to him is his literary one, the scribe or at best the actor whose job it is to make a speech over the body.

Literary and biographical allusion in *Don Juan* form an aesthetic of ambiguity that is purposeful yet indeterminate, relevant and at the same time frustratingly twisted in its logic. Just when a piece seems to finish the puzzle and secure an interpretation, another comes along to throw that momentary totality out of alignment – for allusion is a kind of historical repetition and, as we saw at the beginning of this chapter, such repetition can entail a jolting revision.

Preternaturally alert by the time of *Don Juan* to the potential for inadvertent self-disclosure, Byron engages, through his narrator, in an elaborate and necessarily unending game of misrepresentation. Each episode in *Don Juan* appears as the next step in a staging of the self that will not end because any closure would provide an opportunity for disclosure on the part of another. In the allusive self-examination of the Ravenna assassination stanzas, Byron engages in the 'task of re-creating one's true life' which Proust, one of the few guides equal to the adventure of Byron's art, identifies as 'a most tempting prospect' but one that requires 'courage of many kinds', including the courage of one's emotions, 'for above all it means the abrogation of one's dearest illusions, it means giving up one's belief in the objectivity of what one has oneself elaborated.'[26] Being mistaken, for Proust as for Byron, is the first step in being correct. It is this abrogation of his own illusions, even, in the case of the allusions in the description of the assassination of the

Commandant, the abrogation of illusions that he would eventually die for, that Byron excelled. It is a process from which Byron did not rest, the practice of discovering from within the accumulation of habit and the elaboration of ideals one's own true life. For Byron as for Proust, this true life exists not as the subject defined by biography, but as the narrator imagined by the work. In acting out Mark Antony and Jesus for us over the body of the Commandant, the narrator releases anxiety about the poet's possible political complicity and realizes that despite good intentions the authorial self remains fragmented. A freedom fighter is still a killer, and as all meaning is contextual, so is all human identity. Only in the act of raising doubts about political involvement is Byron the narrator capable of seeking truth, for the unity that ceaselessly evades the human actor is available to the artist through a historically aware self-reflection. Proust says,

> One feels, yes, but what one feels is like a negative which shows only blackness until one has placed it near a special lamp and which must also be looked at in reverse. So with one's feelings: until one has brought them within range of the intellect one does not know what they represent. Then only, when the intellect has shed light upon them, has intellectualized them, does one distinguish, and with what difficulty, the lineaments of what one felt.[27]

5
Marriage, Mobility and the Disavowal of Closure

In the English cantos *Don Juan* modulates towards the novel, while increasing the ratio of narrative digression to plot development. This double strategy results in some of the poem's most intriguing and successful effects – the larger ensemble provides a more variegated canvas for the narrative digressions, which are themselves enlivened by the poet's first-hand knowledge of the society he depicts. Forgoing the adventurous fantasies of Orientalism, the narrative turns to an extravagant nocturne played on the conventions of the country house novel. Once Juan is in England, the poem expands the role of the narrator and elaborates on the circumstances of the telling. In the final stanzas of Canto XV, the narrator's room is shrouded in moody darkness as he prepares his audience for the performance of a ghost story:

> The night (I sing by night – sometimes an owl,
>   And now and then a nightingale) – is dim,
> And the loud shriek of sage Minerva's fowl
>   Rattles around me her discordant hymn:
> Old portraits from old walls upon me scowl –
>   I wish to heaven they would not look so grim;
> The dying embers dwindle in the grate –
> I think too that I have sate up too late:
>
> And therefore, though 'tis by no means my way
>   To rhyme at noon – when I have other things
> To think of, if I ever think, – I say

> I feel some chilly midnight shudderings,
> And prudently postpone, until mid-day,
> Treating a topic which alas but brings
> Shadows; – but you must be in my condition
> Before you learn to call this superstition.

> (XV, st. 97–8)

The ghost story is always more than a story; it is a performance of storytelling as self-display. Telling ghost stories is among the most theatrical of narrative situations. The genre calls direct attention to the sensations connecting the teller to the audience. In the English cantos of *Don Juan* the narrator is drawn deeper into the performative aspect of his role, asking the reader to share nuances of his gesture and tone as if his storytelling were taking place in a luxurious country house like the one his story describes. These cantos temper the poem's antagonism to contemporary British culture by experimenting with a tentative reintegration of the exilic storyteller into British society. Ghost stories are told, conventionally, late at night using fantasy as a parlour game. The night game comes to define the narrator's ambiguous relation to the British society he describes, shadowing the bright, visible half of a culture with the obscure unconscious revealed by his tale.

Emphasizing the nocturnal setting of fantastic storytelling is an aesthetic commonplace that demotes fantasy to a secondary, peripheral status in relation to mimesis. Writers indulging in fantasy in the early nineteenth century ran the risk of a stigmatizing double bind: the presence of the fantastic was read either as a failure in mimesis, or as a ruse of self-display. The aesthetic hegemony of mimetic writing militated against all the non-representational performing arts by casting performance as self-objectification. So feminist educational reformers including Hannah More and Maria Edgeworth argued that the training of women in time-consuming aesthetic accomplishments contributed to the fetishization of their bodies under the male gaze.[1] They understood learning to play the piano, for instance, as pandering to the male desire to watch women perform.

Reading occupies a liminal position in relation to the poles proposed by this ideology of mimesis. The reader is the audience for the performance of the text, and with the novel, the performance of reading is private and interiorized, distant from that which the text represents. Readers are not known by the text: the audience remains abstract. But the English cantos extend the importance of reading beyond social abstraction by staging differences between reader's relationships to reading. Byron shows how women's reading determines control of social vision, providing the basis for meta-performances of how and when to achieve effective self-display, hiding with tact the traces of vanity.

Juan has, through the auspices of his mission on behalf of the Empress Catherine and the recommendation of his own attractiveness and accomplishments, found his way into the heart of fashionable British society. With his ward Leila safely delegated to an appropriate governess, our hero becomes available to accept that most English of invitations, the country house party.[2] The narrator has a grand time introducing the cast and describing the setting, Norman Abbey, a deconsecrated monastery owned by Lord Henry Amundeville, a government minister. The narrator's point in his description of the party tends to be how out of place these city people are in the country, and by implication how out of touch the British aristocracy have grown with their ancestral roles as leaders and benefactors within the local communities centred on their great estates. Juan moves comfortably among this highly artificial group, attracting the attention of his hostess, Lady Adeline Amundeville, as well as that of at least two of the party's female guests, the Duchess of Fitz-Fulke, a well-known (and married) adventuress, and Aurora Raby, an appealingly reticent young Catholic heiress. No sooner has the party begun and the various constituents settled into their familiar roles and pastimes than the equilibrium of both context and hero is endangered by the appearance of what is understood to be the ghost of one of the monks who formerly inhabited the Abbey to Juan in his chambers. We pick up the story shortly after Juan's initial encounter with 'the Black Friar'.

The hostess of Norman Abbey, Adeline Amundeville, represents a departure for the poem in that she is the first character effectively to challenge the role of the narrator, and she does this from the position of a passionate reader. The narrator's account of the Friar's ghostly visit to Juan's rooms is suspenseful, as good as anything in the poem in this vein, but the interpolated ballad of the Black Friar and its performance by Adeline capture the narrator's attention more even than the ghost story itself. Adeline's conversationally polite question over tea and muffins provokes Juan's disclosure of his nocturnal visitation:

> But seeing him all cold and silent still,
>   And every body wondering more or less,
> Fair Adeline enquired, 'If he were ill?'
>   He started, and said, 'Yes – no – rather – yes.'
> The family physician had great skill,
>   And being present, now began to express
> His readiness to feel his pulse and tell
> The cause, but Juan said, 'He was quite well.'
>
>   (XVI, st. 32)

The mystery of Juan's state is not one the physician can solve, and Lord Henry makes things worse by mentioning the family ghost. Juan's condition requires a social remedy which Adeline provides, turning Juan's fright into the occasion for a double performance. First, in order to distract the company from Juan's discomposure, Adeline offers to play a ballad she has written about the friar who haunts her husband's estate. Lord Henry, missing the point of his wife's tactful diversion, demands she add the words to her planned instrumental rendition:

> Of course the others could not but express
> In courtesy their wish to see displayed
>   By one *three* talents, for there were no less –
> The voice, the words, the harper's skill, at once
> Could hardly be united by a dunce.
>
>   (XVI, st. 39)

In the next stanza the narrator opens a debate on feminine performance and the social morality of self-display. He then interrupts himself with the ballad itself, in six stanzas, but he will resume the debate with new intensity:

> After some fascinating hesitation, –
>   The charming of these charmers, who seem bound,
> I can't tell why, to this dissimulation, –
>   Fair Adeline, with eyes fixed on the ground
> At first, then kindling into animation,
>   Added her sweet voice to the lyric sound,
> And sang with much simplicity, – a merit
> Not the less precious, that we seldom hear it.
>
>   (XVI, st. 40)

Adeline's song is a romantic ballad about the last of the friars to resist the deconsecration of Norman Abbey into a country house.

> But beware! beware! of the Black Friar,
>   He still retains his sway,
> For he is yet the church's heir
>   Who ever may be the lay.
> Amundeville is lord by day,
>   But the monk is lord by night.
> Nor wine nor wassail could raise a vassal
>   To question that friar's right.
>
> (XVI, st. 40–5)

Adeline's song provokes the narrator's interest in the conduct-book issue of the morality of women's performance, and he underscores the phrases he adopts from their vocabulary. His response to her singing is to examine her decision to sing:

> Fair Adeline, though in a careless way,
>   As if she rated such accomplishment
> As the mere pastime of an idle day,
>   Pursued an instant for her own content,
> Would now and then as 'twere *without display*,
>   Yet *with* display in fact, at times relent
> To such performances with haughty smile,
> To show she could, if it were worth her while.
>
> Now this (but we will whisper it outside)
>   Was – pardon the pedantic illustration –
> Trampling on Plato's pride with greater pride,
>   As did the Cynic on some like occasion;
> Deeming the sage would be much mortified,
>   Or thrown into a philosophic passion,
> For a spoilt carpet – but the Attic Bee
> Was much consoled by his own repartee.
>
> (XVI, st. 42–3)

The narrator envies Adeline, who can afford to be coquettish and withhold her narrative self-display. Respecting her nonchalance, he resents the attention it gets her. And so he appeals to the men in the audience with an allusion to the anecdotal history of Hellenistic philosophy. Diogenes the Cynic once walked on a carpet and said, 'Thus I trample on the pride of Socrates', to which his interlocutor replied, 'with greater pride'. Byron explains the anecdote in a note, catering to those without knowledge of Greek in a manner that imitates the imputed narcissism of Adeline, but in a masculine register. The note complains that carpets are *for* walking on, and offers a feigned mistrust of memory in place of an explanation of the apparent contradiction. The stanza calls attention to the narrator's easy familiarity with Greek philosophy, reasserting male learning at the expense of the supposed pride of feminine performance.

With masculine control of the story re-established, the narrator can afford to praise Adeline in comparison to other women performers, complimenting her on the intimidating attitude of nonchalance she is able to affect:

> Thus Adeline would throw into the shade,
>   (By doing easily whene'er she chose,
> What dilletanti do with vast parade)
>   Their sort of *half profession*: for it grows
> To something like this when too oft displayed,
>   And that it is so, every body knows,
> Who have heard Miss That or This, or Lady T'other,
> Show off – to please their company or mother.

> (XVI, st. 44)

Adeline can throw dilettantes into the shade because she is more than just a performer. She wrote the song she sang, and her reading enabled her writing. The narrator emphasizes the breadth of her reading, then the depth of her appreciation for form, revealing that her favorite author is Pope:

> In Babylon's bravuras – as the home
>   Heart ballads of Green Erin or Grey Highlands,
> That bring Lochaber back to eyes that roam
>   O'er far Atlantic continents or islands,
> The calentures of music which o'ercome
>   All mountaineers with dreams that they are nigh lands,
> No more to be beheld but in such visions, –
> Was Adeline well-versed, as compositions.

She also had a twilight tinge of '*Blue*',
  Could write rhymes, and compose more than she wrote;
Made epigrams occasionally too
  Upon her friends, as every body ought.
But still from that sublimer azure hue,
  So much the present dye, she was remote,
Was weak enough to deem Pope a great poet,
And what was worse, was not ashamed to show it.

(XVI, st. 46–7)

Adeline's self-possession is made to seem a product of her taste in literature, and her rivals languish in the shadow of her cultivated intellect. It is an indication of the enormous distance traversed by the character of the narrator since Canto I that he can finally allow a woman intellectual status. If the poem's narrative fantasies can be said to organize a screen through which more or less of the social world appears, Adeline is the character through whom the women writers in the poem's audience first become visible. In terms of the dialectic of masculine self-possession, posed as the opposition of Romanticism to women's writing, Adeline's performance represents the narrator's awakening to this cultural opposition and to the social possibilities of women's writing.[3] Recognition of an enabling otherness makes possible the introjection of new images necessary for the integrative transformation of narrative fantasy. A text able to imagine Adeline is a text prepared to modify its own destructive tendencies.

Why was the figure of the woman reader so important? Because a struggle based on gender had begun within the class struggle of the bourgeois cultural revolution. Print culture and consumption were the focal points of both struggles. The rise of the reading public increased the number of women writers and feminized various aspects of discourse.[4] Women's reading contributed to a culture of affective individualism, displacing the eighteenth-century model of marriage with a companionate ideal that was distinguished from a merely social marriage as true 'union'. Women's affective individualism and the new model of the companionate marriage complicated the patriarchal economy of property embodied in such structures as the country estate.

The search for a new social contract among men in effect rewrote the sexual contract between men and women. The philosophical and political elaboration of the rights of man in Western Europe occurred in tandem with a redefinition of the roles of women in civil society. Limiting women's access to the newly re-made spheres of production and community necessarily rendered them the over-determined signifiers of a domesticity apparently divested of politics. As the political text of everyday life became less legible with the rise of capitalism, men were forced to read a new politics of privacy and self-possession into the dynamics of feminine character. Social fantasies of male self-possession came to be embodied in women's 'roles', through coercive representations of women and the overt regulation of their conduct. 'Romantic' in its popular sense has this in common with its academic usage – some varieties of unfreedom must be consecrated for a society to continue to function.

The woman artist at the beginning of the nineteenth century experienced print culture as a double bind. She was absorbed in the figure of 'woman' as it was disseminated by the dominant culture, but unable to mediate this representation without being accused of seeking attention for herself as a commodity.[5] Bourgeois women were brought into conflict with men of their own class by a differential of liberation that left them less independent than they had been before the reforms that freed their male counterparts to travel, work and write as they pleased. The domestic ideology was an attempt to reshape the expectations of a generation of women aroused by the rhetoric of equality. At the core of this reshaping of expectations lay a myth of romantic love as the only legitimate fulfilment of women's affective individualism. As a woman writer in a successful marriage, Adeline Amundeville personifies the ambivalence generated by an excess of individuality under such limited opportunities for feminine self-realization. What she testifies to is the way in which all human identity is forged by relation, and, inevitably, by misdirection:

> Our gentle Adeline had one defect –
>   Her heart was vacant, though a splendid mansion;
> Her conduct had been perfectly correct,
>   As she had seen nought claiming its expansion.
> A wavering spirit may be easier wreck'd,
>   Because 'tis frailer, doubtless than a stanch one;
> But when the latter works its own undoing,
> Its inner crash is like an Earthquake's ruin.

> (XIV, st. 83)

The vacant heart is a very different image from the naked one familiar from the romantic Byronism of the *Childe Harold* period. Adeline promises to be a more complex portrait than those that have come before her in the poem are because, as is apparent from this description, the narrator not only perceives her as possessing a real interiority, however vacant, but he also anticipates that her core will change through her encounter with Juan. The 'inner crash' of her obstinate spirit is somehow linked to the vacancy of her heart, as though the degree to which she remains uncommitted emotionally were the result of a strength rather than a weakness of character. Adeline becomes the locus for the poem's most radical departure from its own philosophy of passion by demonstrating that, under certain circumstances, alienation is more natural than passion, and detachment more indicative of individuality and strength of character than commitment. Unlike Julia, whose platonic system was the symptom of a burgeoning sense of self-possession, Adeline knows herself and her world too well to care that much about them. Where Julia found in Juan the point of departure for the cultivation of her capacity for passion and self-assertion, Adeline sees him as a legitimate object of a more complex emotion: concern. The nuances of characterization here derive from the poet's determination to position his creations within a context the reality of which is derived from an understanding of social psychology. Byron's best characters think and act in response to others like themselves; they are intelligible in so far as they participate in a network of relations. Adeline, whose life is a crucial part of a peculiarly extensive, yet self-contained and artificial social setting, is most alive when she is most concerned.

> She knew not her own heart; then how should I?
>   I think not she was *then* in love with Juan:
> If so, she would have had the strength to fly
>   The wild sensation, unto her a new one:
> She merely felt a common sympathy
>   (I will not say it was a false or true one)
> In him, because she thought he was in danger –
> Her husband's friend, her own, young, and a stranger.

> (XIV, st. 91)

Yet, as will become apparent in the ensuing story line, Adeline's capacity for sympathy conflicts with the limitations imposed on

her by her role as a society wife. She lacks the freedom of move-
ment and expression that would give her sympathetic nature its
proper context. The socialized form of this tragic perception in our
society is patriarchy, in which women's mobility is sacrificed to
consecrate that of men. When Julia writes in her letter of farewell
to Juan that 'Love is of man's life a thing apart', she refers to the
way in which social structures use women to shield men from the
relentless catastrophes and creations of human relatedness.

The primary contemporary structure for the shelter of male psy-
ches is the aspect of life designated 'public'. The word 'public' is
rooted in an imposition which continues to resonate throughout
the history of its derivations – the early Latin word for people,
poplus or *poplicus*, was combined with *pubes*, referring to men who
had passed puberty and been accepted as adults. The metonymy by
which the adult male population comes to stand for the people as
a whole is a familiar one, but less familiar is the degree to which it
governs the vicissitudes of meaning in the derivatives of 'public'.
For instance, the imposition of adult men on society in general is
reinscribed for the nineteenth century when the signification of
the noun 'publicity' is transformed.

The primary meaning of publicity remains that of being open or
known to the public. The secondary meaning, that of calling spe-
cial attention to something, often in an attempt to sell it, has assumed
priority in modern usage. The transition between publicity as a
condition and publicity as an activity occurred in the early nine-
teenth century, the final stage of transformation for today's primary
usage. The Oxford English Dictionary gives Bentham in 1832, 'Pub-
licity is the very soul of justice', and Disraeli next, in 1867, 'The
studious composed their works without any view to their public-
ity.' It would appear that this marks the transition from Kant and
Bentham to Cant and Barnum, the twin avatars of modern public-
ity. Formerly associated with being unashamed of what you have
to say, publicity became the pursuit of the shameless.

The relationship between poetry and publicity necessarily changed
as the meaning of publicity changed. Foucault's theorization of the
epistemic shifts in punishment has given clues for a new under-
standing of the social efficacy of Augustan satire.[6] In an era of 'general'
punishment the poet as a public man was capable of doing justice
simply by bringing injustice to light. The way to regulate anony-
mous literary libels, Pope's 'arrow shot in the dark', was to name
their authors in a satire. Here is the process Bentham invokes when

he calls publicity the soul of justice. The aptness and cultural centrality of satire for the Augustans found its rationale in a system regulated by publicity in the older sense. As this discourse of general punishment gave way to a discipline which operates through the construction of the citizen rather than the punishment of the subject, a different publicity arose, and with it a different role for the poet. The Romantic writer, unable to rely on publicity as the authority of the father in the Augustan manner, was faced with a society the values of which seemed visible only as the forces of the marketplace. In seeking private affirmation in values and persons disengaged from civil life, men created women as narcissistic looking glasses seemingly outside of or in moral opposition to the demands of commerce. In dividing into public and private a life already devalued by the machines of dehumanized industry, this culture, through which men created the private identities and experiences they now felt they had to 'have', institutionalized men's lives as open to work and the public sphere and women's as limited to love and domesticity.

For the Byron of the early career, exemplary in his negotiation of this epistemic rupture, the loss of publicity as the 'soul' of justice meant that public satire had to give way to male fantasy. In *Childe Harold I and II* Byron forged a persona that was confirmed by celebrity in a way that only quest romance could, at that time, articulate. The passions which might have allowed Harold to experience pleasure are imaged at the beginning of his Pilgrimage as empty, satiety itself as unfulfilling, in order that the journey south and east attain the status necessary to counterbalance a perceived impotence of publicity to effect social integration. In a trope that is both imperialist and narcissistic, the adequacy of the known is imaged in farewell, attaining the level of poetic expression as it is being left. What had been regulated by publicity could now only be mastered by abandonment. Other lands are as the pages of a book, and the traveller, like the reader, creates their meaning by turning them one after the other back onto one another. The fullness of satiety maintains a necessary systemic lack, an absence Harold imagines when he sets out not only as his anticipated presence in other lands but also as his absence from his own. A present absence – this is the thought which Romantic fantasy transforms into an experience, and it is pre-eminently a thought of the impossibility of community:

> For pleasures past I do not grieve,
>   Nor perils gathering near;
> My greatest grief is that I leave
>   No thing that claims a tear.
>
> And now I'm in the world alone,
>   Upon the wide, wide sea:
> But why should I for others groan,
>   When none will sigh for me?

(CHP I, ll. 178–85)

The manifest self-pity of these lines from Harold's 'Good-bye' must have been on the minds of many who observed Byron's behaviour in the months leading up to his second departure from England in 1816. That this self-pity is written in a poem within a poem did nothing to lessen the force with which it was held to express the true state of mind of the author, not merely in his youth, but perpetually thereafter.[7] That this absence of the self from the self as an experience of futility became emblematic of an age should surprise us no less than that satire should have acceded so easily to the status of general truth in the age previous. Within a disciplinary discourse founded on the construction of the subject rather than on its punishment, a sense of non-identity and the longing for that which would confirm one without recourse to the system in which one has been constructed has an important function. Denied the power of publicity, the Romantic artist conceals social impotence within a fantasy of anti-social abandon.

Like the personae constructed in the courtly love lyric of the twelfth century, Romantic selfhood is a compromise formation in which a fantasy of individual agency is shared as social fantasy; and so it participates in, rather than conflicts with, the ideology of its cultural moment. The abjection of the courtly lover in the face of the perfection of the beloved is recast in the Romantic ethos as the abjection of social pleasure confronted by Promethean yearning. The imperialist impulse to enlist others while subordinating them is embodied in a fantasy which expresses and confounds satiety in movement – we go out of the country to get out of ourselves because that which is worthy in ourselves cannot be what was satisfied at home. Harold presages the modern 'existential' tourist, a pilgrim made holy by internal strife rather than by the intrinsic sacredness or object of his quest.[8]

The English cantos of *Don Juan* are concerned with the organization of enjoyment in a society that is stifled by its own pleasures. Like the alienated socialite Adeline and the existential tourist Harold, the members of Society are frustrated by their inability to imagine anything outside of themselves. The circuit of their lives and loves is, whether they acknowledge it or not, confining.

> And hence high life is oft a dreary void,
>> A rack of pleasures, where we must invent
> A something wherewithal to be annoy'd.
>> Bards may sing what they please about *Content*;
> Contented, when translated, means but cloyed;
>> And hence arise the woes of sentiment,
> Blue devils, and Blue-stockings, and Romances
> Reduced to practice and perform'd like dances.
>
> (XIV, st. 79)

Thus Byron's last attempt at an erotic allegory of Utopia takes place in a uniquely challenging context. A rack of pleasures presents an entirely different set of problems for the fantasist than an island or a harem. Where everything is already too comfortable, and love is an invention employed like other toys to pass the time, a useful fantasy will require an approach that takes into account the modern dilemma of ennui. How is one to imagine an instructive fantasy treating the advent of modern leisure? By imagining the one thing that at this point no one expects – Juan *not* in love.

Despite all the temptations which surround him in the English cantos, the multiplicity of interesting women with whom he is confronted, Juan retains some emotional distance from even the most idealized of them. In the context of the earlier episodes, this is what seems fantastic. Many explanations have been offered for the higher ratio of digression to plot in this sequence, but none as compelling as the idea that the narrator has become inhibited about allowing his hero to fall in love.

In his review of Charles Maturin's play *Bertram*, Coleridge spins a fantasy about individuation which is paradigmatic of the way in which women's emotions are exploited by patriarchal thinking:

> There is no danger (thinks the spectator or reader) of my becoming such a monster of iniquity as Don Juan! *I* never shall be an atheist! *I* shall never disallow all distinction between right

and wrong! *I* have not the least inclination to be so outrageous
a drawcansir in my love affairs! But to possess such a power of
captivating and enchanting the affections of the other sex! to be
capable of inspiring in a charming and even a virtuous woman,
a love so deep, and so entirely personal to *me*! that even my
worst vices, (if I *were* vicious) even my cruelty and perfidy, (if I
were cruel and perfidious) could not eradicate the passion! To be
so loved for my *own self*, that even with a distinct knowledge of
my character, she yet died to save me! this, sir, takes hold of
both sides of our nature, the better and the worse. For the he-
roic disinterestedness, to which love can transport a woman, can
not be contemplated without an honourable emotion of rever-
ence toward womanhood: and on the other hand, it is among
the mysteries, and abides in the dark ground-work of our na-
ture, to crave an outward confirmation of that *something* within
us, which is our *very self*, that something, not *made up* of our
qualities and relations, but itself the supporter and substantial
basis of all these. Love *me*, and not my qualities, may be a vi-
cious and insane wish, but it is not a wish wholly without a
meaning.[9]

Coleridge's vision here of a redeeming love that discounts a man's
faults and distills his essential selfhood is a kind of narcissistic sac-
rament. This fantasy of utter, unqualified acceptance makes male
self-possession the gift of the woman. One could see this as a hu-
manized version of the redemptive faith Wordsworth expresses to
his sister in the 'Lines Written Above Tintern Abbey', that 'Nature
never did betray the heart that loved her'. The crucial difference is
that Coleridge is speculating on a specifically male fantasy as it
might be held in the mind of a man, rather than inculcating the
fantasy as a doctrine that could be taken up by a woman, as
Wordsworth offers his faith in Nature to Dorothy.[10]

Where in the Don Juan legend does this fantasy originate? Al-
though much is made of the Don's skill as a seducer, I can remember
no scene in which a woman could be said to have identified his
'*very self*', much less venerated it. Shadwell's Don John, if he is in
fact the one Coleridge has in mind, is more partial to force and
deceit than to seduction, and can hardly be said to inspire much
devotion in the women he abuses. Coleridge is almost surely blending
his memories of Don John from Shadwell or perhaps from *Much
Ado About Nothing* with the much stronger ones he must have had

of the group of stage villains he takes up next in his essay, male characters from Shakespeare. This slippage is understandable – Shadwell's John is a poor copy of Shakespeare's Edmund in his philosophy of nature.

And Edmund is, of course, against all odds and to the sublime dismay of audiences and readers, 'belov'd' (*King Lear*, V.iii. 240–3). This awkward fact divides the play's audience, as good readers disagree about the line and the relationships. What precisely do Goneril and Regan feel for this man? Lear demands that his daughters confess their loves. Their words turn out to be empty, but they nevertheless do love *someone* more even than their husbands – not Lear, but Edmund. One of many uncanny symmetries in Lear, the link created between Lear and Edmund by the unanimity of Goneril and Regan in betrayal and in love, suggests the fantasy of woman's redemptive love, in that Lear's guilt appears projected as Edmund's evil. Abdicating absolutism finds its double in usurping illegitimacy.

What Coleridge's fantasy presents as women's heroic disinterestedness does exist in social reality, but there it is called dependence. We are witnessing one early example of what will become a generic proliferation of dependent women depicted as ennobled by their dependency. (The chorus of Nancy's lament in the musical *Oliver!*, 'As long as he *needs* me', sung about the less than sympathetic Bill Sykes, exploits this paradigm for the idealization of women's dependency.) Women are excluded from production and their dependency is fetishized as beauty, as love and as the sanctity of the home. Men turn from the competitive world of the marketplace towards their wives and sweethearts as secret bowers, havens in a heartless world, but in this turning to their women they deny women's capacity for choice. If there exists a central target of the satire in the exceedingly capacious and diverse *Don Juan*, it would be this complex. In his own very different idiom, Byron agrees with Wordsworth that the furthest reaching consequences of the industrial (and military) revolution will be in the sphere of human affections, and that the locus for this emptying out of feeling will be the family. Because of social conditions women are dehumanized by their love. This is a very severe piece of social criticism. Don Juan remains a repellent legend because he points to the inadequacy of the family to its own social function. Like Shakespeare's tragedy in relation to the supposed 'Elizabethan world-view', *Don Juan* asks if the social formation with which it coincides is working, and answers in the negative. Lear's imagination of the happy prison in which he and Cordelia may remain as birds in a cage, 'God's spies', is uncannily prophetic of the panoptics of married complacency.

Dudù and Haidee especially represent narcissistic male fantasies in that they are identified with the abstract categories men have designated as outside of or in opposition to political economy – Art and Nature. A trio of the poem's other heroines are, however, invested with all that society adds to the complexity and genuine otherness of men's imagination of love. In Donna Julia, Gulbeyaz and Adeline Amundeville, Byron has constructed and deconstructed the social fantasy of women's stronger and more intransigent love and explored the romanticization of women's dependency as a force in specific relationships.

One reason that these three women represent a more socialized and complex idea of woman's love is that they are all married. Julia's letter, Gulbeyaz's stylized and homicidal despair, Adeline's repression of her motives for coming between Juan and Fitz-Fulke – these are the moments in which Byron delves most deeply into the construction of woman as the one who feels love, as opposed to the loved one. (Haidee's traumatized, catatonic wasting away in the dénouement of her episode would qualify as well if it were not so pure and close a reflection of Lambro's jealous tyranny.) All three cases demonstrate a sympathy for the occlusion of women by their social roles; but they all also suggest strains of selfishness and delusion in the ways these women recognize and deal with their own circumscription.

Gulbeyaz is, of the three, the least complex, chiefly because in her position Byron seeks to imagine the extreme limit of male tyranny, and in her person its corrupting effect on the constrained woman. The luxury of Gulbeyaz's boudoir is like its vases 'of porcelain' which 'held in the fettered flowers, / Those captive soothers of a captive's hours' (VI, st. 97). The narrator inverts this commonplace later, at the end of a stanza in which Gulbeyaz registers her shock upon learning of Juanna's night in the harem. Hearing that Juanna was with Dudù, her 'heart's dew of pain sprang fast and chilly / O'er her fair front, like Morning's on a lily' (VI, st. 105).

The comparison with Dido that follows is as predictable as that of the flower, but more ironic, in that this Dido nearly becomes homicidal. At this point, however, the description of Gulbeyaz's misery slows to a standstill. The static nature of her simple, narcissistic jealousy makes it hard to render her suffering as anything but a pose. Byron repeats an image from the opening lines of one stanza to the opening lines of the next: the first begins, 'Her face declined and was unseen; her hair / Fell in long tresses like the weeping willow', and the next adds that 'Her head hung down, and her long hair in stooping / Concealed her features better than a veil.' Featureless, immobile, the story is stuck – even the narrator bogs down and registers his problem as an impatience with his medium:

> Would that I were a painter! to be grouping
>   All that a poet draws into detail!
> Oh that my words were colours! but their tints
> May serve perhaps as outlines or slight hints.

(VI, st. 109)

Gulbeyaz suffers passively because her process of self-fashioning, dependent as it is on arousing the admiration and dependence of another person, is breaking down. Her dilemma is like Adeline's in that she cannot move or change her sympathies because the social system in which she exists has no space for her to do so. England, unlike Gulbeyaz's city of Ismail or even Spain, allows women the freedom to circulate, but in England this circulation is constantly in danger of becoming commodified.

The opportunity to change one's focus and sublimate what otherwise may become overwhelmingly frustrating is the theme of Julia's letter to Juan in Canto I. There the fate of the adulterous young wife appears from her own perspective. Julia touches on a familiar topic when she declares that 'To love too much has been the only art / I used', begging the question of whether the 'too much' in this hackneyed, seemingly indestructible phrase refers to *how* she loved, or *what*.

Adeline Amundeville represents the most complex and satisfying investigation of this topic that Byron achieved in *Don Juan*. Her situation is more interesting and multifaceted than that of Julia because it arises out of her concern that Juan will fall to the charms of another married woman, Fitz-Fulke. Adeline senses that Fitz-Fulke is practising a kind of entrapment:

> Her Grace too pass'd for being an Intrigante,
>   And somewhat *mechante* in her amorous sphere;

> One of those pretty, precious plagues, which haunt
>   A lover with caprices soft and dear,
> That like to *make* a quarrel, when they can't
>   Find one, each day of the delightful year;
> Bewitching, torturing, as they freeze or glow,
> And – what is worst of all – won't let you go
>
> The sort of thing to turn a young man's head,
>   Or make a Werther of him in the end.
> No wonder then a purer soul should dread
>   This sort of chaste *liaison* for a friend;
> It were much better to be wed or dead,
>   Than to wear a heart a woman loves to rend.
> 'Tis best to pause, and think, ere you rush on,
> If that a '*bonne fortune*' be really '*bonne*.'

(XIV, st. 63–4)

By insinuating his own analysis of Fitz-Fulke's character within the motivations of Adeline, the narrator lends Adeline credibility without rendering her completely conscious of the meaning of her feelings for Juan. The feelings of the narrator and Adeline alike are implicated in the process of opposing Fitz-Fulke, because even altruistic actions cannot arise in an emotional vacuum. Fitz-Fulke's emotional entrapment is presented as the inverse of the self-deception Adeline practises in seeking to prevent it. In the English cantos, *Don Juan* balances characters against one another and deepens the dramatic situation with novelistic perspectivizing. The subsequent conversation between Adeline and her husband, Lord Henry, is a significant step beyond the simple mismatch of Julia and Don Alfonso, in that it depicts people who mean to communicate finding themselves unable to do so. The problem of 'women who love too much' becomes less one of male–female antagonism than of the evanescence of passion.

Adeline is motivated by her sense of social truth and the desire to share it with someone. Her husband no longer engages with her on this level, and it is the emptiness of his response to her interest in the way the world goes, more than any loss of attractiveness, that saps their marriage of its vitality. Lord Henry has only commonplaces to offer his wife, and better things to do than discuss with her the intricacies of seduction. But, as the narrator soon remarks, 'Intense intentions are a dangerous matter'. Without dwelling on its origin in Lord Henry's unromantic, businesslike distraction, the narrator moves on to a five-stanza digression on the relation between Love and Idleness. These stanzas are among the very best in *Don Juan*. Subtly and appositely the narrator eases dependency out from under the sign of gender where it has remained in every other consideration we have encountered. Although love may be the product of idleness, 'Thrice happy they who have an occupation!' Although women may have a more complex relationship to love through their socialization, love is not well rooted in our world for either sex because 'violent things more quickly find a term' (94). 'Would you have endless lightning in the skies?' we are asked in this stanza, recalling the 'silent thunder' of the quiet Dudù, and stressing the point that real love strains the capacities of society and representation, requiring that we tolerate unnatural states and paradoxical ideas. The narrator refuses us closure on the matter of Adeline's involvement with Juan – he wishes to keep 'the atrocious reader in *suspense*'. But then he assures us that even though 'It is not clear that Adeline and Juan / Will fall ... if they do, 'twill be their ruin.' Rhyming 'Juan' with 'ruin' is a not so subtle reminder of the fates of Julia, Haidee and Gulbeyaz; but by including him as a potential victim as well the narrator indicates that this episode promises a departure from the pattern of the past. In Adeline, Byron has raised the cultural stakes of women as objects in and subjects of male fantasy, and involved us at a higher level than before in considering the problem of human dependency.

The suspense in which the atrocious reader is left with regard to Adeline and Juan is never truly satisfied, only displaced onto the episode of the Black Friar. The Friar comes to Juan first as an apparition, then as Fitz-Fulke – a woman dressed as a man whose very existence is questionable. The eminently practical Fitz-Fulke becomes Fitz-Fulke-as-friar, turning a dead man who appears to be alive into a woman who appears to be a man, knowing that these ambiguities will be cleared up by sexual consummation. As usual, the poem offers only ambiguity where the sexual event, the fulfilment of the fantasy, should be. The teasing format of the Friar's appearances recapitulates the pattern in which an event only takes on a finite meaning in retrospect. Not having known what he saw on the first night, Juan can either assign the meaning of the second incident to the first and have done with it, or leave the peculiar experience open to possibility and speculation. This is the final formulation of fantasy *Don Juan* offers.

Fantasy is an event, the repetition of which, as representation or 'reality', necessarily either reveals the fantasy to be false or inadequate or takes advantage of its form to impose itself – and the social roles it implies – upon us. There is no possibility of closure for *Don Juan*, for the poem has shown that consummation can be represented only through absence, that narrative closure is just a fantasy waiting to be inverted, contradicted or undone by its repetition. The literary uses of fantasy, and in particular the articulation of the crucial passage from fantasy itself to its application in a gendered, politicized social world, are nowhere more fully explored than in Byron's *Don Juan*.

6
Don Juan as a Defence of Liberty

> Nature had not formed him for a Liberal peer, proper to
> move the Address in the House of Lords, to pay compli-
> ments to the energy and self-reliance of British middle-class
> liberalism, and to adapt his politics to suit it. Unfitted for
> such politics, he threw himself upon poetry as his organ.
>
> Matthew Arnold, 'Byron'

Arnold's recourse to the argument from Nature here, the idea that
some force greater than historical circumstances or personal choice
can be held responsible for the fact that Byron was 'unfitted for
such politics', is peculiarly un-Byronic in its manner of dealing with
the historical world in which the poet's life played itself out. The
impulse to try to understand Byron's poetry as a kind of politics by
other means is, however, a good one, and it is by bringing to-
gether careful attention to the organ of choice, poetry, with an
equal curiosity about cultural politics outside not only the House
of Lords but the whole British system that the true measure of
Byron as a defender of liberty may be taken. Unlike most other
aristocratic intellectuals who enjoyed the privileges of English free-
dom in his day, Byron knew the ironic cost of his own liberty in
the systematic subjugation of working-class and colonial peoples.
Even before he was conclusively 'unfitted' for the House of Lords,
Byron explored alternative outlets to the parliamentary system for
his political impulses. In Chapter 3 I looked at his formal address
on the Luddites, discussing the memorable and pregnant phrase
'superfluous heads', but to understand the relation of 'Byron' to
liberty it will be necessary also to recall the street-ballad he wrote
on behalf of the frame-breakers at the same time. In this early political

poem Byron mocks the celebrated British tradition of freedom by pronouncing 'Liberty' in ironic intonational quotation marks.

> Men are more easily made than machinery –
> Stockings fetch better prices than lives –
> Gibbets on Sherwood will heighten the scenery,
> Showing how Commerce, how Liberty thrives.[1]

The sympathy Byron extended to the Luddites, founded in his awareness of the dialectical ironies of British Liberty, was not limited to them or to the other political constituencies with which we commonly associate it, such as the enslaved Greeks of the Turkish occupation or the Italian Carbonari. The missing links in the chain of interests necessary to understand Byron's political impact are the men and women who travelled the colonial world by ship.[2] In this final chapter I will re-identify and to a large extent literalize the importance of the ocean in *Don Juan* by asserting that shipping and international travel were not only the necessary material conditions of the poem's production, but also that the denizens of the sea, the members of the oceanic diaspora, were an important constituency for Byron's political message.[3] In order to provide a new perspective on the historical significance of Byron's commitment to the cause of liberty I will look not only at how he forsook parliamentary politics for poetry, but also at how he forsook land for sea by adopting a transnational political identity at a time when the most influential British poets were determinedly nationalistic. In the following stanza from the original Dedication to *Don Juan* what is ordinarily read as a simple denigration of the provincialism of the Lakers sounds quite different if we grant the existence of an inverse, transnational, sea-going political identity and community.

> You, Gentlemen! By dint of long seclusion
>   From better company have kept your own
> At Keswick, and through still continued fusion
>   Of one another's minds at last have grown
> To deem as a most logical conclusion
>   That Poesy has wreaths for you alone;
> There is a narrowness in such a notion
> Which makes me wish you'd change your lakes for ocean.
>
>   (Dedication, st. 5)

As is so often the case in *Don Juan*, the designations 'metaphorical' and 'literal' prove unstable. While it is unlikely that Byron intended to attract Wordsworth, Coleridge or Southey to his own nautical mode of existence, the proposition that they change their lakes for ocean has a specific historical material basis. The entire system of colonialism depended for its very existence on men and women who made the change here suggested in reality. By declining to become conscious participants even in the discourse of ocean-going commerce, the Lakers built their poetic systems on an ideology that ignored the material basis of the British Empire. Or so it seemed to Byron. In fact, Wordsworth and Coleridge did write and think about the ocean and about mariners, and they did so in ways that indicated that they were interested in the centrality of sea-travel to the culture of the era. Yet Byron has a point, and it is one that becomes more intelligible when we put his work in a larger literary context that also includes the poetry of contemporary women writers.

Charlotte Smith's Elegiac Sonnet XLII depends on an analogy between the speaker and an émigré who appears to be a castaway.

> The unhappy exile, whom his fates confine
> To the bleak coast of some unfriendly isle,
> Cold, barren, desart, where no harvests smile,
> But thirst and hunger on the rocks repine;
> When, from some promontory's fearful brow,
> Sun after sun he hopeless sees decline
> In the broad shipless sea – perhaps may know
> Such heartless pain, such blank despair as mine:
> And, if a flattering cloud appears to show
> The fancied semblance of a distant sail,
> Then melts away – anew his spirits fail,
> While the lost hope but aggravates his woe!
> Ah! So for me delusive Fancy toils,
> Then, from contrasted truth – my feeble soul recoils.[4]

Smith imagines the disappointment of her castaway at the melting away of his hopes of rescue as a way to express both her own need for a refuge in the fantasy world of her writing and Fancy's inevitable failure to delude. Byron often identified with the women writers he read and freely adapted their rhetorical strategies for coping with social marginality. Smith's clever conflation of the poet's Fancy and the castaway's hope of rescue leaves little doubt about her sense of the public role of the woman writer. By playing upon the sense of internal exile called up by social marginality, both Smith and the early Byron courted the identification of their sentimental audiences. But for Byron, the persistence of this theme of exile, chosen in his youth for its tragic pathos, was to become both a determining fact of his later life and a source of sublimely anti-sentimental fiction.

The shipwreck of the *Trinidada* in Canto II of Don Juan is one of the most remarked-upon sequences in the poem. Its impact on Byron's contemporaries was enormous and almost entirely negative. Andrew Cooper, the shipwreck sequence's best modern interpreter, defines the essential aspect of this negative reception as an experience of mortification. 'So with regard to the shipwreck episode, what is most striking about first readers' reactions is not their horror, but specifically their *mortification*, as though they felt Byron had personally duped them somehow.'[5] He goes on to quote the *Blackwood's* reviewer, who described the episode as 'the insulting deceit which has been practised upon us'. Without going into too much detail, let me say that the episode contains elements drawn from a wide range of sensational accounts both true and fictional of what can happen to people who are stuck together in a lifeboat without adequate food. In Byron's version of this popular tabloid legend, it is Pedrillo, the tutor who has been sent to watch out for young Juan as he makes his grand tour, who is killed and eaten by the others in the boat. Juan refuses to participate in the cannibalism, and is rewarded at least negatively when those who have eaten human flesh go crazy and die while drinking seawater. The narrator has just explained that it was not to be expected that Juan would consent to 'Dine with them on his pastor and his master'.

> 'Twas better that he did not; for, in fact,
>   The consequence was awful in the extreme;
> For they, who were most ravenous in the act,
>   Went raging mad – Lord! how they did blaspheme!
> And foam and roll, with strange convulsions rack'd,
>   Drinking salt-water like a mountain-stream,
> Tearing, and grinning, howling, screeching, swearing,
> And, with hyaena laughter, died despairing.
>
>   (II, st. 79)

The worst, however, is yet to come, for the narrator takes this opportunity to engage in his now familiar tactic of following tragedy with comedy, and breaking up even his most sombre effects with moments of unexpected levity. A single example of this tactic will suffice. Even after the death of the original cannibal contingent, some of the passengers in the longboat are forgetful and hungry enough to consider a second attempt.

> And next they thought upon the master's mate,
>   As fattest; but he saved himself, because,
> Besides being much averse from such a fate,
>   There were some other reasons; the first was,
> He had been rather indisposed of late,
>   And that which chiefly proved his saving clause,
> Was a small present made to him at Cadiz,
> By general subscription of the ladies.
>
> (II, st. 81)

In the same month, July 1819, that saw the initial publication of *Don Juan*, the French artist Géricault completed his best-known work, the gigantic 'Le radeau de la Méduse', which now hangs in the Louvre. It depicts the victims of a disastrous wreck as they hail a distant ship just visible on the horizon. The picture derives from an actual event of three years previous, when the French frigate *Méduse* went aground on a reef while making its way to Senegal. The dramatic story of the escape by raft from the doomed frigate includes episodes every bit as lurid as the events described in Byron's poem, up to and including the detail that provoked the most resistance from Byron's audience, the practice of cannibalism in the interest of survival. The wreck of the *Méduse* became a *cause célèbre* in France, as the violence of the days at sea on the raft came to stand for the carelessness with which Napoleon had treated the sailors on his ship of state. The iconographic power of the picture can be attributed to the resonance of both its art-historical and its political precedents – the antediluvians left behind by Noah's Ark in Michelangelo's Sistine ceiling, and the people of the barricades left behind by the evolution of imperial France.[6] John Keats and his friend Joseph Severn are representative of the reception of Byron's handling of the motif – it disgusted them, and it reminded them of the wreck of the *Méduse*.[7] The mortification that many readers experienced when they encountered the shipwreck in *Don Juan* Canto II can be traced to Byron's handling of the volatile elements introduced into public discussion by the wreck of the *Méduse*.

Years later, Eugene Delacroix, one of the models who posed for Gericault's composition, painted the longboat scene from *Don Juan*. This painting can also be seen in the Louvre. Juan sits in the stern of the boat, pale and exhausted but more awake and aware than many of the others. These two giant canvases of peril at sea form a sequence when viewed in light of Byron's treatment of this highly charged material. From the heroic desperation and physical aspiration of the men on the raft of the *Méduse* to the stoicism of Juan's survival through self-control, the progression is from a last view of antediluvian man to a first look at the post-covenant pilgrim.

Clearly the value of the debate over what was appropriate behaviour for people adrift in longboats was not entirely practical. While the various discussants, artists and writers who tackled this motif were concerned about the fate of mariners lost at sea, their plight would not have played so vividly on shore-bound imaginations if it had not held some significance in terms of other, less consciously available anxieties than the ones to which the actual situation could be expected to give rise. The shipwreck story in *Don Juan* ends with Juan alone surviving. As the lone passenger from the *Trinidada* to make it to shore alive, Juan takes on the aura of a mythical hero. He washes up on Haidee's island still clutching the single oar with which he floated to safety. It is one of the rare moments in the poem when the narrator makes a direct statement about the protagonist's beauty.

> And as he gazed, his dizzy brain spun fast,
>   And down he sunk; and as he sunk, the sand
> Swam round and round, and all his senses pass'd:
>   He fell upon his side, and his stretch'd hand
> Droop'd dripping on the oar, (their jury-mast)
>   And, like a wither'd lily, on the land
> His slender frame and pallid aspect lay,
> As fair a thing as e'er was form'd of clay.

> (II, st. 110)

There are a number of ways to read the shipwreck as a metaphor. In the poem 'Letter to Maria Gisborne', Shelley, for whom this metaphor would soon become all too real, wrote

> You are now
> In London, that great sea whose ebb and flow
> At once is deaf and loud, and on the shore
> Vomits its wrecks, and still howls on for more.
> Yet in its depths what treasures!
>
>   (ll, 193–7)

This is suggestive, but it is more of a statement about the city than it is an account of the shipwreck metaphor it employs. The reading offered by Elizabeth Boyd in her book on *Don Juan* takes us closer to what we need.[8] Ms. Boyd remains perhaps the best student of Byron's extensive reading. She points to what was in Byron's day a well-known passage from Lucretius' philosophical poem *De Rerum Natura*. I quote from the modern translation of Rolfe Humphries.

> When nature, after struggle, tears the child
> Out of its mother's womb to the shores of light,
> He lies there naked, lacking everything,
> Like a sailor driven wave-battered to some coast,
> And the poor little thing fills all the air
> With lamentation – but that's only right
> In view of all the griefs that lie ahead
> Along his way through life. The animals
> Are better off, the tame ones and the wild,
> They grow, they don't need rattles, they don't need
> The babbling baby-talk of doting nurses . . .[9]

Juan's passage through the vortex of the wreck of the *Trinidada* strips him of all his cultural baggage and enables him to emerge on the shore of Haidee's island as if reborn, having jettisoned his former identity and ready to be raised again into a different language and culture. The passage form Lucretius is useful in that it makes clear the connection between the regressive fantasy of Juan's recuperation and the more traumatic one of the shipwreck. Without a sufficiently destructive episode to precipitate his entrance into his next adventure Juan would remain in thrall to the colonial system of which he remains a representative. The ubiquitous fantasy of the 'lone survivor' underwrites a denial of the real conditions in which European adventurers ordinarily encountered the women of subject populations. Without a dangerous shipwreck to deprive

Juan of his social context, we might see his encounter with Haidee for what it must have corresponded to in Byron's and many other men's historical experience – the exploitation of native populations.

It is an apt historical irony that made William Wilberforce and his Society for the Suppression of Vice the antagonists of Byron's later career. Consider the following sequence in which Byron addresses the great reformer with whom we began this study on the subject of his better-known involvement with abolition.

> Oh Wilberforce! thou man of black renown,
>   Whose merit none enough can sing or say,
> Thou hast struck one immense Colossus down,
>   Thou moral Washington of Africa!
> But there's another little thing, I own,
>   Which you should perpetrate some summer's day,
> And set the other half of earth to rights:
> You have freed the *blacks* – now pray shut up the whites.

(XIV, st. 82)

The next two stanzas follow through on this fantasy of the colonial world turned upside down, imagining the 'Holy Trio' shipped to Senegal, among other things. There is something sublimely insolent about this that exceeds even the most daring flights of Oscar Wilde's campaign to shock the late Victorian bourgeoisie.

'You have freed the *blacks* – now pray shut up the whites' may not be terribly clever, but it is truly a conversation stopper. Coming late in the poem, this splendidly lunatic fantasy of vengeful role-reversal, far from being the exception, is instead the rule of the narrator's stance towards his former country and its culture in the last six cantos. The desire to confront and reform the audience who had made him world-famous runs straight through the latter part of *Don Juan*, often surprising even the modern reader with the intensity of its exuberant irreverence. The most important freedom for Byron as a poet was the inner freedom he only found later on, the liberty of thought and emotion that came with his genuine and permanent detachment from English society. It is impossible to know if this distance was the product of *Don Juan* as a process of working through his past feelings and attachments, or if the poem is merely the record of something that happened on another, yet more personal level. John Speirs concurs in this assessment of the poet's attitude in his commentary on Byron's handling of the London social scene and the 'hopes and fears which shake a single ball' in Canto XI, stanza 71.

> The gay humour and amusement – not merely nostalgia and contempt – with which these past scenes are evoked seem again to arise from the poet's new-found detachment from them. Such a tone and attitude towards the world have clearly been made possible for him by a liberation from it – from the oppressive conventionalities and falsities underlying its dazzling, glittering surface, its sparkling evanescence. He can recall it now with a certain enjoyment and zest as a remembered brilliant spectacle, with delight in its absurdities, because he is at last himself freed from it.[10]

For the modern reader this detachment lends a quality of nonchalance to the narrator's tone in the later cantos that is most noticeable when he chooses to address one of his contemporaries directly. The peevishness of the direct addresses earlier in the poem is gone, replaced with a more playful and genuinely startling imaginative freedom. At the end of Canto X the narrator calls out to another of the day's most famous reformers, Mrs Elizabeth Fry, a Quaker who was the first woman to enter England's prisons as a missionary. The narrator warns his reader that in the next canto he will tell him 'truths *you* will not take as true, / Because they are so.' He says that he intends to be 'a male Mrs. Fry' before launching into this.

> Oh, Mrs Fry! Why go to Newgate? Why
>   Preach to poor rogues? And wherefore not begin
> With Carlton, or with other houses? Try
>   Your hand at hardened and imperial sin.
> To mend the people's an absurdity,
>   A jargon, a mere philanthropic din,
> Unless you make their betters better: – Fie!
> I thought you had more religion, Mrs Fry.
>
> (X, st. 85)

Byron's outrageous identification with the formidable Elizabeth Fry clearly cost him some anxiety, or else why 'a *male* Mrs Fry'? – which seems to protest too much. But it was also not always an entirely facetious move, as in the letters Byron wrote just before embarking for Greece and the planned revolt against the Turkish it reappears as a serious analogy for what he expects to have to do there. The imagined exigencies of Mrs Fry's prison mission work were one of the ways in which Byron imaged to himself the profound changes that had overtaken the public role of the imaginative writer in his lifetime. *Don Juan* is his attempt to put poetry at the centre of this new international public sphere. Byron perceived these changes in a way that no other British Romantic writer did, with the exception perhaps of William Blake, and he acted on them by seizing any and all available models for effectual engagement with what was clearly a different political and economic world. The era of courts and castles was gone never to return. In its place a vast and indeterminate system working in many ways and places at once had sprung up seemingly overnight, and this system depended for its vitality and circulation on the sailors and ships that travelled the world's oceans. The ocean is thus more than a metaphor for the uncertainties of human life in this poem. It is a positive material presence, the regular successful navigation of which made the publication of Byron's work after 1816 possible. By writing so effectively about England and everywhere else from Italy, Byron became an international artist whose medium and home, whose version of the public sphere, was the system of colonial trade itself, rather that any of the stations of accumulation within it. Like the latterday remittance man, Byron lived out his life on the basis of his ability to withdraw value from the imperial centre against the relentless flow of goods and resources into it.

Byron shared with Wordsworth an abiding sense of the deep contradictions inherent in British liberty. Both poets knew well the roots and branches of that other symbolic tree, the thorn of popular resistance, or, as the historian Christopher Hill has termed it, 'liberty against the law'.[11] This tradition arose among those made vagrant and vagabond by the seventeenth-century enclosure of common lands, but it is equally the political philosophy of those who plied the seas without the benefit of rank or merchant capital. When liberty is defined by property rather than by life, the result is a basis for public policy that is nothing more than fantasy. In *Don Juan* Byron pits a poetics of private reverie against the excesses of the public fantasy that is conventional history. The hypocrisy which made it all right to conduct public policy as though the people were nothing more than a beast with many heads could not tolerate the public expression of the kind of fantasies that underwrote its own attitudes. Byron could not tolerate this. He called it cant, and used *Don Juan* to expose the inherent contradictions of a system that operated on the basis of public fantasies it could not acknowledge as such. Fantasy in *Don Juan* is judged not according to the standards of propriety, but rather by how it affects those for whom it becomes reality. Even ideals, such as the ideal of service to one's country, can become vicious when the abstract concept of one's bureaucratic position precludes a human connection to one's actions.

In the stanzas that follow those on Southey and Wordsworth in the poem's Dedication, Byron attacks the current Foreign Secretary, Robert Stewart, Viscount Castlereagh, for betraying his humanity. Castlereagh served as Foreign Secretary from 1812 to the time of his suicide in 1822. To Byron he was the epitome of all that was false and vicious in his country's foreign policy. A former Irish peer, Castlereagh helped destroy the Irish rebellion in 1798 and form the colonial regime of the Irish Union in 1801. In 1814 he used his authority against international liberty when he withdrew support for the revival of free Italian cities and sided with the Congress of Vienna in subjugating Italy. Cold and calculating in his tactics, Castlereagh made a mockery of political leadership by drawing support through the espousal of the cause of freedom, only to abandon liberty once the advantage of the appearance of such support had been gained. The attack on Castlereagh in the Dedication begins when the narrator asks if Milton would have obeyed 'the intellectual eunuch Castlereagh'. In the stanzas that follow Castlereagh the eunuch is referred to by the pronoun 'it' rather than 'he'.

> Cold-blooded, smooth-faced, placid miscreant!
>   Dabbling its sleek young hands in Erin's gore,
> And thus for wider courage taught to pant,
>   Transferr'd to gorge upon a sister-shore;
> The vulgarest tool that tyranny could want,
>   With just enough of talent and no more,
> To lengthen fetters by another fix'd
> And offer poison long already mix'd
>   . . .
> If we may judge of matter by the mind,
>   Emasculated to the marrow, *It*
> Hath but two objects – how to serve, and bind,
>   Deeming the chain it wears even men may fit;

> Eutropius of its many masters – blind
>   To worth as freedom, wisdom as to wit –
> Fearless, because *no* feeling dwells in ice,
> Its very courage stagnates to a vice.

(Dedication, st. 12, 15)

I see two principles here extending throughout the poem. The first is the principle of *ad hominem* attack on those who have abdicated their essential humanity in the service of abstractions. Byron always resisted laying the blame for political tyranny at the feet of abstractions, whether class, state or form of government. The culpable flaws he detected within the fallen world were the fault of powerful individuals, and he considered it the duty of respectable people to call them out for violating the public trust. To call Castlereagh 'the vulgarest tool that tyranny could want' is thus a precise description of the problem. Tools are the exact opposite of what free human beings should be. Whether we are dealing with weavers or statesmen, we must always hold to this distinction. In *Culture and Anarchy* Matthew Arnold employs the same central idea:

> What is alone and always sacred and binding for man is the making progress towards his total perfection; and the machinery by which he does this varies in value according as it helps him to do it.[12]

Castlereagh becomes a human tool in Byron's eyes because he has lost this sense of purpose. This brings me to the second point I wish to draw from this passage. This concerns the name-calling involved in the use of the pronoun 'it' and the term 'eunuch'. Byron is on bad terms with late twentieth-century readers whenever he uses gender or sexual preference as the basis for political attack. Castlereagh is likely to have been what we call homosexual. That his suicide was a response to disclosure of this is all but an established fact. Is Byron gay-bashing here?

He certainly knew and was taking advantage of rumours about Castlereagh. As someone who was actively bisexual, he also must have known and felt how dangerous it was to be identified in this way at the time. Nevertheless, his motivations for using this information against Castlereagh are multiple. *Don Juan* is about being a man. It is the first major poem in English explicitly to thematize masculinity. In it the poet confronts the masculine bias of European culture on many fronts. In the process of reckoning with the consequences of this unacknowledged bias the poem valorizes the self-awareness of those men who accept and appreciate their privileges and limitations as men in a somewhat less than definitively male-dominated world. To Byron at least, Castlereagh was an example of what this unacknowledged masculinism could become when it assumed the form of an abstract universality. For Byron, political, philosophical, aesthetic and ethical claims to universality were undermined fundamentally when they assumed the masculinity of the subject. When men such as Castlereagh wrote the rules for everything from Ireland and Italy to the sublime, they did so as nothing more than men. To paraphrase Lacan, men are the best things we have – of their kind. For better or worse, men are men *only* – until something better comes along for them to be.

In *Don Juan*, gender and sexual desire are the principle ways in which we humans experience our fallen state. Like the severed halves of original double-sided wholes in Aristophanes' fable of the origin of desire in the *Symposium*, men and women in *Don Juan* experience gender and sexual desire as a fundamental lack in their being. This lack causes them to seek fulfilment outside themselves. The poem opens with the famous cry, 'I want a hero.' The unfolding irony of this notoriously ironic text is that the most interesting, compelling figures in the poem are not heroes but heroines. The ostensible hero, Don Juan, is little more than an excuse for the narrator to produce an international gallery of intriguing women. Juan adapts to the changes in his fortune and location by accepting the attentions of a series of heroines. It is their desires and predicaments that give form to the narrative's central conflicts.

In Canto XVI this method reaches a climax of self-consciousness in the introduction of the concept of psychosocial mobility. Lady Adeline Amundeville provides the narrator with a point of departure.

> So well she acted, all and every part
>   By turns – with that vivacious versatility,
> Which many people take for want of heart.
>   They err – 'tis merely what is called mobility,
> A thing of temperament and not of art,
>   Though seeming so, from its supposed facility;
> And false – though true; for surely they're sincerest,
> Who are strongly acted on by what is nearest.

(XVI, st. 97)

Adeline is certainly a fine example of this quality, but anyone who has managed to get this far in this very long poem has got to be aware that mobility is an even more apt term for the career of Juan. He has been remarkably mobile, both in his affections and his person. The wide geographical sweep of the poem – from Spain to Greece and Turkey, then to Russia and now England – is the result of his travels. Not only is Juan capable of moving swiftly across the continent, he seems to fit in every where he goes.

Byron supplies his own gloss in a note on this stanza.

> In French, '*mobilité.*' I am not sure that mobility is English, but it is expressive of a quality which rather belongs to other climates, though it is sometimes seen to a great extent in our own. It may be defined as an excessive susceptibility of immediate impressions – at the same time without *losing* the past; and is, though sometimes apparently useful to the possessor, a most painful and unhappy attribute.[13]

Following on modern accounts of the phenomenology of perception, I would identify this supposedly uncommon attribute with all spontaneous perceptual activity. We are all mobile in our perceptions, at least to the degree that we are free from habit and stock responses. Mobility, then, far from being the special attribute of a select few, is the basic experience of all of us, mediated by our internal sense of identity. Adeline and Juan are exceptional in that they seem to lack a core to which their identities may return. *Don Juan* is of interest to readers today, on the eve of the twenty-first century because it so often seems to predict the breakdown of psychosocial boundaries we identify as characteristic of our era. Juan's 'donjuanism' is very different from the phallic style of his namesake, and very similar to the serial monogamy now more and more accepted as the norm for adult sexual behaviour. The painful and unhappy aspects of mobility are the result of problems that arise in relation to the past that, as Byron specifies, is not lost, no matter what the appearance. Liberty in mobility can only be achieved through reconciliation of the disparate identities imposed by outside contexts within the individual psyche and in relation to the active aspects of the past.

It is a paradox that it is only through our capacity to remember that we experience the sensation of loss. In Freudian terms, the loss of any love-object contributes to the mounting severity with which the superego judges the ego. To proceed, the ego must establish and retain a sense of itself which is not dominated by this severity, which is understood as the reality principle. This capacity for ego-growth is called creative apperception. It is the total set of mental processes through which we retain a background sense of ourselves without the imposition of an unhealthy or impractical consistency. Cultural creative apperception is romantic memory. One's romantic memory is what knows that, despite all apparent changes and contradictions of the unromantic record, somehow one always remains the same person. Without some sense of romantic memory, human beings would be tempted to disown rather than reflect upon earlier versions of themselves. If it had not mattered so much to Wordsworth that he be always the same person, he might simply have disowned the earlier selves he works so hard in his poetry to understand and incorporate into his current identity. Romantic memory, far from being a principle of falsification, is that feeling which makes us resist the temptation to say of our past actions: 'that wasn't me – I didn't do that.'

Creative apperception became important in psychology when doctors began to study infantile development. In the first years of life changes come so quickly that a sense of self-unity can be hard to establish and maintain. The most prominent element in theories of infantile creative apperception is the transitional object. Whether this is a favourite blanket or toy, it is endowed with a fantastic status that aids the child in retaining her sense of identity. Fantasies involving the transitional object are what allow that identity to evolve actively and flexibly. In adulthood, this role is internalized. We use the creative apperceptive sense we developed as children in our adult daydreams. The literary protagonist is the most highly evolved cultural aid to successful mature creative apperception. One's romantic memory grows in proportion to the depth and intensity of one's literary experience. Every encounter with narrative generates an identification which either feeds or starves the individual's capacity for flexible self-realization.

Byron understood this function of romantic memory. In *Don Juan* he set out to create a hero who would be a pure transitional object, with as few obstacles to identification as possible. Unlike previous versions of the Don, Juan is mostly passive and nearly always silent. His affairs stem from a single quality, his continued susceptibility to real emotion.

Juan is not a man or even a little boy, as Peter Manning has suggested, but a figure. He is the poetic figure through whom the narrator can describe the real historical world of the Mediterranean in the late eighteenth century. 'Don Juan' allows Byron to explore its social structure through the invention of a series of politically representative heroines. Byron used Juan to go places, such as Russia, that he never saw for himself. The flexibility of the hero as a vehicle for imaginary adventure is, in *Don Juan*, the poetic equivalent of the oceanic diaspora of eighteenth- and nineteenth-century colonial history. By being 'no place' the ocean gave place to all the 'nobodies' created by colonialism. Through the myth of Don Juan, Byron gave a form and an expression not only to his own experience, but also to the experiences, real and imaginary, of a generation and more of these transnational subjects. Focusing on the historic importance of the condition of women under these circumstances gives the poem's satire of masculinity its edge. The poem does not defend promiscuity or sexual licence. It does defend the liberty of such licence for the daydreaming imagination, and allies this liberty to literature's capacity to reflect on and judge daydreams. By sending an ostentatiously fantastic protagonist into a carefully delineated historical context, Byron unbalances the ingrained critical bias towards mimesis operative in western culture since Aristotle. The result is a work that resists categorization. Repeated readings fail to resolve the difficulties presented by the tone of many passages. As with the transitional object, about which the question, 'is it real or is it imaginary?' is never appropriate, *Don Juan* resists our attempts to know whether or not to take it seriously.

The difficult art of making the most important points without ever being entirely serious, like mobility, is a product of an era that knew an unprecedented acceleration in the dynamic generation of new wants. Utilitarian accounts of consumerism cannot explain the inordinate proliferation of desires in modern consumerism because they ignore the crucial role of pleasure or hedonism. It is hedonism, and not utility, pleasure and not satisfaction, that are the goals of the modern consumer. To understand fully this romantic difference, we should follow Colin Campbell in distinguishing between modern and traditional hedonism. According to Campbell, 'this modern, autonomous, and illusory form of hedonism commonly manifests itself as day-dreaming and fantasizing.' Campbell sees a necessary connection between the Protestant ethic described by Weber in his theory of the rise of capitalism and a Romantic ethic of autonomous, illusory hedonism in his own theory of the rise of modern consumerism.

By recognizing that social conduct is typically a composite product of hedonistic self-interest and altruistically inclined idealism, with an overriding concern with self-image serving to articulate the two, it becomes possible to see how the spirit of modern consumerism and the romantic ethic might be connected; hedonistic concerns leading into self-idealism and ethical preoccupations creating opportunities for hedonism. Indeed, the two forms are not merely connected, but must be seen as inextricably interlocked, bound together by processes through which a desire for pleasure develops into a genuine concern for ideals, and ethical preoccupations creating opportunities for hedonism.[14]

In other words, the hedonistic male fantasies of *Don Juan* can be understood as part of the process through which Byron developed an idealized self-image that led him to a genuine, active involvement with the cause of liberty in Greece. The marketable vice of literary daydreaming can, for author and reader, issue through self-idealization in a commitment to virtuous action in the real world. The fantasist gradually becomes responsible to the person he or she already is in daydreams. The freedom enjoyed in reading and in fantasy is potentially the freedom to become the idealized person one dreams of being.

In the unfinished Canto XVII the narrator proposes an existential category that sums up, insofar as this is possible, the evolving position of this extraordinarily capacious and self-contradictory poem on the intertwined questions of identity and subjectivity.

> The world is full of orphans: firstly, those
>   Who are so in the strict sense of the phrase;
> But many a lonely tree the loftier grows
>   Than others crowded in the Forest's maze –
> The next are such as are not doomed to lose
>   Their tender parents, in their budding days,
> But, merely, their parental tenderness,
> Which leaves them orphans of the heart no less.
>
> The next are '*only* Children,' as they are styled,
>   Who grow up *Children* only, since the old saw

      Pronounces that an 'only''s a spoilt child –
        But not to go too far, I hold it law,
    That where their education, harsh or mild,
        Transgresses the just bounds of love or awe,
    The sufferers – be't in heart or intellect –
    Whate'er the *cause*, are orphans in *effect*.

(XVII, st. 1–2)

The idea of the 'orphan in effect' corresponds nicely to the two main themes I have been developing both in the present chapter and throughout this study of *Don Juan*. The regressive fantasies at the core of much adult behaviour and even of public history are the consequences of having been weaned, as it were, too soon from either the tender parents or the parental tenderness of a truly adequate cultural and social context for proper human development. Since this is inevitably the fate of all of us to some degree in this best of all possible worlds, it is important to accept and deal with the ways in which the infantile, the pre-Oedipal and the fantastic continue to shape and inhibit the pleasures and pains of our existence. The purpose of play, especially of that play which is known as 'literature', must always be understood as a more or less poor substitute for that education within the just bounds of love and awe that even the most studious ordinarily evade. The second theme for which the metaphor of the 'orphan in effect' is appropriate is that of the responsibility we all feel to participate in the world beyond our own imaginings, the 'real' world of action and potential change. It is only through establishing an adequate romantic memory through creative apperception that any modern subject can hope to be as flexible and as manifold in selfhood as consequential participation in the 'oceanic' modern world demands. The 'Byron' of *Don Juan* demonstrates that the pattern of human growth can lead out of, rather than into, the kind of fixed identity that ordinary narrative forms of human recognition seem to require. It is with this end of perpetual self-reinvention and multiplication in mind that I conclude this study.

Notes

Introduction

1 Robinson Blann, *Throwing the Scabbard Away: Byron's Battle against the Censors of Don Juan* (New York: Peter Lang, 1991) p. 21.

2 Quoted in R.W. Harris, *Romanticism and the Social Order, 1780–1830* (New York: Barnes and Noble, 1969) p. 128.

3 Colin Campbell, *The Romantic Ethic and the Rise of Modern Consumerism* (Oxford: Basil Blackwell, 1987) p. 37.

4 Sir James Mackintosh, 'Vindiciae Gallicae' (1791), quoted in Malcolm Kelsall, *Byron's Politics* (Brighton: Harvester Press, 1987) p. 23.

5 See Robert Ryan, *The Romantic Reformation: Religious Politics in English Literature, 1789–1824* (Cambridge: Cambridge University Press, 1997). 'The new attention to domestic evangelism seems to have arisen partly as an afterthought to the fervor for foreign missions that emerged rather suddenly among the Dissenters in the early 1790s', p. 24. Also, for a good discussion of the politics of Byron's orientalism, see Marilyn Butler, 'Byron and the Empire in the East', in *Byron: Augustan and Romantic*, ed. Andrew Rutherford (Basingstoke and London: Macmillan, 1990). 'The amendment of the East India Act, so that Christian churches were permitted to proselytise in India, was an important symbolic defeat inflicted on the ruling aristocracy by the still-disfranchised middle classes. And it may have been largely as an aristocrat that Byron resented it, as *The Giaour* suggests he did', p. 72.

6 Ryan, p. 121.

7 Campbell, p. 89.

8 Jerome J. McGann, 'The Book of Byron and the Book of the World', in *The Beauty of Inflections: Literary Investigations in Historical Method and Theory* (Oxford: Clarendon Press, 1985) pp. 286–9.

9 See Kelsall, pp. 87–90, and Marilyn Gaull, *English Romanticism: The Human Context* (New York: Norton, 1988) pp. 147–53.

10 Michael Nerlich, *The Ideology of Adventure: Studies in Modern Consciousness, 1100–1750*, Vol. 2 (Minneapolis: University of Minnesota Press, 1987) p. 5.

11 David Simpson, ed., *The Origins of Modern Critical Thought: German Aesthetic and Literary Criticism from Lessing to Hegel* (Cambridge: Cambridge University Press, 1988).

12 D.A. Miller, *Bringing out Roland Barthes* (Berkeley: University of California Press, 1992) p. 46.

13 Miller, p. 54.

14 Antony Easthope, *Poetry and Phantasy* (Cambridge: Cambridge University Press, 1989); Karl Kroeber, *Romantic Fantasy and Science Fiction* (New Haven: Yale University Press, 1988); Kathryn Hume, *Fantasy and Mimesis: Responses to Reality in Western Literature* (New York: Methuen, 1984);

Tsvetan Todorov, *The Fantastic: A Structural Approach to Literary Genre*, trans. Richard Howard (Cleveland: Case Western University Press, 1973); and Christine Brooke-Rose, *A Rhetoric of the Unreal: Studies in Narrative and Structure, especially of the Fantastic* (Cambridge: Cambridge University Press, 1981).

15 Hermann Fischer, *Romantic Verse Narrative: The History of a Genre* (Cambridge: Cambridge University Press, 1991) p. 47.

16 Nigel Wood describes the poem as 'an interrogative work in its constant questioning of the illusions that keep the great literary ideas comprehensible'. Nigel Wood, ed., *Don Juan* (Milton Keynes and Bristol: Open University Press, 1993) p. 11.

17 Donald W. Winnicott, *Playing and Reality* (New York: Basic Books, 1971) pp. 89–103.

18 Frances Ferguson, 'Romantic Memory', *Studies in Romanticism*, 35 (Winter 1996) p. 509.

19 See Nancy Armstrong, *Desire and Domestic Fiction: A Political History of the Novel* (New York: Oxford University Press, 1987).

20 Caroline Franklin, *Byron's Heroines* (Oxford: Clarendon Press, 1992) p. 101.

21 Georg Lukács, *The Historical Novel* (London, 1962).

22 My remarks here on the effect of the Napoleonic Wars on British culture were influenced by Marilyn Gaull's lecture on Keats's 'Otho the Great', 'Little, Unremembered Acts of Kindness and of Love', delivered at the 1995 Wordsworth Summer Conference, Grasmere.

23 From the Finale – Iolanthe, the Queen and Phyllis sing:

> Though as a general rule we know
> Two strings go to every bow
> Make up your minds that grief 'twill bring
> If you've two beaux to every string.

(William Gilbert and Arthur Sullivan, *Iolanthe*, 1882) *The Complete Annotated Gilbert and Sullivan* (Oxford: Oxford University Press, 1996) p. 445.

24 G. Wilson Knight, *Byron and Shakespeare* (New York: Barnes and Noble, 1966).

25 This is borne out by Truman Guy Steffan's intriguing account of the poet's accretive matrix method of composition. See his essay on 'The Anvil of Composition', in *Don Juan. A Variorum Edition*, Vol. 1 (Austin: University of Texas Press, 1957).

26 Several critics have cited the term *arabesque* as an appropriate one to describe this formal characteristic. It appears in Mellor, who derives it from Schlegel (pp. 17–18, 57), and in Peter Graham (pp. 7–8). For a particularly enlightening discussion of arabesque as a critical concept, see Alan Liu, *Wordsworth: The Sense of History* (Stanford: Stanford University Press, 1989) pp. 41–3.

27 My theoretical formulation of social fantasy is indebted to Lacan and to the politicized Lacanian analysis of Slavoj Žižek, especially *The Sublime Object of Ideology* (London: Verso, 1989) and *Looking Awry: An*

Introduction to Jacques Lacan through Popular Culture (Cambridge, MA: MIT Press, 1991).

28 Laura Claridge, *Romantic Potency* (Ithaca, NY: Cornell University Press, 1992).

1 Learning to Say Juan

1   For a view of this pronunciation as entirely unremarkable and consistent with early nineteenth-century English custom, see Bernard Beatty's review of 'Romanticism: The Next Wave', a special issue of ANQ in *The Byron Journal* 23 (1995) 86.

2   See Alan Y. Liu, *Wordsworth: The Sense of History.* (Stanford: Stanford University Press, 1989) and James Chandler, *England in 1819* (Chicago: University of Chicago Press, 1998) for particularly thorough accounts of the Romantic sense of history phenomenon, but also Paul de Man, 'Time and History in Wordsworth', in *Romanticism* ed. Cynthia Chase (London and New York: Longman Group, 1993) for an important dissenting view.

3   Lord Byron, *The Complete Poetical Works Volume V, Don Juan*, ed. Jerome J. McGann (Oxford: Clarendon Press, 1986) p. 3. All references to *Don Juan* in this text are to this edition.

4   John Guillory, *Cultural Capital: The Problem of Literary Canon Formation* (Chicago: University of Chicago Press, 1993) p. 131.

5   See also J. McGann, *Don Juan in Context* (Chicago: University of Chicago Press, 1976); Frederick L. Beaty, *Byron the Satirist* (De Kalb: Northern Illinois University Press, 1985); *Byron: Augustan and Romantic*, ed. Andrew Rutherford (London: Macmillan, 1990); and A. B. England, *Byron's Don Juan and Eighteenth-Century Literature* (Lewisburg: Bucknell University Press, 1975).

6   George Ridenour, *The Style of Don Juan* (New Haven: Yale University Press, 1960) p. 7.

7   Moyra Haslett, *Byron's Don Juan and the Don Juan Legend* (Oxford: Clarendon Press, 1997) pp. 144–5.

8   See Marcus Wood, *Radical Satire and Print Culture, 1790–1822* (Oxford: Clarendon Press, 1994): 'The passage in *Wilkes's Catechism* which is most heavily reworked is the parody of the Ten Commandments', p. 117.

9   Wood, p. 107.

10 *Beppo* in *Byron*, ed. Jerome J. McGann (Oxford and New York: Oxford University Press, 1986).

11 Wallace Stevens, *Opus Posthumous* (New York: Vintage, 1990) p. 205.

12 Elizabeth French Boyd, *Byron's Don Juan* (New York: The Humanities Press, 1958) p. 104.

13 Quoted in R.W. Harris, *Romanticism and the Social Order, 1780–1830* (New York: Blandford Press/Barnes and Noble, 1969) p. 349.

14 Haslett, 113.

15 William Hazlitt, *Lectures on the English Comic Writers* (1819) (New York: Doubleday/Dolphin Masters edition, 1965) p. 17.

16 Hazlitt, pp. 14–16, passim.

17 Quoted in Paul Hammond, *John Oldham and the Renewal of Classical Culture* (New York: Cambridge University Press, 1983) p. 31.
18 Mikhail Bakhtin, *The Dialogic Imagination*, translated by Caryl Emerson and Michael Holquist (Austin: University of Texas Press, 1981) p. 59.
19 Bakhtin, p. 46.
20 *'In the Wind's Eye': Byron's Letters and Journals*, Vol. 9, 1821–2 (London: John Murray, 1979).
21 Peter Graham, *Don Juan and Regency England* (Charlottesville: University Press of Virginia, 1990).
22 Antony Easthope, *Poetry As Discourse* (London and New York: Methuen, 1983).
23 Easthope, p. 93.

2 The Feminization of Male Fantasy

1 Nigel Leask, *British Romantic Writers and the East: Anxieties of Empire* (New York: Cambridge University Press, 1992) p. 33.
2 Jessica Benjamin, *The Bonds of Love: Psychoanalysis, Feminism, and the Problem of Domination* (New York: Pantheon, 1988) p. 127 and note. Benjamin's book, coming out of psychoanalytic and object-relations theory and an awareness of feminism and the Frankfurt School, can provide literary scholars with an exceptionally suggestive introduction to the transition from older 'intrapsychic' models of individuation to more recent 'intersubjective' theories of development. Two other useful collections on which I have drawn are: *Essential Papers on Object Relations*, ed. Peter Buckley MD (New York: New York University Press, 1986) and *Between Reality and Fantasy: Transitional Objects and Phenomena*, ed. S. Grolnick, L. Barkin and W. Muensterberger (New York: Jason Aronson, 1978).
3 Jerome Christensen, *Lord Byron's Strength: Romantic Writing and Commercial Society* (Baltimore: Johns Hopkins University Press, 1993).
4 Jerome Christensen, 'Theorizing Byron's Practice: The Performance of Lordship and the Poet's Career', *Studies in Romanticism* 27.4 (Winter 1988) pp. 477–90.
5 Martin Meisel, *Realizations* (Princeton, NJ: Princeton University Press, 1983) pp. 302–21. Robert Rosenblum, 'Caritas Romana after 1760: Some Romantic Lactations', *Art News Annual* 38 (1972) pp. 43–63.
6 Meisel, *Realizations*, p. 318.
7 See Simon Schama, *Citizens: A Chronicle of the French Revolution* (New York: Knopf, 1989) pp. 145–9.
8 *Rebel Daughters: Women and the French Revolution*, ed. Sara E. Melzer and Leslie W. Rabine (New York: Oxford University Press, 1992), see Joan B. Landes, 'Representing the Body Politic: The Paradox of Gender in the Graphic Politics of the French Revolution'.
9 *Rebel Daughters*, p. 55.
10 *Daughters*, p. 70
11 Schama, pp. 212–21, 391–2. See also the essays collected by Lynn Hunt in *Eroticism and the Body Politic* (Baltimore: Johns Hopkins University Press, 1991).

12 Susan Winnett, 'Coming Unstrung: Women, Men, Narrative, and Prin-ciples of Pleasure', *PMLA* 105.3 (May 1990) p. 509.

13 Sonia Hofkosh, 'The Writer's Ravishment: Women and the Romantic Author – The Example of Byron', in *Romanticism and Feminism*, ed. Anne K. Mellor (Bloomington: Indiana University Press, 1988) pp. 93–114.

14 *BLJ*.

15 *CPW Byron vol. V, Don Juan*, p. 694.

16 In *Godiva's Ride: Women of Letters in England, 1830–1880* (Bloomington: Indiana University Press, 1993) Dorothy Mermin writes that '[Lady Godiva] represents to the highest degree, and in a singularly enabling form, the multifarious contradictions that encompassed women writers in early and mid-Victorian England' (p. xvi).

17 Quoted in Jerome J. McGann, *The Romantic Ideology: A Critical Investigation* (Chicago: University of Chicago Press, 1983) pp. 113–14. McGann comments on the quotation as follows: '[Shelley's] remarks serve to highlight the function of such poetry, especially as it operates in decadent and morally imperialist cultures, or as it is judged by sensibilities which maintain and defend the ideologies of those cultures. Eroticism, Shelley argues, is the imagination's last line of human resistance against what he elsewhere called "Anarchy": political despotism and moral righteousness on the one hand, and on the other selfishness, calculation, and social indifference.'

3 The Fantasy of Superfluous Heads

1 Jerome J. McGann, 'The Book of Byron and the Book of the World', in *The Beauty of Inflections: Literary Investigations in Historical Method and Theory* (Oxford: Clarendon Press, 1988) p. 268.

2 Susan Wolfson, '"Their She Condition": Cross-Dressing and the Politics of Gender in *Don Juan*' *ELH* 54.3 (Fall 1987) pp. 585–617.

3 Horace, *Ars Poetica*, translated by A.S. Dorch, in *Classical Literary Criticism: Aristotle, Horace, Longinus* (London: Penguin, 1965) p. 87.

4 *Don Juan in Context*, p. 168.

5 'Openly displaying and freely discoursing of his mothered body, Barthes shares with, say, the clone whose much different body is devoted to signaling its various sexual availabilities this common refusal: of the desirability, even the possibility, of the male body's autonomy.' D.A. Miller, *Bringing out Roland Barthes* (Berkeley: University of California Press, 1992) p. 33.

6 Jacques Lacan, *Feminine Sexuality: Jacques Lacan and the école freudienne*, ed. Juliet Mitchell and Jacqueline Rose, trans. Jacqueline Rose (New York: W.W. Norton and Co., 1982) p. 143.

7 Anne K. Mellor, 'Romanticism, Gender and the Anxieties of Empire', *European Romantic Review* 8.2 (Spring 1997) p. 149.

8 Byron's scepticism is less a definitive philosophic rationalism than a perpetual process of pragmatic adjustment. Hence, it completes itself only in the reader's mind (not the narrator's, whose thought, however various, remains determined by what Byron actually wrote), as over and over we are made to confront, examine and revise our prior responses

to the poem, To a scepticism so paradoxically thoroughgoing in its tentativeness, an affirmation any less indirect is bound to appear merely self-approving.' Cooper, p. 262.

9 Richardson, p. 22.

10 Byron's maiden speech to the House of Lords, quoted in Pinto, p. 14.

11 Malcolm Kelsall, *Byron's Politics* (Brighton: Harvester, 1987).

12 Michael Foot, *The Politics of Paradise: A Vindication of Byron* (London: Collins, 1988).

13 Theodor Adorno, 'Commitment', in *The Essential Frankfurt School Reader* p. 318.

4 Mortal Fantasies

1 Nicola J. Watson, *Revolution and the Form of the British Novel 1790–1825: Intercepted Letters, Interrupted Seductions* (Oxford: Clarendon Press, 1994), and 'Novel Eloisas: Revolutionary and Counter-Revolutionary Narratives in Helen Maria Williams, Wordsworth, and Byron', *European Romantic Review* 3.1 (Summer 1992).

2 Watson, *Revolution and the Form*, p. 184.

3 Watson, 'Novel Eloisas'.

4 Caroline Franklin, *Byron's Heroines* (Oxford: Oxford University Press, 1992).

5 Franklin, pp. 163–4.

6 Franklin, p. 8.

7 Slavoj Žižek paraphrases Hegel on the transition from Caesar to caesarism: 'The Truth thus arose from failure itself: in failing, in missing its express goal, the murder of Caesar fulfilled the task which was, in a Machiavellian way, assigned to it by history: to exhibit the historical necessity by denouncing its own non-truth- its own arbitrary, contingent character' (*The Sublime Object of Ideology*, London: Verso, 1989, p. 60).

8 Claude Lévi-Strauss, *Structural Anthropology*, 2 vols (New York: Basic Books, 1963) 2: p. 184.

9 In 1728 the most frequently sung ballad among highwaymen was a celebration of drink:

> Now we are arriv'd to the *Boozing-Ken*,
> And our Pockets are full of Cole;
> We pass for the best of Gentlemen,
> When over a flowing Bowl,
> Our Hearts are at ease,
> We kiss who we please:
> On Death it's a Folly to think;
> May he hang in a Noose,
> That this Health will refuse,
> Which I am now going to drink.

Peter Linebaugh, *The London Hanged: Crime and Civil Society in the Eighteenth Century* (Cambridge: Cambridge University Press, 1992) p. 216.

10 See Louis Crompton, *Byron and Greek Love: Homophobia in 19th-Century*

England (Berkeley and New York: University of California Press, 1985) for a comprehensive treatment of Byron's sometimes elaborately encoded references to his sexual activities with other men.

11 *Lord Byron's Strength*, p. 306.
12 *Strength*, 'the Romantic recovery of strength entails the capacity to deal death casually yet with unwavering conviction, blithe fascism', p. 314.
13 *Strength*, p. 333.
14 *Strength*, p. 329.
15 Lacan's discussion of the *vel* of alienation reads almost like a commentary on this episode. Here is its conclusion:

> Freedom, after all, as you know, is like the celebrated freedom to work, for which the French Revolution, it seems, was fought. It can also be the freedom to die of hunger – in fact, that's what it amounted to throughout the nineteenth century, which is why, since then, certain principles have had to be revised. You choose freedom. Well! You've got freedom to die. Curiously enough, in the conditions in which someone says to you, *freedom or death!*, the only proof of freedom you can have in the conditions laid out before you is precisely to choose death, for there, you show that you have freedom of choice.

At this moment, which is also a Hegelian moment, for it is what is called the Terror, this quite different division is intended to make clear for you what is, in this field, the essence of the alienating *vel*, the lethal factor. *Four Fundamental Concepts of Psychoanalysis* (New York: W.W. Norton, 1981) p. 213.

16 I recognize that this is a crude formulation in the face of the complex and multifold set of relations called up by the term *pharmakon*. Good use might be made of the work of Jean-Pierre Vernant and Pierre Vidal-Naquet on ancient tragedy in opening up the subject of the function of the hero in the nineteenth century. I am thinking in particular of the remarks of Jean-Pierre Vernant in his essay 'The Tragic Subject: Historicity and Transhistoricity', in which he distinguishes between the hero of lyric and epic, who is a model, and the hero of tragedy, who is a problem. *Myth and Tragedy in Ancient Greece*, trans. Janet Lloyd (New York: Zone Books, 1988) p. 214.
17 Quoted in Linebaugh, p. 50.
18 In his study of the idiosyncratic German theologian and philosopher J.G. Hamann, Isaiah Berlin traces this refutation of scepticism to the influence of David Hume. 'Nature is like the Hebrew alphabet. It contains only consonants. The vowels we must supply for ourselves, otherwise we cannot read the words. How do we supply them? By that faith – or belief – of which Hume had spoken, without which we could not live for an instant; by our unbreakable certainty that there exists an external world, that there exists God, that there exist other human beings with whom we are in communication – this is presupposed by all other knowledge. To suppose it to be false, to doubt it, is nothing but self-refuting scepticism, *the denial of that consciousness without which we could*

not even have formulated the doubt' (*The Magus of the North: J.G. Hamann and the Origins of Modern Irrationalism* (London: John Murray, 1993) p. 86). Byron represents a similar insistence on the primacy and integrity of language as a living medium composed by creative action, and therefore inimical to the universalizing claims of an abstract scepticism.

19   *Four Fundamental Concepts of Psychoanalysis*, p. 104.

20   Truman Guy Steffan, *Byron's Don Juan: The Making of Masterpiece* Volume 1 of the Variorum *Don Juan* (Austin: University of Texas Press, 1957).

21   G. Wilson Knight, *Byron and Shakespeare* (New York, 1966) p. 89.

22   Jonathan Bate, *Shakespeare and the English Romantic Imagination* (Oxford: Oxford University Press, 1989).

23   Frederick L. Beaty, *Byron the Satirist* (De Kalb: Northern Illinois University Press, 1985) p. 140.

24   A.D. Nuttall, *A New Mimesis: Shakespeare and the Representation of Reality* (London: Methuen, 1983) p. 110.

25   'A droll story is told us, among others, of Jesus Christ having driven a legion of Devils into a herd of pigs, who were so discomfited with these new enemies that they all threw themselves over a precipice into the lake and were drowned. These were a set of hypochondriacal and high-minded swine, very unlike any others of which we have authentic record . . .

   Such is the tone of Shelley's 'Essay on the Devil and Devils', although in fairness to him it arises far more out of the subject of the title than out of the subject of Christ, for whom as an historical figure Shelley had a great feeling, if not an excess of reverence.' (From *Shelley's Prose*, ed. David Lee Clark (London: Fourth Estate, 1988) p. 271).

26   Marcel Proust, *Remembrance of Things Past*, trans. Kilmartin and Moncrieff (New York: Random House, 1981) Vol. III.

27   Proust, p. 933.

5   Marriage, Mobility and the Disavowal of Closure

1   Katharine Green, *The Courtship Novel* (Lexington, KY: University Press of Kentucky, 1991) p. 113.

2   The credentials of Leila's new governess are impeccable:

> Besides, he had found that he was no tutor:
>   (I wish that others would find out the same)
> And rather wished in such things to stand neuter,
>   For silly wards will bring their guardians blame:
> So when he saw each ancient dame a suitor
>   To make the little wild Asiatic tame,
> Consulting 'the Society for Vice
> Suppression,' Lady Pinchbeck was his choice.
>
>   (XII, st. 42)

3   Marlon Ross, *The Contours of Masculine Desrire: Romanticism and the Rise of Women's Poetry* (New York: Oxford University Press, 1989).

4 Gary Kelly, *Women, Writing, and Revolution* (Oxford and New York: Oxford University Press, 1993).

5 Mary Favret, *Romantic Correspondence: Women, Politics and the Fiction of Letters* (Cambridge: Cambridge University Press, 1993).

6 See, for example, Jerome Christensen, '*Marino Faliero* and the Fault of Byron's Satire', in H. Bloom, ed., *Lord Byron* (New York: Chelsea House, 1986) pp. 150–3.

7 Andrew Elfenbein, *Byron and the Victorians* (Cambridge: Cambridge University Press, 1995) p. 20.

8 'It was in the character of the disappointed pilgrim that Byron first became known to the world. The word pilgrim was used with some irony when it was first applied to the disreputable Childe Harold, who, having found nothing at home to satisfy his hungry heart, sailed off to the Eastern Mediterranean to drink from the fountains of European art, philosophy and religion. But the title of pilgrim was one that Byron claimed more and more as his right as he redefined its meaning for a culture just beginning to articulate the modern conception of alienation' (Ryan, p. 129).

9 S.T. Coleridge, *Biographia Literaria* ed. James Engell and W. Jackson Bate (Princeton, NJ: Bollingen Press, 1983) pp. 216–17.

10 Would it have been possible for Coleridge or his contemporaries to imagine this particular fantasy with the genders reversed? Could a man fall completely and forever in love with the essential self of a degraded and villainous woman? Is this the point of Keats's 'La Belle Dame Sans Merci'? Coleridge's tone, with its italics and mid-sentence exclamation points, must represent his amanuensis's attempt to render what was surely an animated effusion on the part of the critic.

6 *Don Juan* as a Defence of Liberty

1 Quoted in Vivian de Sola Pinto, *Byron and Liberty* (Folcroft, PA: Folcroft Press, 1969) p. 15.

2 Peter Linebaugh offers a useful account of the role of the ship in the formation of the colonial system. 'Do not think of the form of cooperation among these Atlantic communities as the rigid 'triangular trade' as if it were commodities doing the cooperating... Instead, imagine your hand as the ocean and the fingers the continents: the index finger is England, the middle finger Africa, the ring finger the West Indies, and the little finger North America. They cooperate to build a tremendous community. The thumb connects them all: it is the ship. It moves and oceans are crossed, diseases endured, danger overcome. From the cooperation of the people in these modes of production the triangle is produced, 'an instance of programmed accumulation of wealth such as the world has rarely seen', as C.L.R. James has written.' 'All the Atlantic Mountains Shook', *Labour/Le Travailleur*, 10 (Autumn 1982) p. 108.

3 'There is another constituency of Byron's readers who deserve a mention... After the end of the war many British people settled on the Continent, where the cost of living in sterling terms was a fraction of British levels.... Some had strong personal reasons for leaving England,

but the majority of people in these British communities across the channel were simply trying to survive on fixed incomes ... On the whole their lives were dull, for they had nothing to do and no role in society. But one thing they did have in plenty, to help while away their days – in France, Belgium, Germany and elsewhere you could buy locally-pub-lished editions of Byron very cheaply.... It is clear from the sheer numbers, not only that these books were immensely popular among the expatriate rentier class, but that many copies found their way to this country.' William St. Clair, 'The Impact of Byron's Writings: An Evaluative Approach', in *Byron: Augustan and Romantic*, ed. Andrew Rutherford (Basingstoke and London: Macmillan, 1990) p. 19.

4   Charlotte Smith, Elegiac Sonnet XLII, in *British Literature 1780–1830*, ed. Anne Mellor and Richard Matlak (Fort Worth: Harcourt Brace, 1996) p. 227.
5   Andrew Cooper, 'Shipwreck and Skepticism: *Don Juan* Canto 2', in *Lord Byron's Don Juan*, ed. Harold Bloom (New York: Chelsea House, 1987) p. 118.
6   Julian Barnes, *A History of the World in 10 1/2 Chapters* (London: Jonathan Cape, 1989). 'In the Sistine Chapel the Ark (now looking more like a floating bandstand than a ship) for the first time loses its composi-tional pre-eminence; here it is pushed right to the back of the scene. What fills the foreground are the anguished figures of those doomed antediluvians left to perish when the chosen Noah and his family were saved. The emphasis is on the lost, the abandoned, the discarded sin-ners, God's detritus ... Whatever the reason, Michelangelo reoriented – and revitalized – the subject. Baldassare Peruzzi followed him, Raphael followed him; painters and illustrators increasingly concentrated on the forsaken rather than the saved. And as this innovation became a tradi-tion, the Ark itself sailed further and further away, retreating towards the horizon' (p. 138).
7   *The Keats Circle* II (1969) p. 134.
8   Elizabeth French Boyd, *Byron's* Don Juan: *A Critical Study* (New York: The Humanities Press, 1958) p. 120.
9   Lucretius, *The Way Things Are*, trans. Rolfe Humphries (Bloomington: Indiana University Press, 1968) pp. 165–6, ll. 221–31.
10   John Speirs, *Poetry Towards Novel* (London: Faber and Faber, 1971) p. 249.
11   Christopher Hill, *Liberty against the Law: Some Seventeenth-Century Con-troversies* (London: Penguin, 1996).
12   Matthew Arnold, *Culture and Anarchy* (Cambridge: Cambridge Univer-sity Press, 1932).
13   Lord Byron, *The Complete Poetical Works. Volume V. Don Juan* (Oxford: Oxford University Press, 1986) p. 769.
14   Colin Campbell, *The Romantic Ethic and the Spirit of Modern Consumer-ism* (London: Allen and Unwin, 1989).

Index